RAMJET

MY SECRET LIFE WITH PTSD

To Marvica
Be well!
Roger

BY

ROGER BLAKE

OUTSKIRTS PRESS, INC.
DENVER, COLORADO

•

Life is a puzzle with many missing pieces.

•

<u>DEDICATION</u>

To all veterans, service members,
and their families that have proudly served
and now suffer from PTSD.

ACKNOWLEDGEMENTS

It is my honor to say thank you
to those kind souls who have helped me
with this enterprise –

First, to my family who provided helpful and encouraging comments as I bashed along. Special thanks go out to Brian who gave me treasure troves of family history to use.

To my classmate Steve who did an incredible job of proofing the text for military accuracy. I think I got it right, Steve.

To Clark whose proofing, encouragement, and frequent tweaking kept me focused till the end.

To the Navy Department Library for keeping important historical records and photos accessible for use by the public.

Special thanks to the entire staff at the Veterans Hospital in Albuquerque for keeping me together – body and soul.

To John Wiley & Sons, Inc. that gave me permission to use the American Psychological Association's definition of Post-traumatic Stress Disorder.

Saving the very best for last – to Sandy. Thank you for the countless hours of proofreading and editing that you spent plowing through my typos and mistakes. Beyond that, your unbending support and enthusiasm kept me at my computer when the story became too difficult, and I really wanted to walk away. Thank you so much – again and again – and to Ron who gracefully let me borrow her for the duration.

In Memory of
Cowboy Jerry Lee
1939 – 2012

TABLE OF CONTENTS

TABLE OF CONTENTS (Continued)

TABLE OF CONTENTS (Continued)

ILLUSTRATIONS

All photos and artwork are by the author except as noted in the text.

ILLUSTRATIONS (Continued)

Inspiration

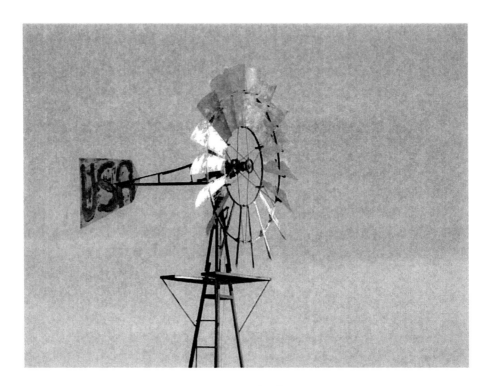

USA Windmill

INTRODUCTION

RAMJET is an autobiography. It is the story of my secret life with PTSD – Post-traumatic Stress Disorder. I dealt with this syndrome most of my adult life without knowing that it had taken root in my mind. The disorder has many evolving descriptions. The American Psychiatric Association's definition of PTSD is:

> "... a severe anxiety disorder that can develop after exposure to any event that results in psychological trauma. This event may involve the threat of death to oneself or to someone else, or to one's own or someone else's physical, sexual, or psychological integrity, overwhelming the individual's ability to cope. Diagnostic symptoms for PTSD include re-experiencing the original trauma(s) through flashbacks or nightmares, avoidance of stimuli associated with the trauma, and increased arousal – such as difficulty falling or staying asleep, anger, and hyper vigilance. Formal diagnostic criteria require that the symptoms last more than one month and cause significant impairment in social, occupational, or other important areas of functioning." *

In WWI, PTSD was called "battle fatigue." During WWII and the Korean War it was commonly known as "combat fatigue" or "shell shock." During the Vietnam War, it was called "delayed stress." After the war ended, it was diagnosed as "Post-Vietnam Syndrome" and finally "Post-traumatic Stress Disorder" – or simply "PTSD."

Many who have not experienced combat or a traumatic event first hand are skeptical that the disorder actually exists. In fact, there is a sad history of reprehensible treatment of PTSD victims – as in the notorious incident between a soldier and General Patton who slapped and berated him for being a coward. I hope the reader will suspend his or her own reality and experience mine – all the events, decisions, and emotions that made up my life – and gain an understanding of the enormous impact that PTSD has had on me. I will lay my life before you to show that this affliction is very real and has devastating long-term effects on those who suffer its consequences. My perspective has not been easy to write about. PTSD is invisible unless the warning signs become severe. It can fester within the mind and be undiagnosed for years. Then some triggering event will make it develop

* American Psychiatric Association, *DIAGNOSTIC & STATISTICAL MANUAL OF MENTAL DISORDERS, DSM IV-TR*. Used with permission by John Wiley & Sons, Inc.

unexpectedly into a full-blown, psychological disability. The symptoms can be mild or mortally dangerous. In my case, I lived with its subtle symptoms for 35 years without having a clue that it was affecting my every thought and move. Sometimes I was able to work through my problems, but many times I was dysfunctional. I am currently receiving therapy and treatment provided by the Veterans Administration and am much better. Truthfully, I would not be alive today if it had not been for the intervention of the VA's caring and professional staff.

There are treatments – but no certain cure – for PTSD. I sincerely wish I could flip a magic switch and turn it off. Some people have told me, "Just get over it!" If only it were that simple, but that is not how any mental disorder works. About all we can do is to adjust our lives to accommodate it.

As I am writing this book, I am seeing PTSD etched on the faces of the Japanese survivors of the recent earthquake/tsunami/nuclear disaster. News clips of children and civilian victims of war and other traumatic events show the agonizing effects of their horrific experiences. The media is full of reports of how it is seriously affecting our recently returning veterans of the Gulf and Afghanistan wars. Ask any of the survivors if PTSD exists. Its costs go way beyond the monetary expense of treatment. The human loss in terms of squandered productivity and creativity and of broken families and wasted lives is astronomical beyond computation.

As I wrote *RAMJET*, I started to ask myself if my tale was believable or would it appear that I was being dramatic for the sake of achieving a more interesting story. I assure the reader that all these events are true as I remember them. If anything, I could not find words to adequately describe the horror of my calamitous accidents – or the emotional agony of my personal tragedies – or the joys of the many pleasures I have known.

I have wondered if my experience was much different than what most flight officers in the Navy went through at the time – or any other military personnel who have to fight in combat situations. The details vary, but extreme events happen in warfare all the time. There are also differences in the degree that each of us is capable of coping with these traumas. My PTSD has been exacerbated by chronic physical pain that is the result of my injuries and serves as a constant reminder of my accident.

I was a crew member – not the pilot – in an aircraft when the accident occurred that changed my life. My PTSD might not exist if I had been the pilot that had control of the plane. I tried with all my might to stop this impending calamity, but could only watch as my life came within inches of being terminated before my eyes. Trauma rises to a higher level entirely when you can see your imminent death and are powerless to prevent it from happening.

To some degree or another, PTSD is reflected in almost everything I do. I can cite many examples. If I go out to dinner, I always select a quiet place. I don't go to concerts because I am uncomfortable being in crowds. I don't go to war movies or films that depict violence for its own sake. I have walked out of previews because their mind-splitting noise and flash-bang special effects are intolerable. I cringe when a fire engine or ambulance speeds by with its sirens screaming. It isn't just the noise that bothers me, but also the gruesome faces of imagined victims that flash through my mind. If I am stuck in a crowded space, I always make my way as far as possible to the back. I need to observe everybody and everything for some hidden threat. I avoid confrontations by just walking away. I have quit jobs because I could not tolerate the directions of a higher authority. I shied away from other jobs because I could not handle the stress or responsibilities of the position. Sometimes my decisions were made despite PTSD. I struggled with myself to successfully overcome my anxieties and function in difficult family, social, or professional situations. I was – and still am – happiest alone or with a dear friend walking through some deep woods or through a high mountain meadow filled with wild flowers and the constant hum of insects.

Many positive and happy moments have indeed happened since my accident, and many of them are covered – in delicious detail – in this book. But happiness was hard to find and even harder to maintain. PTSD was not the sole determining cause but was certainly a major influence in everything I did. The simplest way I can express the depth that PTSD affected and continues to affect my life is to describe it as a detrimental influence that remains intertwined with all the other elements that determine who I am.

One way that I believe PTSD molds the mind is that it makes us dwell on negatives. Positives are suppressed and pushed aside. Much like depression, these negatives shape my life. PTSD is like a demon lurking under my bed, always there and waiting for an opportunity to sneak out, to grab my legs, and to pull me under.

I did not know this disorder was part of me all these years. When my actions were illogical or dysfunctional, I thought they just reflected who I was. I simply shrugged them off and blamed my behavior on some undefined character flaw. Only two people – my first wife Marge and a good friend Catherine – pushed and said that I ought to seek help. Marge continually asked me to see a counselor and quit drinking so much. I took her concern as criticism that I did not want to hear. My excuse was always that I needed to escape the stress of my job, and there was always stress in my job from which I had to escape. Catherine – who was a nurse – told me that she thought I was depressed. I simply could not see that I had a problem.

RAMJET is not a scholarly dissertation about PTSD. I have occasionally backed out of the story to discuss this problem objectively, but only to point out how it has affected my life. I leave it to the readers to recognize each occurrence as it may relate to them. The events speak for themselves.

A note about all the medical terminology, and the military anachronisms and abbreviated terms used in the book. If you would like further information, just type the term into Google or Wikipedia for more than you ever wanted to know.

Most of the names in the book are the characters' real names. There are a few instances, however, when I couldn't recollect a person's name or thought it would be best to create a substitute. I apologize if I have offended anyone in the process. I have also tried very hard to be even-handed in the presentation of these events. I have shown that I was culpable in many instances. On the other hand, I have not hesitated to place blame where I perceived that it rightfully lies.

The opinions I express here are based entirely on my own observations and sentiments. My memories may very well not be correct or reflect opposing recollections and opinions which are just as valid as mine. I have not written any of this out of meanness or desire to get back at anyone. The truth will always shine where it may, regardless of the distress it may cause. If I have been unfair or misstated the facts, I sincerely apologize. My intentions were entirely the opposite.

The title of this book comes from the "call sign" – also known as the "handle" – that my squadron mates gave me after I first arrived for duty. Every aviator in the Navy was given one because you didn't want your real name to be heard by the enemy over the airwaves. Your fellow aviators would try to come up with the most macho or ridiculous or disrespectful term possible. There was a popular cartoon character on the radio during the 60s called "Roger Ramjet." With my first name being Roger, my handle came easily. It had to be Ramjet. A ramjet is a jet engine that uses the speed of the plane, or any object attached to it, to compress – or ram – the incoming air into the engine before it is ignited in the combustion chamber. A regular jet engine has turbines that compress the air.

I liked my new handle, and it stuck to me. Hence the title of this book – *RAMJET.*

Notes to the Wall

PREFACE
Some Necessary History

MY MOTHER AND FATHER were both born in 1912. It was the year that the TITANIC sank, but there was probably no connection. Mom grew up in one of the most privileged families in North America. Her father was heir to a family fortune built by generations of powerful financiers and railroad entrepreneurs. Their main house was a mansion in Gramercy Park, New York, with opulent, marble-floored, columned interiors decorated with Italian tapestries and tiger and polar bear rugs.

Gramercy Park Mansion - Alcove

There was also an estate on Long Island and a country home in Andover, Maine, built in 1791. When the family traveled to Maine, they leased two entire railroad cars. All the butlers, maids, housekeepers, nannies, and family members would travel together in an overnight sleeper car. The luggage, trunks, carriages, wagons, horses, and their drivers would be hauled behind in a freight car. There was no train to Andover, however.

The family would make the 85 mile, three day trip from Portland on the coast on rugged dirt roads to the wilds of the interior in its caravan of buggies and wagons. It must have been quite a sight!

Mom's father was a well-known financial attorney. In 1931, he became embroiled in the Ivar Kreuger Affair, a ponzi scheme that ruined many lives. It was the lawsuits which ensued – not the Great Depression – that destroyed the family wealth and reputation. My grandfather committed suicide by shooting himself with a shot gun in 1932 as most of the family assets were being liquidated to settle claims against the estate.

My mother, Ruth, was only 20 years old. Through family contacts, she got a job as house keeper and companion for Georgia O'Keefe at the Ghost Ranch in New Mexico. She said that Miss O'Keefe was very demanding and difficult to work for. Every detail had to be meticulously planned. Mom would have to get all of the equipment set up perfectly wherever Georgia decided to go painting. The only anecdote she ever told me about Miss O'Keefe was that the lady was deathly afraid of rattlesnakes. Georgia would sit in her Model A Ford while Mom went around with a broom stick to beat the brush and chase any critters away.

Ruth met my father, Forrester, at a community playhouse in Santa Fe where they both had bit acting parts. Dad came from an Oklahoma and Michigan family with an established history of remarkable characters. One of the most notable was John Y.F. Blake – "... a dashing West Pointer with the 'Galloping 6th' U.S. Calvary Regiment who commanded a company of Indian scouts in Arizona and New Mexico, fighting Apache Chief, Geronimo. Colonel Blake went on to use tactics learned in the Indian wars as the commander of the renowned Irish Brigade in South Africa's Boer War of 1899 to 1902." **

Forrester wrote western novels about the early trail rides and mountain men that opened the territories before the mass settler migrations arrived. Mom was enamored by his writing and the romantic idea of traveling around Texas and Oklahoma to do research for his books. They were married in 1933. Unfortunately, this was the dust bowl era and her romantic hopes became a terribly difficult experience.

My older twin brothers, Brian and John, were born in 1940. Then World War II came. Dad enlisted in the Army on December 8, 1941 – the day after Pearl Harbor. I was born in 1943 and my sister, Priscilla, followed in 1946. My half-brother, Tony, was born in 1955 to Mom and my step-father, Reggy.

**Blake family history provided courtesy of my brother, Brian Blake, whose book *UNDER BRILLIANT STARS* is a major work in progress.

Forrester spent most of the war in England as an administrative technician. Records show that he did get to Europe, but stayed behind the front lines. As far as we know, he did not see combat except that he nonchalantly wrote in one letter that he was "... in London being chased by buzz-bombs." Perhaps he was more traumatized by the attacks than he let on. Maybe he was shocked by the sights of wounded coming back from the front lines. We will never know for sure. The fact is, however, that his mind was significantly damaged after he came home.

Ruth left Forrester in 1948 and married my step-father in 1951. His name was Reginald T. Townsend. The middle initial also stood for Townsend. Reginald Townsend Townsend was from a prominent and wealthy Rhode Island family whose fortune was lost during the Great Depression. He had known my mother since she was eight years old. Reggy's poor eyesight kept him out of the military, but he got himself to France through the Red Cross and played a secretive role in the French resistance. He spoke perfect French. For his extraordinary contributions, France honored him with the French Legion of Honor Medal, which is the highest civilian award given by the French Government. After the war, he was in the advertising and publishing business, and then became an executive for Radio Liberty which made broadcasts into the Soviet Union and its satellite countries. Radio Liberty was a CIA front. Reggy's apartment in New York was a safe house for Soviet Union refugees. Many times, strange visitors would also appear at our country home north of New York City. They generally came with dark, haunted expressions on their faces and could hardly speak English. Reggy always wined and dined them and made them feel comfortable – probably for the first time that many of them could remember.

Reggy was also a socialite who knew almost every significant player in New York City. He was a "club man." At one time he was a member of 20 different clubs and president of many of them. A story is told that Reggy once tried to cut back on his number of affiliations. He resigned from one, but was told that he couldn't because he had just been elected President!

Growing up, I was unaware of Ruth and Reggy's extraordinary backgrounds. Those worlds were gone, and they did not talk about them. Reggy was still an important man in New York City, however. I was dressed up in rented tuxedos and paraded through grand debutant balls at the Waldorf Astoria Hotel. I hated it! We went into the city to see Broadway plays and museum openings. Some of his clubs had Christmas shows that I always had to go to. That kind of elegant style never stuck to me, however. Perhaps I took after my father's preferences for a more rugged existence. Regardless of the reason, the older I got, the more authoritarian Reggy became, and we frequently argued. I was always being sent to my room in tears and threatened with "reform school" for disagreeing with him about some minor thing. We were both obstinate, but Reggy was the boss and he beat me down with his dominance. As soon as I was able, I got out of the house. I went to camps in the summer time and finally Pomfret School in Connecticut. I never spent more than a few weeks home a year.

When it became time for college, I wanted to go to the Boston Museum School – one of the finest art schools in the country. My painting and drawing instructor at Pomfret had encouraged me to apply. I was accepted and excitedly told Reggy about it. He had other plans for me, however.

"I will not pay for 'art' school. You will starve! What you need is a solid liberal arts education."

He would not consider any other position. Two years later, I dropped out of Middlebury because I had my mind set on art and nothing else. Reggy gave me the same response about going to art school. Regrettably, I did not have the force of will to change his mind or do it on my own. Besides, there were important events happening in the world, which I wanted to be part of. This was 1963 and the Vietnam War was escalating into a major conflict. I signed on with the Navy to get away from Reggy, to avoid the draft that would have nabbed me since I was no longer in school, and to become involved with a cause greater than myself. At least in the Navy, I would not have to fight as a soldier or marine in some leech-infested swamp that nobody had ever heard about.

Flight training lasted until the summer of 1964. Events of that year were as important as any in our recent history. President Johnson was our new President after Kennedy had been assassinated the year before. China exploded its first nuclear bomb. The Civil Rights Act of 1964 was signed into law against an ugly back drop of racial riots and violence. The Beatles shook the world with I Want To Hold Your Hand and All My Loving. Other bands and performers like The Rolling Stones, The Supremes, The Grateful Dead, and Bob Dylan, to mention only a few, set the tone for a generation. Cassius Clay beat Sonny Liston and changed his name to Muhammad Ali. Gas was 30 cents a gallon. A new car might cost $3500. Ford produced the first Mustang. Postage was 5 cents. The average annual salary was $6000.

1964 was also the year that I received my commission as ensign and my wings as a Naval Flight Officer – just as Congress approved the Gulf of Tonkin Resolution that authorized war against North Vietnam.

As it is said, "The rest is history." My life from that moment on is the subject of this book.

Officer Candidate Airman Blake – 1964
US Navy Photo

A Detour To Shake Hands With The Past

PRESSING REALITIES SWEPT ASIDE the romantic aspirations of my youth. Two years spent trying to study subjects which didn't interest me had been enough. Important events were happening in the world, and I was missing the action. I left the insulated, academic halls of my small New England college – and to avoid being drafted – I preemptively signed on with the Navy.

Basic training and flight school were behind me, and I had just pinned on my wings and would be flying the back seat of the F4B Phantom II – a supersonic fighter/bomber that had been recently introduced to the fleet. My orders were to leave the East Coast and report to my first squadron in San Diego in 30 days. With time on my hands, I decided to go by way of San Francisco and do some sightseeing.

Just before the trip, I bought a glorious, flat-finned, 1960 Chevy Impala convertible – flint black with flaming red leather interior, a 348 Tri-Power Engine, and Power Glide automatic transmission. Open highway – here I come! My destiny lay somewhere beyond the horizon, and I was looking forward to what my journey had in store.

At Salt Lake City, I took a break for coffee and was planning the rest of my route from a map of the western United States. Pocatello, Idaho popped out at me. The last anyone in the family had heard, my father was a professor of American Literature at Idaho State University in Pocatello. Mom had corresponded with him, but none of us had seen him since she had gotten her divorce 13 years ago.

Dad had come back from WW II and locked himself in the basement of our Denver home. Mom had to take most of his meals down to him, plus manage the household and raise the kids by herself. She continually warned me to be quiet and steer clear of our father.

"Be very careful not to disturb Daddy. He's not feeling well today."

I still remember the one occasion he let me down there to see him. I was only about four years old. Mom had to yell and bang on the locked door to get his attention.

"Forrester! He's your son. You need to spend some time with him. Let him come in!"

After a few, silent minutes, Dad came up the stairs. He was trying hard to be friendly and nice. He picked me up, and we descended into his dark, private domain, which felt like crawling into a cave. It took a moment for my eyes to adjust to the darkness. The reading lamp by his typewriter and a narrow casement window provided the only light in the large room. The bright shafts only served to darken the shadows that dominated the space.

The first thing I noticed was a big mound of furs on the floor. There were skins of all types – buffalo, beaver, deer, coyote, and the like. Of course, it was the perfect playground, so I pawed my way to the top. I sat proudly on the hides and then something caught my attention that was propped up against the wall.

"What's that, Daddy? Can I hold it?"

"That's a rifle – an old Hawkens muzzle-loader. The mountain men of the old west used it to hunt and protect themselves. It's special, so be very careful."

I stood up unsteadily, and he put it in my hands. It weighed about half as much as I did. I tried for a moment to hold on, but toppled over and dropped the gun on the side of the pile. It rolled down the furs and clattered on the concrete floor. My father erupted in a barrage of relentless insults and curses that brought Mom rushing down to protect me.

"What do you think you're doing letting him play with that? It's not his fault – you should know better!"

She whisked me away and slammed the basement door behind us. I curled up, whimpering, in the safety and comfort of my favorite arm chair. So much for spending time with Dad.

My father did come out occasionally for trips and excursions. I saw him then, but always had to be "seen and not heard." I learned to be very quiet, or I would get yelled at for no reason – at least, for no reason that I could figure out. Even though I was young, I remember feeling that my father resented my presence. Other than my sister – who was strangely excluded – Dad had the same attitude toward my two older brothers and especially Mom. The family was an unacceptable drag on his life.

My trip to California was way ahead of schedule, and Pocatello was only the width of three fingers off my route on the map, so why not try to track him down? Perhaps his attitude toward me and the family might have mellowed after all these years. Maybe he would open up and tell me his version of the story. At worst, he might slam the door in my face. That response would be enough to tell me all I really wanted to know anyway.

I climbed into the Chevy, turned northwest, and hit the road for Pocatello. I arrived at Idaho State, but was informed that Forrester was off somewhere on summer vacation. With a little persistence I found his be-sequined secretary.

"I'm so sorry, but he's gone to Seattle on vacation. All I can give you is the forwarding address he gave me for his mail."

The syrupy-sweet lady started to dig through a pile of papers on her desk to find the note he had left her. She looked up and gave me a confidential smile.

"I'm really fond of him you know. It is so wonderful of you to go out of your way to find him! In all the time I've known your father – my goodness, over ten years now – he's never told me about his family. Extraordinary!"

"Yes. Very odd."

"Ah – here it is!"

She copied the address and pressed it into my hand with an affectionate squeeze.

"If you find him, please say 'Hi' for me."

OK, Seattle was a good eight fingers width from San Francisco. But why not? I jumped in the Chevy and took off heading for the Pacific Northwest. I had the top down, the car and I were in over-drive, and the changing vistas kept urging me on. I soon pulled up in front of a dilapidated boarding house near the waterfront. The weathered woman who answered the doorbell looked as if she had hauled too many crab pots on the stormy Pacific seas.

"Sorry to bother you, Ma'am, but I'm looking for Forrester Blake. I was told he might be here."

She looked at my car and tossed her unruly mane of gray hair. She clearly did not want to be bothered.

"Forr'ster left 'bout two days ago."

She turned and started to disappear behind the door.

"Excuse me – I'm his son. Do you have an address or telephone number of where he was going?"

"Son – eh?"

She sized me up some more before deciding that I was on the level.

"Nope – sho' don't."

Her mouth moved like her teeth had to be set before she spat out the next word.

"But he did talk a coupla' of times 'bout heading some place – let me think here. Hmmm."

She scratched her mossy lip for a moment. I figured that if I said anything it might interrupt her "thinking" so I just waited.

"Oh yeah! Butte – Butte, Montana. Now I remember! He said he knowed someone 'dere who rents rooms in some fancy old mansion on a hill. Now – dat's all I can tells ya'."

Her information was sketchy, but how difficult could it be to find such a building? I checked my map again. Butte was five, maybe six fingers width behind me. That wasn't so bad, but did I have time to go there and get to San Diego? That was a long way. I had come this far, however, and didn't want to give up the hunt. Again – why not? I wheeled my high-desert, top-down, fire-breathing, rocket-man mobile around and blazed a trail back east. What a great way to see the country! A few days later, I stopped on a rise outside Butte.

I scanned the downtown for a "fancy old mansion on a hill." I saw it! It could only be that imposing Victorian house overlooking the city from its lonely perch close to the business district. A few minutes later, I parked in front of the building. It was late afternoon when I climbed the long set of concrete steps leading to the entrance. There was a row of battered mail boxes with the names of the tenants taped on them. No Forrester Blake, however. The thought crossed my mind that this search may have become an unfortunate lost cause, but I wasn't about to just turn around and drive away. I went inside to see if I could find anyone who knew of my father.

The entry was framed by a pair of tall, stained-glass windows. The wall paper, that once was a decorative floral design, was faded and dimly lit by a brass ceiling fixture where a fine chandelier must have once hung. The musty odor of mildew rose from the thin carpet. Nobody on the ground floor answered when I knocked on the doors. This was not looking good. Then I heard several excited, young voices coming down the stairs. Their shoes clattered and clunked on the wooden steps and a colorful group rounded the corner.

"Excuse me – would any of you know if Forrester Blake is staying here?"

They looked at each other, pulled a blank, and shook their heads.

"Nope – not that we know of."

They were walking out when one of them turned back.

"Come to think of it, a man moved into the attic up on the third floor yesterday. Maybe that could be him."

Bingo! I climbed to the second floor and found another, narrower stairway that led to a small landing. I made my way up as quietly as I could. It felt like I was climbing a medieval tower filled with mysteries and dark unknowns. I was not used to the elevation of Butte and had to wait at the top to catch my breath. The clatter of steady typing came from the room. I knocked lightly and waited. There was no response, so I knocked again – harder this time. The typing stopped, and the sounds of footsteps came towards me.

"Who is it?"

"It's Roger – your son, Roger."

A deadbolt turned, and a chain lock slipped through its channel and rattled as it fell against the wood frame. The door swung slowly open to the inside. All I could see was the dark form of a man – lit from behind by the soft twilight sun. Somehow, I knew that he was my father.

5

Relic

Knowing My Father Became Knowing Myself

"MY GOSH! – Roger! – Well, so you are!"

"I was just passing through and thought I'd look you up, Dad."

"Of course. Of course. Come on in."

We shook hands stiffly, and he stepped aside to let me enter. The single open window let in a beam of light that filtered through mists of dust as we moved about. The bulb in the ceiling fixture was burned out. A pair of dingy, smoke-stained drapes fluttered easily in the evening breeze. An old typewriter, some manuscript papers, and a reading lamp were set on a desk next to a single bed. A tiny mirror was all that hung on the walls – which were mottled tones of beige. A dirty area rug, a threadbare blanket, and a tiny bathroom completed the apartment. All the rest merged with the darkening shadows of the setting sun. I felt as if I had stepped back in time to our unhappy episode together in the basement.

"Gee – I have so many questions. Are you really just passing through? How on earth did you find me? What brings you here? Please, have a seat. My goodness, you look just like I imagined – just like your mother!"

Dad was an inch or two taller than my 5'10". He wore a faded tan shirt and brown khaki slacks which had shrunk – making them too short for his legs and too tight for his girth. His brown, wide-brim hat was tossed on the bed along with a well-worn, hip-length, brown, leather jacket. The muted shades of brown created a drab, monotone appearance – a first impression that proved consistent with his personality.

I don't know what his leather coat would be called. It had a belt that buckled around the waist. Maybe it was a country or hunting or campaign jacket. Whatever – he always wore it and his hat when we went outside. His old, polished boots came above his ankles, and were cracked from years of wear. From the way he dressed, he could have been a hunter of ancient tombs, or an explorer of untracked wilderness, or a seeker of timeless truths that could only be told by the land and by fragments that had been left behind. Actually – my father was all those things.

His face was full and puffy, and he carried a few extra pounds, which seemed natural for him. He looked exactly like my grandfather in a photo I later saw of them together – right down to the shiny metal frames of their thick glasses and the neckties that they always wore in public. I felt fortunate that – as Dad had said – I looked like my mother. There was nothing else physically notable about him that I remember – except his nervousness when we were together.

"Here – have a seat on the desk chair. I'll sit on the bed."

I told him about my new assignment in the Navy and that I just had a whim to track him down.

"All I have are vague memories of us together from when I was a kid. I guess I would like to get to know you now that I'm older. That's all."

"Of course. Of course."

We talked about where my search had taken me, and how I had finally found the "fancy mansion." We then went to his favorite café for dinner. As we walked outside, he spotted my Impala.

"That yours? It sure is an impressive machine,"

He pointed out his old Woody station wagon parked a few spaces away, and a memory popped into my head.

"Is that the same wagon that we almost wrecked crossing a bridge in about – when was it – around 1948?"

That was 15 years ago, and I must have been about five years old at the time.

The whole family – Dad, Mom, older twin brothers, baby sister, and I – was packed into the wagon on a deeply-rutted dirt road in Estes Park high in the Colorado Rockies. We paused at the top of a long hill that ran down to a rough, plank bridge spanning a stream and then a difficult climb up the other side. Dad took the car out of gear and coasted to gain as much speed as possible. Unfortunately, we ended up going much too fast. The rear axle snapped when we hit a pothole abutting the bridge, and we skidded to a stop – dangerously close to going over the edge. We were stuck until a rancher came by on a tractor and towed us back to his barn. He and Dad managed to wire up a strong timber to support the axle – they actually did use baling wire – and Dad gingerly drove the long, slow way back to Denver.

He looked at me and smiled proudly.

"Yup, this is that same wagon."

The café he took me to felt like home because one of my favorite pastimes used to be sitting in small diners, drinking coffee, and chatting with acquaintances who happened to drift by. We walked through the door, and a waitress looked up with a bit of surprise. Dad had obviously been there many times before.

"Hi, Pat. You're late – we thought you might have found some other place to eat. Now, who's that young man you have with you?"

I remembered that my mother had labeled old photographs with my father's nickname "Pat."

"This is my son, Roger. He's in the Navy – going to California to ship out overseas."

"My goodness – you never told us you had any children!"

She came over to the booth we had selected and looked back and forth between us to see a resemblance.

"What a surprise, Roger! Your dad sure knows how to keep a secret."

He just smiled awkwardly and buried his head in his menu. During dinner, Dad was reticent to answer any questions that pried into his personal life or feelings, so we talked mostly about what I had been doing. When I offered to fill him in a bit about Mom and the rest of the family, he looked down and shook his head. OK, he didn't want to discuss them, so I shifted to college and my desire to be an artist, which he found interesting. He asked for more information about the Navy and how that was going. I explained that I would be flying in F4B Phantom jets off of aircraft carriers as a Radar Intercept Officer (RIO.) Dad nodded politely, but not proudly or supportively. I had no big expectations, however his lack of enthusiasm was still disappointing.

"I've never heard anything about your experience in the Army – or about the War, Dad. That must have been rough. Can you tell me something about it?"

He visibly stiffened and silently went off in some distant world. He stared at his plate, pushed a few bits of food around that were left, and slowly shook his head. I needed to change the subject again.

Café Still Life

"I saw in the apartment that you are writing something. Are you working on another book?"

He took a deep breath and came back from his thoughts.

"I'm typing up some information I've found on Indian War battles here in Montana. Investigating historic locations is how I spend my summers. The story hasn't come to me yet, but the research usually leads me somewhere. Maybe you would like to come out to one of the sites tomorrow?"

"Absolutely, Dad."

We went back to his room after pulling out an army cot from the wagon. He insisted on sleeping on it and that I take the bed.

"I'm used to it."

The next day, Dad first had to check on the stock market at his local brokerage office. It was clear that he was not a poor man – just extraordinarily frugal. The antique Woody, his musty room, his well-worn clothes, and meager lifestyle all exemplified his belief that no unnecessary

10

dollars should be spent on comfort or appearances. We went for breakfast, and he then drove us far out onto the trackless prairie.

We stopped on a desolate knoll with tall grass waving in the strong winds. It could have been the middle of nowhere. Dad spent a long time describing where the Indian camps had been and how Army troops had surrounded and massacred them all. He pointed to a bend in a creek that weaved through the rolling hills where the last battle had been fought. He was immersed in the details of the story as he laid out the historical account for me.

"The soldiers were a band of marauding, blood-thirsty killers. They murdered everybody – men, women, and children – and showed no mercy. The Indians did not have a chance. The troops were killing for pleasure – there's no other way to portray it."

Dad looked out over the vacant prairie and shook his head.

"These were peaceful tribes that had lived on this land for centuries. What right did the white man have to come in and take it all?"

I too sympathized with the Indians, but believed that there was ample cruelty on both sides. I did not, however, want to start an argument with my father.

"It is a sad history, indeed."

We hiked along the creek looking for arrowheads, bullets, spent cartridges, or anything interesting to be found. We rested under a shady cottonwood tree for a light lunch and then hiked separately. Dad was engrossed in his project. I kicked dirt, turned over rocks, and lost myself in my own world. I enjoyed the feeling of being blown by the constant wind – as if I was a schooner with billowing sails cruising across distant seas. It was late afternoon when Dad and I returned to the car with a few bits of historic treasure in our pockets.

He seemed happy with the day. Dusk was falling when we got back to Butte and stopped at the café for dinner. We seemed to be hitting it off well, except for his resistance to any personal questions about himself.

"There is another site I can take you to tomorrow if you're interested."

"I'd like that. I really enjoyed today. Thanks a lot."

Dad ate for a while lost in thought. Then, for some unknown reason, he totally changed the subject.

"Don't ever lose that body, Roger."

"What do you mean, Dad?"

"Look at you. You're fit and trim. I used to be like that."

He looked down and wrung his hands regretfully.

"... in the Army. Now, I'm spreading like a fat lump of lard."

His description was a cruel and exaggerated one. Yes, he could lose some weight, but he did not look nearly as bad as he had suggested. Whatever led to his comment, it was the only time he ever mentioned the Army. I believe now that his remark revealed an unsound sense of low self-esteem. In any event, we finished our meal and turned in. I was tired from all the fresh air and exercise, and sleep came easily.

Very early the next morning, I was awakened by the click of the latch as the door closed. The old stairs gave Dad away as he tried unsuccessfully to go quietly outside. I sat up and had to shake the sleep away. The grey light of dawn was beginning to shine through the window. Dad's cot and typewriter were gone. I went to the window and saw him just as he closed the back of the wagon. He climbed into the front seat, stuck his elbow out the window, and drove away. I noticed $40 and a note lying on the desk.

"Roger, I'm sorry. I can't deal with this – Forrester."

That was it. He did not say, Dad. Not love. Just Forrester. Not even good to see you or goodbye. The note, $40, and a few memories of our brief time together were all he left behind. I first felt sad for myself, then sad for Dad because he needed to isolate himself from the family, then sad because I had intruded on his reclusive life.

My brother, Brian, who has studied our family in considerable depth, discovered a history of serious mental illness through several generations. Dad had, in fact, exhibited many psychological problems – probably related to depression – before he went off to WWII. Mom once told me, however, that Forrester was a "changed man – much for the worse" after he returned from the war. I have to believe that he experienced some traumatic event while he was overseas – something that severely aggravated whatever pre-existing conditions he may have had. What I later came to realize was that his dysfunction met all the criteria of PTSD. Isolation, anxiety, and depression are classic symptoms of the disorder. I may have also been predisposed to similar psychiatric problems, but I knew none of this at the time.

In any event, my only meeting with my father as an adult was probably my first real exposure to PTSD.

There was no reason for me to stay longer in Butte. I packed up my gear and turned southwest toward San Francisco. No more fooling around. I would only have a few days to spend sightseeing around the "City by the Bay" before I had to continue on to San Diego.

•

Let sleeping history lie.

•

Northwest Highway

Marge

TERRY, A PRE-FLIGHT BARRACKS ROOMMATE and close friend, had told me that I should look up his parents near San Jose if I ever got to the Bay Area.

"At least, they will be worth a free meal."

I called his folks a few days before I arrived and was invited to stay for as long as I wanted. I drove up, got out of my awesome, cross-country cruiser, and introduced myself. While I was talking with Terry's dad, his wife excused herself for a moment. She told us when she returned that she had called her daughter, Marge, at work and told her to get home – "right now!"

A little while later Marge drove up, swung out of her VW Bug, and introduced herself – all sparkly-eyed and beaming. Damn! Terry had neglected to mention anything about his sister. She was a California girl, born and raised – soft brown hair streaked with blonde highlights, freckled, tanned to perfection, lively, athletic, and bright. During our conversation, I mentioned that I intended to do some sightseeing in the area over the next couple of days. Marge jumped on the opening.

"Wow! Why don't I show you around? I know all the places and these freeways are pretty tricky to figure out."

"Well ..."

I had wanted to explore San Francisco by myself.

"What about your job? I don't want to inconvenience you."

By this time, I was looking Marge over more closely. I typically felt awkward around girls. Yes, I have to admit that I came shamefully late to the party. With Marge, however, I felt the opposite. Her warm personality and natural smile made me feel completely relaxed and comfortable. She was working at Cal-Tech with her father, and her Mom and Dad chimed in right on cue.

"The job's not a problem!"

So, they settled the matter. I wasn't to be allowed out by myself. I was sure Marge just wanted a ride in my car. Anyway, she and I agreed to set off in the morning.

It was a one-day, whirlwind tour and romance. By the time we had seen the main attractions in San Francisco and driven to the misty top of Mt. Tamalpias in Marin County we were hopelessly in love. It was that fast, but it happened. The next day, we walked hand-in-hand through some towering redwood groves. With Marge by my side, my whole world seemed as it was meant to be.

It was time for me to head down to San Diego, but Marge and I were anxious – drooling – to get together again. The flight from San Francisco to San Diego was an easy commute. Her grandmother had a lovely ranch-style home about fifteen minutes from Naval Air Station Miramar and only three blocks from the sand and surf of La Jolla Beach. At her first opportunity, she flew down for the weekend. Saturday night, I snuck her into the bachelor officer's quarters, and we made mad, wild, passionate love until we – or more accurately, I – couldn't take it anymore. It was a glorious event to be celebrated many times in the future.

Marge's grandmother got used to us going out at night. She would ask with a knowing twinkle in her eye, "Is the fog thick on Mt. Soledad tonight?" or "Going out for ice cream again?" We could only smile and wave as we went out the door. Marge was amazing. We soon graduated to floors in front of a fire, the back seat of my Impala, or any place that was available. Comfort was not a requirement.

Our most outrageous afternoon was in some no-name motel in Anaheim close to Disneyland. The room had glowing stars stuck on the ceiling, red fuzzy wallpaper, and burnt-orange carpeting. Wrought-iron Mexican lamps with globes of blown, yellow glass were especially tacky. Black-velvet paintings hung over a pair of bouncy, queen-sized beds. We brought in a quart of Bacardi, a 6-pack of Cokes, and a bucket of ice. Foreplay became jumping naked from bed-to-bed while trying to hit each other in midair with pillows. We finally collapsed in a heap of feathers and laughed 'til we cried – then we had sex!

After a couple of months, Marge told me that she was concerned that she had missed her period, but that it might just be all the sex or stress of the new relationship. A few weeks later, we were sitting in her car after I had arrived for another wonderful weekend in San Francisco. She took a deep breath and broke the news.

"Roger, I'm pregnant."

"No question?"

Marge rubbed her hands together nervously.

"I went to the doctor. The tests were positive."

"I guess you're telling me it's mine?"

I looked at her with a smirk. Marge rolled her eyes at my attempt at humor.

"Yes, Roger. There's been no one else."

"I'll be shipping out soon and be gone a long time – and with the war, I may not be coming back. This is really a bad time. Maybe you should get an abortion."

"I've thought of that, Roger, but I really want to have your baby – even if you don't want to marry me."

I let her words sink in. I had no doubt that she loved me, and I could not imagine loving anyone more than I loved Marge. There would certainly be problems, but I did not want to lose her. I reached over and held her hand.

"Then I guess we better get married."

Our wedding was on December 30, 1964, culminating what had been, indeed, one helluva year! My new father-in-law never forgave me for "stealing his tax-deduction!" Our first son was born seven months later, or nine months after our stay in that sleazy motel.

•

Life is a lesson that we learn too late.

•

Vacancy – Sorry

One Accident, Two Accidents, Three Accidents ...

MY SQUADRON WAS VF 114 – the "Fighting Aardvarks." We had BC's image of a long-snouted aardvark painted on the tail of our planes. I was riding tandem behind the pilot in the front cockpit. I had been recruited to be a pilot, but my eyes betrayed me. They failed to test 20-20 after an intense weekend of shore leave when I was in pre-flight training. They must have been bloodshot or cross-eyed or something. I was given the choice of flying as a Radar Intercept Officer (RIO) or becoming an enlisted seaman. RIO sounded more exciting so I stuck with aviation.

Unlike the Air Force, the Navy did not install a dual set of flight controls and throttles in the back seat. So, I had no direct command of the aircraft, but it was my job to tell the pilot where to go, how to get there, and what to do when we arrived. Despite the fact that the pilot and I were a well-oiled team, after flying the F4 for four years, and after putting my life in someone else's hands a couple of times a day every day, my nerves had worn a bit thin. Actually, they lay shattered on the cockpit floor. In my opinion, whoever made the decision not to include a dual set of controls for the RIO had made a huge mistake. If I had them, I'm sure I could have prevented a few accidents and also saved myself from a lifetime of distress and pain.

When I wasn't being shot at or crashing, I was having a damn good time. Maybe I should also exclude standing at attention for inspection and making a night landing in a typhoon. Those times were not fun either. The scenery was amazing, however, as we ripped along on our low-level training routes over the southwestern US. A typical exercise would consist of flying 300 knots or greater at 50 feet off the deck, popping over a ridge, flipping inverted, pulling the aircraft back as close as possible to the ground, and finally rolling back upright to get set for the next ridge. We would be so low that our jet blasts kicked up a trail of dust over the desert or a rooster tail of spray over the water. My apologies to the residents of Big Bear and Arrowhead Lakes who were on our course and no doubt dove for cover every time we blasted past.

The towering clouds, the mellow sunrises and sunsets, the deep canyons and valleys – they were all spectacular wherever I was flying. I've flown more than twice the speed of sound and high enough to see the curvature of the earth. And flight operations off a carrier had a sense of incredible power and majestic beauty all their own.

Part of the fun of being a jet-jockey was getting away with stuff that we were not supposed to do – like sneaking under the span of the Golden Gate Bridge on a foggy morning, or cruising through the Grand Canyon beneath the rim, or meandering low-level up Yosemite Valley. In the '60s, those flights were like rites of passage – and we did them as much for the bragging rights as for the thrill of the flights themselves. Flying jets was special, and I loved it.

I was now teamed up with a pilot I will call "Nitro" for the upcoming cruise. My call sign, or "handle," was Ramjet. Nitro controlled the F4 with intense finesse. His formation flying was precise, bombing runs were accurate, and carrier landings were impeccable. It was a pleasure to ride in his back seat, and I had no reservations about going into combat with him.

One night we were flying back to San Diego after a training exercise. Below we saw a freight train making its slow way across the desert.

"Fair game, Ramjet"

I agreed with a thumbs-up.

"Let's wake 'em up,"

We turned off our running lights and flew up behind the train just above the railroad tracks. As we passed over the locomotive, Nitro hit both afterburners, and we climbed straight up to about 10,000 feet – lighting up the sky for a hundred miles. Nitro threw in a few barrel-rolls for good measure.

"Geez, look at that – sure got his attention!"

I looked down and watched the sparks shooting off the train's wheels as they skidded down the tracks. The engineer probably thought he had been attacked by a UFO and was so surprised that he had hit his emergency brakes.

"Gosh, I hope we didn't give the poor guy a heart attack."

I logged that as a successful intercept, and we moseyed on home. Most of the time, however, flying was serious business. During those six years, I squandered more lives than the Navy normally dispenses to anyone. Not counting close calls – like dodging surface-to-air missiles, or getting back to the carrier with bullet holes and flak damage in the aircraft – I had survived three serious landing crashes which could have been deadly and a combat accident which almost blew my young butt out of the sky. One time, we even flew into Japan and landed with a fresh bullet hole in our port engine. The only time the hole could have gotten there was during landing at our "friendly" ally's airbase. Simply stated, I oughta' be dead – many times over.

The first incident happened after a training flight on a very hot day while landing on a short runway at Fallon, Nevada. The heat and the high altitude required a faster landing speed than normal, we had a heavy load of ordinance, and our brakes simply could not slow us down.

"Hold on, Ramjet – can't stop. We're going off the runway!"

We stopped with our landing gear stuck deep in the soft sand just before we buried our nose in the opposite side of a drainage ditch. It was one of those moments when events seem to happen in slow motion – like I was watching the accident unfold before me from outside the aircraft. All I could do was to hang on and brace myself for whatever happened. A bit more speed or a slightly shorter distance, and the accident would have been much worse.

My second training accident happened a few months later. We were the last aircraft in a flight of four coming in for landing. Again, it was a brutally hot day – this time at the Marine Corps Training Center in Yuma, Arizona. Just before touchdown we were caught in the jet wash of the aircraft ahead of us. The air burble dropped our left wing, and our tire hit the runway – blowing it instantly. We left the concrete doing about 130 knots and careened across the desert.

"We're going for a ride, Ramjet!"

"Yee-haw!"

We rocked and bucked through clumps of yucca, brush, and mounds of drifted sand. I could only hope that the plane held together, didn't flip over, or catch fire.

Jack rabbits, rattlesnakes, and cactus were flying in all directions. We plowed through a few thousand feet of desert before coming to a stop with our landing gear buried up to the bottom of the wings. The engines had ingested a few tons of debris, and the frame of the aircraft was twisted beyond repair. I was getting used to going off the runway, however, and the accident didn't bother me much. Just another day at the office flying the hottest aircraft in the skies!

"I would have paid good money for a ride like that, Nitro."

"Yeah, but one of those rides is enough."

The next accident, however, was much more intense and serious. I was the junior back-seat driver in the squadron – "junior" meaning expendable – and was given the dubious honor of flying with a lieutenant commander as he tried to qualify for jet carrier landings. He was a veteran of the Korean War and had hundreds of combat missions and carrier landings to his credit. But these were all in propeller-driven aircraft, and he had never flown jets before. He was slated to be our squadron executive officer – in line to become our skipper – but only after he became jet qualified.

The problem was that carrier landing techniques are different for propeller aircraft as opposed to jets. In a prop plane, you follow the glide slope down until you fly over the fantail at the stern of the ship. Then you cut power, float down, and usually catch one of the arresting cables stretched across the flight deck. As soon as you touch down, you go to full power so that the plane can take off if necessary.

In a jet, if the pilot cuts power over the fantail, you sink like a 20,000 pound hunk of metal and splatter on the deck. The proper technique is to keep the power on all the way to touch down, then hit the afterburners and go to full power. That way the aircraft can get airborne again in case the tail hook fails to catch a wire. Complicating the problem is that the landing speed of a jet is about twice that of a prop-driven aircraft.

So the commander and I practiced and practiced and made over a hundred simulated carrier landings on airport runways. We trained at night, in foul weather, and on bright, clear days. My job was to feed him approach information as we descended on the glide path. Finally, everybody agreed that he was ready for the real thing. The sky was clear, the seas were calm, and the ship was not pitching and rolling as it does in foul weather. We banked into the break and came around to the downwind leg. I read through the check list as we turned on our approach behind the ship. The pilot lowered our flaps, gear, and dropped the tail hook. All was ready. The landing signal officer began talking us down.

"You're in the groove – a little high – take some power off – easy – keep your nose up – don't chase the ball – you're drifting left – bring it back – slow corrections – give me some power – you're doing good – just fly it down."

I watched the whole performance as we came down and coached him from the back seat – trying to sound as calm and re-assuring as possible.

"Keep the power on – you're doing fine – just keep the power on."

We flew over the fantail in good shape. Then, of course, the idiot commander pulled the throttles back. I yelled, "POWER! POWER!" but it was too late.

Sure enough, he had cut the damn engines back to idle. Without power, we stopped flying and down we went – SPLAT! The landing gear collapsed, and we flattened the F4 on the deck like a pancake. By some improbable stroke of good fortune, our tail hook caught a wire, and we came to a sliding, skidding, screeching halt just before we dribbled off the angle of the flight deck.

I just sat in my seat speechless and shaking. The fire team rushed over with extinguishers and sprayed the engines down with foam. My cockpit crew chief climbed up and opened the canopy.

"Nice landing, Sir!"

It took me a while, but I finally looked up at him. I was still shaking.

"Ye – yeah. Right!"

The commander was faster getting out than I was. He came over as I was climbing down. He was trying to act nonchalant and friendly.

"Sorry 'bout that. You OK?"

I'm sure he was more concerned about his flight status. I totally lost my temper.

"Never fucking better! And that's the last time I'll get in a cockpit with your sorry ass!"

Some gross insubordination was appropriate at that moment – not that I gave a damn. My adrenalin was pumping in high gear as I stomped away. I don't need to repeat what I was thinking as I tossed my gear down in the ready room. It took some senior officers and a couple of shots of medicinal brandy to calm me down. Wherever the commander's mind was when he pulled the throttles back, he damn sure wasn't thinking about landing an F4.

I was not senior enough to know how accidents were handled as part of an aviator's record. I also do not know at what point a pilot (or air crew member for that matter) loses his wings. In my opinion, however, the first two "incidents" should not have been considered the pilot's fault and probably had no negative effect on his records.

The Commander's performance, however, most certainly went to an accident board and was determined to be pilot error. He disappeared for a period of retraining, but came back months later and assumed his position as executive officer. He must have gotten himself straightened out, however no – I never flew with him again. Clearly, the Navy did everything possible to keep their aviators in the air. They would lose a huge investment in training and experience if they let any warm body go that could be thrown against the enemy.

One fine afternoon, Nitro and I were in the middle of a dogfight training exercise. We were twisting upside down and turning in a dive to get on the tail of the opposing aircraft (or bogey) so we could simulate getting off a missile to shoot it down. The bogey was trying its best to do the same to us. The flight was turning into a regular free-for-all when I heard a message over the radio's emergency frequency.

"Miramar Tower calling Ramjet – come in Ramjet – over."

I had to catch my breath for a moment.

"Roger, Tower – Ramjet here – what can I do for you?"

"Ah – Ramjet, your squadron ops officer called. It seems Mrs. Ramjet is having your baby. She asks if you might be able to come home and take her to the hospital."

"Copy, Tower. Damn! You sure? – She was supposed to hold it 'til tonight!"

"Funny, Ramjet, but I think you better hurry home – now!"

"Oh. OK, Tower – on my way – be right there!"

We broke off the dogfight and slammed the beast into afterburner. La Jolla Shores got hit with our sonic boom, and the next thing I knew we were trying to slow down enough to land before we got to Arizona. That night, Jeff came kicking and screaming into the world. It was the first time a baby was flown in by an F4 rather than a stork.

•

Unfortunately, Navy-issue babies do not come starched, pressed,
and obedient to commands.

•

24

Into The Jaws Of War

A FEW MONTHS LATER, it was time to deploy and head to the South China Sea. I had managed to survive training in one piece. Saying goodbye to Marge and Jeff was a difficult and anxious moment. Last year she had been a carefree, twenty-year-old with few worries or responsibilities. Now, she was a mother of our son and the wife of a Naval Aviator. Our futures were intertwined, but mine was far less certain. Marge put on a very brave face. There were kisses, tears, promises, and lots more kisses. One thing was certain, however. Our love would span the oceans no matter how far we were apart.

Our carrier was the USS KITTY HAWK – CVA 63. The cruise west was time spent mostly with lectures and training manuals. Tactics were intensely reviewed and retrained. We received intelligence briefings about current events in Southeast Asia. Somehow, the material in our classified briefings frequently had no resemblance to the information we were fed on the news. We studied the geography of Vietnam, Laos, and Thailand. The carrier would first be assigned to Dixie Station off South Vietnam where we would provide close air support for allied ground forces. Then we would rotate north to Yankee Station in the Tonkin Gulf and make bombing raids against North Vietnamese assets. We would also fly combat air patrol (CAP) against any MIGs operating out of Hanoi that might test our air defenses.

I was assigned the additional billet of Power Plants Officer, which meant that I was responsible for all squadron engine maintenance. I did not know much about engines, but I had a great chief who assumed that chore for himself. He basically told me to butt out.

"I'll take care of the engines, Sir. You just fly the airplanes."

That was fine with me.

"Great, Chief, but if you need backup for any reason, I want to know about it. I'm here to be useful if I can."

Our squadron did not lose a single aircraft from engine failure the whole cruise. I salute all the fine work that our maintenance crews did –especially my Chief Knowles. I gratefully thank you all!

The KITTTY HAWK had readiness trials scheduled when we reached the waters off Hawaii. The squadron tests involved bombing, missile firings, air-to-air intercepts, and carrier landing skills. The results were a critical indicator of our abilities and also an evaluation factor of our skippers and the executive teams. We could not allow ourselves to get a low rating and had practiced until every tactic and drill had become second nature.

One "problem," however, came up that I did not expect. Because we were going to a war zone, the carrier was loaded with extra aircraft to replace some that had already been lost, and there were too many aircraft aboard to conduct flight operations. The only solution was to fly some of the planes off to Hawaii for the duration of the exercise. Much to my surprise, as I was the junior flight officer in our squadron – and the one most likely to screw up – I had to fly one of the planes ashore. I objected strenuously, of course, but eventually had to give in. Drat! I was billeted for a week at the Fort De Russy Military Reservation in Honolulu – right on Waikiki Beach. Toughest duty I've ever had. I swam in the surf, drank Mai-Tais, and stared at the bikini-clad wahinis. I rented a jeep and drove around the island. I went to Pearl Harbor and saw the Arizona Memorial. It was the best damn way to go to war that I could imagine!

Somehow, the squadron scored well in the exercise without me, and it was time to continue heading west again. Strange things seemed to be the norm in Western Pacific waters. It was not unusual for the fleet to get a flyover by Russian Bears – long range, heavy bombers specially equipped with photo-reconnaissance gear. Their mission was to get photographs of the fleet, so they could count ships and aircraft and maybe spot other gear that we might have onboard. Our mission was to escort them in and fly underneath their camera bays to prevent them from getting pictures. The Russians must have a special folder somewhere with lots of photos of us giving them the finger. We had two aircraft and crew constantly hooked up to the catapult and ready for immediate launch if any inbound hostile contact was spotted on the ship's radar.

One calm night as the carrier plowed west through the ocean swells, I was one of the CAP crews on duty. Sure enough, the ship identified an unknown contact, 70 miles out and closing. We started the engines, cranked up our radar, and blasted off into the night. Already this was strange because how were the Russians going to get pictures at night? Perhaps they were testing some new infra-red photography or radar imaging technology. As soon as we got airborne the ship's combat information center (CIC) started giving us vectors, distance, and altitude to the bogey. We accelerated in afterburner and headed to intercept the target. My radar came up, and I started to sweep the area. I should have been able to pick up anything airborne inside of 50 miles.

"Let us know when you have him, Ramjet."

"Roger – nothing yet."

"He's bearing 290 – 45 miles from you, Ramjet. We've got him at about 25,000 feet."

"Copy Control – still don't have anything."

"Ramjet – target now inbound at 40 miles – 290 degrees – descending – elevation 23,000 feet. We've got a hard paint on him. We're launching the second CAP."

I'm trying frantically to find the contact. The radar is working fine. I'm getting returns from everything else – like clouds, ocean waves, and ships. I should be able to pick it up without a problem.

"Control, this is Ramjet – I've got nothing – you sure it isn't a bug in the system?"

"Negative, Ramjet. We're tracking a clear target. You're almost on top of him. Let us know if you get a visual. It's now five miles out – coming by on your port side."

The moon was bright and visibility was good. We started to bank and swerve to try to see anything.

"Still nothing – sorry,"

"Roger, Ramjet, return to the ship. Let us know if you see anything on the way in."

The second CAP came on the air. They also could not find anything except thousands of miles of ocean, the moon, and millions of stars. I never heard anything else about it, but maybe the ship reported it as a UFO. It was a mystery.

I had one other incident while sailing west to Dixie Station. Nitro and I were flying under the ship's control in thick storm clouds at night. We had been grinding around in a racetrack pattern experiencing heavy turbulence for over an hour. Suddenly, without warning, a blinding flash – brighter than any spotlight – lit up the sky and shone directly in our eyes. Nitro was as shaken as I was. He immediately banked hard and pulled down to avoid a collision. Nothing happened. He leveled out and got the light shining off our

27

port wing. We had been circling all night in murky darkness and had unexpectedly come out of the clouds. The moon had caught us by surprise, and we damn near flew right into it!

Larger Than Life

Chapter 6

Bombs Fell Like Rain From Angry Clouds

WE EVENTUALLY ARRIVED at Dixie Station and commenced combat operations. I typically flew two missions a day, occasionally three. We would launch at dawn with a load of rockets and 250 pound bombs for close air support. On our way in, we were transferred to a forward air controller (FAC) who was flying in a light aircraft low over the jungle to spot enemy activity. When he saw something, he would mark the spot with smoke or white phosphorous flares and direct us in. We would make multiple runs with the FAC telling us where to adjust our drops.

When we were done, the FAC would fly over the area and give us a count of bodies, vehicles, thatched buildings (hooches), or even water buffalo that we had hit. We had to report those numbers back to the ship's intelligence officer. He had to report them to command and, eventually, all the numbers from all the flights and all the commands were compiled, and our Defense Secretary, Robert McNamara, reported them on the stateside evening news.

Speaking of McNamara's War, our re-supply logistics were so bad that sometimes we barely had enough bombs or rockets to fly a mission. But the mission count was critical to McNamara – and to other bean-counters in Washington – and we were frequently loaded with only two 250 pounders, when we could carry approximately 16,000 pounds of missiles, rockets, and bombs. They might as well have armed us with firecrackers. It made no sense because they were endangering two flight crew members and a $3,000,000 aircraft for one or two runs on a suspected target. We would have to make a direct hit to do more than dent a tin can or scare whoever might be down there. "Stupid!" is the only way I can describe it. The more this happened, the more I resented it, and I was not alone. I had no problem risking my neck in combat – just give me the fire power to make it worthwhile.

Occasionally, we were lucky enough to get a full load of ordinance. Early one morning, we were transferred to a FAC immediately after flying over the coast. He had a compound manned by South Vietnamese Army troops that was close to being overrun by the Vietcong. We flew over and could see the intense battle unfolding on the ground. The VC were about to breach the barbed-wire fence line of the compound with a vastly superior number of troops, but the South Vietnamese had so far held them off from their dugout positions. The FAC told us that the situation was critical – our forces would soon be out of ammunition. His strained voice reflected the urgency of the situation.

"F4s – drop the bombs right on the fence line."

"That's awfully close to our troops."

"No option. Roll in when ready."

"Copy – on the fence line."

There were four aircraft in our flight, and we each made four bombing runs. All of the ordinance landed on target, and the VC were decimated. The few who survived made a swift retreat into the jungle. The FAC flew over the compound and gave us the body count. Then he came back on the radio.

"The commander would like to thank you guys for saving their asses. Great shooting!"

We flew low over the compound dipping our wings, and the troops were waving back at us. This made it personal. If ever I felt good about what I was doing in the war – this was the time.

•

The world needs a law to require any of our esteemed leaders
that would drag us into a war on false pretenses to stand on some high ground
between the opposing armies and fire the first shot. I'll provide a T-shirt with
bright red targets printed front and back so everyone will know who it is.

•

The Height Of Absurdity Is When Combat Becomes Routine

AFTER OUR 30 DAY TOUR on Dixie Station, we headed north to the Tonkin Gulf to operate from Yankee Station. These flights were much different. We were usually directed to interdict the enemy's supply lines along the Ho Chi Min Trail or to hit primary targets such as bridges or barges that intel had identified from reconnaissance flights the day before. Anti-aircraft sites could pepper the skies with flak at any moment. Enemy MIGs were out there, but they would always scamper back to their airfield when we turned to pursue them. They were bait – trying to lure us into their ground fire. North Vietnamese airfields were off limits to our bombers, and we couldn't attack their aircraft once they were on the ground. This was the Administration's version of a limited war. OK, they were concerned about giving China an excuse to join the war, but what kind of baloney was that!

Sometimes, we participated in strikes on significant targets in and around Hanoi. These were called "alpha strikes" when the Air Force, Marines, and Navy were all involved against a major asset like the Hai Phong Bridge or a large power plant. I participated in one such strike near Hanoi that became a major gaggle. We had every attack aircraft on the ship that was flyable (some 60 planes) in the air. Another carrier, the USS RANGER CVA-61, sent a comparable number of planes, and the Marines and Air Force each committed another 25 aircraft or so. The Air Force assigned even more planes for air cover, and the Marines were responsible for flak suppression. Army helicopters provided search and rescue for any downed aircrews.

The strike had been meticulously planned. The flights had windows of only a few minutes to make their runs and then depart the area. The timing was critical because the next group could not start their attacks until the previous flight got out of the way. If that didn't happen, the following flight would have to wait and circle until it could commence its attack on the target. However, getting that many aircraft turned around in an orderly formation while being blasted by anti-aircraft fire proved to be impossible. The first Air Force flight arrived late and everybody else got backed-up accordingly. We rolled in for our run going in the opposite direction from what we had planned and had to dodge other planes that were still in their dives. At the peak of the attack, two A5 Vigilantes – supersonic Navy reconnaissance aircraft – came screaming through to get photos of the bomb damage. Unfortunately, bombs were still falling on the target and it was obscured by thick clouds of smoke. Nitro looked at me in his mirror and shouted into the intercom.

"Which way out of here?"

I was as turned around as he was, but remembered from our briefings that 110 degrees was the quickest route to the Gulf.

"Hit the deck – head 110!"

We got right down on the roof tops and screamed over Hanoi at about 450 knots. The North Vietnamese were hanging out their windows, shooting pistols, and shaking their fists at us. I remember how strange it felt – seeing them and the beautiful planters of flowers on their French-colonial balconies as we raced by. We were soon over water and headed southeast to the ship. It took us awhile to get back in formation, but we made it – and by some unlikely stroke of good fortune – nobody was missing. For all that, however, the target was hit, but not destroyed.

Every few weeks while on Yankee station, our air group would lose an aircraft and its crew. It was easy for me to imagine myself as one of those missing-in-action airmen. I would visualize myself exploding in a fireball as we were hit by anti-aircraft fire, or flew into a "cloud full of rocks" – as we were fond of saying. It was clear that even if I had been the best RIO in the fleet, I could not protect myself from some unpredictable accident. The feeling began to make me very uncomfortable and queasy. Perhaps that was normal, but the effect was very real. Some nights it was difficult to clear my head and get to sleep. Fatigue was setting in. Daily operations and back-to-back strikes were becoming a stressful ordeal.

When we were not doing flight operations, I was fond of climbing to the deck and standing at the bow as the ship rose and plunged with the waves. The speed of the carrier would generate stiff winds and I could lean into them, spread my arms, and believe I was flying. (This was before the movie TITANIC, thank you.) If the weather was stormy, spray would soak me like I was in a hurricane. Other times I would stand on the stern and look forward. When seas were rough, I could watch the bow rise above the horizon – then fall and bury itself in the waves. The midsection of the 1068-foot carrier would bend upward as a wave passed under the hull or twist as a swell hit the ship from an angle. Such incredibly dynamic and powerful forces always gave me a real sense of my irrelevance – as if the carrier was a force of nature all by itself.

President Johnson declared a "stand down" over Christmas and New Year's 1965-66 as a goodwill gesture to Hanoi. It was a good time to catch up on paperwork, write letters, and rest. When I wrote to Marge, there was not much news I was allowed to report, so they were just "I Miss You" and "I Love You" letters. After my chores were done, there was little to do but lay in my rack for hours and think of my family back home.

•

Loneliness sleeps with its cousin, Depression.

•

On Christmas Eve, I was in my bunk and imagining what special things Marge had done for Jeff on his first Christmas. I scattered the photographs I had received on my pillow and looked at them for the hundredth time. She had sprinkled perfume (Shalimar) on her portrait, which created a string of lonesome memories every time I looked at it. I finally got tired, rolled over on my back, and turned out my light. But it was hours before I got to sleep. Images of my family continued to play in my mind. I longed to be with them. I imagined being close to Marge, but the distance between us always dragged me back to reality. If there was any place in the world I would rather not have been, it was stuck in that steel box on the wrong side of the planet. Those few days of stand-down were the loneliest days of my life.

Phantom on Patrol
US Navy Photo

The Fruits Of War Are Bitter To The Core

THE STAND-DOWN DID NOTHING except allow both sides time to take on supplies and rearm. After New Year's, we returned to combat with a vengeance and were allowed to attack objectives around Hanoi that were previously off limits. That was good, but they were in the most heavily defended areas of North Vietnam.

Many of our missions, both day and night, were to hit the North Vietnamese supply lines along the Ho Chi Min Trail. The objective of night attacks was to catch the large convoys that traveled only after dark. If nothing else, we would keep everybody awake down there and make them tired the next day. With specific objectives, we might be loaded with 500 pound bombs or larger – up to 2000 pounders. Other times, we were loaded with cluster bomb units (CBUs) or sometimes 2.75 inch (70mm) rocket pods. The rockets were not accurate, but they could spray a deadly pattern around a target.

The CBUs (a little larger than hand grenades) could be set with timers to explode up to 24 hours after they landed. "Clusters" of them were launched from tubes, and they had small fins that snapped out when they were deployed so they would disperse over a large area. Some North Vietnamese soldier (or poor farmer) could be walking along a footpath, and one of these bombs would go off next to him without warning. Sometimes, we would weave our way over the Trail releasing strings of cluster bombs without timers as we went. Then we would fly back on our course and watch as they floated to the ground. The entire valley would light up with blasts and secondary explosions. CBUs were recognized as an indiscriminate weapon and never used on residential areas.

One time, we made a daytime strike with a full load of 250 pound bombs. Nitro and I were the fourth aircraft in a usual flight of four. We were transferred over to a FAC who had spotted a truck park underneath a thick jungle canopy. We couldn't see the trucks from our altitude, but the FAC swore they were there and fired a smoke flare to mark the location. Even though we dropped our bombs right on target, we saw no return fire or secondary explosions after any of our runs.

Nitro and I rolled in to make the flight's final drop. We pulled out at the bottom of our dive and intense ground fire erupted from the jungle. The VC could easily see as we pulled out when we had no ordinance left with which to hit them. They jumped out of their holes and fired everything they had at us. A hail of tracers zipped past our canopy. The aircraft got hit several times, and we had to fly to Da Nang to get our hydraulic system repaired, but the F4 was a damn tough bird to bring down.

The North Vietnamese began to introduce surface-to-air (SAM) missiles, which were dangerously proficient at blasting our aircraft out of the sky. Our only defense was to see the missile coming at us before we were hit. They were compared to "flying telephone poles," and the F4 could out-maneuver one if the aircrew saw it in time. Different strike tactics had to be developed. Aircraft always flew in pairs to get better visibility and would swerve and weave to watch each other's tail – a maneuver called "jinking." We also flew in at low altitude, below the enemy's radar, all the way to the target. The North Vietnamese were listening to our attack transmissions to determine our locations – so we observed strict radio silence.

A row of colored warning lights was mounted in the cockpit. A white light showed that a SAM radar site was searching the area. Yellow indicated that the launch site radar was tracking an aircraft, and red meant that a missile was in the air and homing in on its target. If we saw any of these lights, we were to call out "CODE WHITE," "CODE YELLOW," or "CODE RED." Any other communication could give away our position to the North Vietnamese.

On one strike, Nitro and I were flying in over the coast with two flights of four – a total of eight aircraft. Our target was close to Hanoi, so we expected to see SAMs and everything else the North Vietnamese could fire at us. Our only communication was to be through hand signals – total radio silence except in an emergency. Weaving tactics were great between us and our wingman, but keeping track of the other aircraft in the flight was more difficult. We had not received much ground fire, and the radios were quiet.

Suddenly – all our warning lights came on, and three SAM sites launched missiles at us at the same time. Instead of "CODE RED," someone blurted out over the air:

"IT'S A FUCKING SAM! – DIVE! – DIVE!"

All eight planes dove every which-way for the deck. It's tough trying to evade missiles when you're laughing so damn hard and trying to avoid your own aircraft. Adrenaline quickly brought us back to reality, however. Radio silence was blown, so we were free to communicate as needed.

"Watch it, 401 – we're passing under your nose." (All aircraft in our squadron were numbered starting with 400.)

"Flak eleven o'clock! – Hard right! – Hard right!"

"411 – We took a hit! – Backup electric only."

"This is Number One. 411 – Break off and head for the ship. 405 – Follow him back – good luck!"

No crippled aircraft was ever left to fly solo over North Vietnam.

"Target – One o'clock – Rolling in."

F4s were crisscrossing and flashing by in all directions. Missiles swooped harmlessly overhead – our altitude was too low for their radar to effectively track us. Anti-aircraft fire filled the sky with flak. Streams of tracers from their bunkered sites made the guns easy to spot and dodge around. Our bombs successfully found the target despite the heavy barrage thrown against us. Tactics and training were important, but a measure of good luck often made the difference in getting safely home.

•

Real luck – not the kind that we make for ourselves – is a fluke of fate.

•

F4B Phantom II – On the Cat
US Navy Photo

Chapter 9

Last Strike And I'm Out

OUR DAYS SEEMED TO BLEND TOGETHER – one after the other – after the other. Five months into the cruise, I racked up my 100th combat mission. Half of those strikes were over North Vietnam, and most of those were at night.

On one ordinary strike – like all the others – it happened. Nitro and I had a piece-of-cake target – a line of barges right on the coast south of Hai Phong Harbor. As usual, we were the fourth aircraft in our flight. The sky was so hazy that there was no visible horizon for reference. I guided us in to our entry point by radar, and we popped up to our roll-in altitude right over the beach. By the time the barges were in sight, however, it was too late to get a good position for our dive because the other aircraft had to roll in first. We were much too close to the target and that made our dive too steep. What happened next I have to call pilot error – specifically "target fixation." Nitro was so intensely engrossed on the barges that he was not aware of anything but the target – not me, the aircraft, or even the ground. He didn't hear me yelling over the intercom:

"We're too fast! We're too steep! Dammit – WE'RE TOO LOW!"

We blazed through 800 feet in a 50 degree dive doing about 450 knots, and I'm now screaming:

"PULL OUT! – PULL OUT!! – PULL OUT!!!"

Seconds later at about 500 feet, Nitro finally woke up and yanked back on the stick. The aircraft shuddered and strained against the violent forces trying to pull it apart – forces far beyond its design limits. I fully expected the plane to shake to pieces, but it held together, and our nose slowly pulled up above the horizon.

We were still rapidly losing precious altitude and had only seconds before we plowed into the ground. Vapor trails streamed off the wings. I have no idea how many Gs we actually pulled, but the meter was pegged at maximum. Our wings were bending up in an unnatural curve, and if they didn't break off, I was certain we would crash anyway. To make matters worse, Nitro had been releasing bombs in our dive. Normally, gravity separates the bombs from the plane as it pulls out. Now, however, because we were so steep, we were following them down as they fell beneath the aircraft!

I was holding my breath, grasping the rails of the canopy in a death grip, and bracing myself for impact – which would be fruitless if we crashed into the ground at 450 knots. Ejecting at this speed was not an option. My parachute would have been torn to shreds when it opened – if it even had time to open. The only thing left of me would be a bloody smudge at the bottom of a blackened pit in the sand.

At the last possible second, we mushed through the bottom of our dive. The ground was so close I could reach out and touch it, and our bombs started to explode beneath us. I heard and felt them.

"THUD – THUD – THUD."

Shrapnel from the blasts ripped through the fuselage, tore off large pieces of our wings, and blew our starboard engine completely out of the aircraft!

Ironically, the bomb blasts, which could have killed us, may have actually saved us. The explosions created extra cushions of air that lifted us just enough to clear the beach. We were already forcing a compression wave against the ground – called "ground effect" – that was helping us recover from the dive. I felt the extra pressure pushing us up each time a bomb went off underneath the aircraft. We bottomed out so low that we were literally flying through beach grass growing on top of the dunes. We weren't really flying – it was more like staggering home drunk on one leg. We were in serious trouble!

Our one remaining engine was on fire, but it had to be kept in afterburner to keep us airborne. It could have disintegrated or exploded at any moment. Jet fuel and hydraulic fluid were pouring out of holes and cracks in the wings and fuselage, the electrical system had failed, the emergency power generator was inoperable, the cockpit was full of smoke, and a circuit breaker panel beside my leg was shooting out sparks and flames. The metal frame of my seat was so hot that it burned a hole through my leather glove. That was not good because it was mounted just forward of a tank filled with 2000 pounds of jet fuel. Sections of our wings had been torn away, and they had indeed been permanently bent up as we had pulled out. I was shaking so badly that I had trouble unstrapping my survival radio from my vest. When I finally got it out of its pocket, it was useless because my fingers could only fumble around the buttons.

How we made it over the coast, I honestly don't know. I'll give Nitro credit for an incredible feat of flying – but only after he almost killed us. Without hydraulic pressure and electrical power, he had to muscle the flight controls to keep us airborne. If we lost our second engine there would be no time to eject. My first reaction was to get out as we were now somewhat stabilized. I looked outside the canopy, however, and saw a fleet of North Vietnamese junks with sailors firing machine guns at us. We flew through a hail of tracer fire and were so close to the junks that I could see the fierce expressions on the faces of the sailors as we flew by. I'm sure they hit us, but we were so full of holes already that it did not make any difference.

Oh well, I remember thinking to myself. One way or another I'm going to die in this damn airplane.

Any death would be preferable, however, to being captured and spending years wasting away in some North Vietnamese prison camp. I had made the decision before I flew my first combat mission that I would die before being captured. I felt totally hopeless and did not expect to make it back to the ship in any event. I had already accepted my death, so if I crashed it didn't matter. I stuck with the plane and waited for the worst.

Miraculously, we stayed airborne – just barely skipping over the waves – and flew beyond the range of the junks. The smoke gradually cleared from the cockpit, and I was able to take better stock of our situation. We had no radios or intercom, so Nitro and I had to use hand signals to communicate. I noticed the fuel gauge in the front cockpit steadily unwinding as fuel kept pouring out of our damaged wings. I stared grimly as the numbers wound down and prepared to eject when the engine went silent. The dials hesitated a moment as they hit zero – and then just started to unwind again from the top. The engine kept running, but there was no way of knowing how much fuel was left in the tanks. We were flying, and that was all that mattered.

The aircraft gradually gained a few hundred feet of altitude and limped back to the carrier. There was no way, however, that we could land because the landing gear would not come down, we were still losing fuel, the flaps were inoperable, we were flying with manual controls only, and – oh yes – our one engine was still on fire. A wingman flew alongside and signaled for us to eject. Nitro and I agreed through hand signals, and I prepared to go out first – standard procedure as we were trained to do.

But not so fast. It was only then that I realized that I had another major problem. I could not lower my seat prior to the ejection as we had no electrical power. I always flew with my seat adjusted as high as possible in combat situations because the visibility was much better. My helmet was almost touching the top of the canopy. This configuration meant that the force of the explosive charge on the seat would be severely amplified. My head would probably hit the canopy as I went out causing serious injury. I knew that, but again – I did not have much of a choice. The plane would not float, and nobody had ever survived a ditching in an F4. The only thing I could do was position myself as low as possible in the seat and hope for the best.

I arranged myself, took a deep breath, and pulled hard on the ejection handle. NOTHING happened! The sequence should have been instantaneous. I waited – and waited some more. Damn! My heart sank in despair. I had visions of myself trapped in the cockpit – gasping for my last breath as water flowed in around me and the aircraft sank to the bottom of the Tonkin Gulf. It took me a moment to get my wits about me and figure out what went wrong. The handle had caught on the visor of my helmet because the seat was so high. That prevented it from coming out far enough to activate the ejection sequence. But my seat was possibly armed, and I could be blown out of the aircraft at any second.

I thought briefly of using the alternate means of ejecting. I could have pulled an emergency lever on my canopy and blown it clear of the aircraft and then pulled a secondary handle located in the seat between my legs. That is precisely what I should have done. But I was concerned that the primary handle, which I had already pulled, would flop around and hit me in the head as I went out. That should have been a minor concern because I was wearing a helmet, but I was not thinking clearly.

I left the alternate means as a last resort and decided to try the original sequence again. I scrunched down as low as possible and desperately pulled the handle with all my might. This time I made sure that it came out far over my helmet visor. Unfortunately, the fabric that attached the handle to the ejection seat pulled my head down as I yanked it forward. This caused my neck and back to be bent over as the charge exploded in the seat and blasted me free of the cockpit.

Excruciating pains ripped through my neck and lower back as muscles tore and vertebrae mashed together. The ejection handle snapped back and hit my helmet with such force that it cracked the heavy fiberglass shell. My head may have also hit the canopy as I went out, but in any event I was knocked unconscious. The next thing I remember when I came to was that I was swinging uncontrollably in the parachute.

The carrier was close by on one side, and a rescue helicopter was following me down on the other. I saw Nitro eject in the distance and watched the crippled aircraft fall into the sea. I managed to inflate the float rings around my waist. Then I realized that my left shoulder was separated, and my arm was flopping painfully at my side. I grabbed my left arm with my right and held on as I swung up almost horizontally to the ocean. I came down with a bone-jarring smack as I hit the calm water – every bit as hard as a concrete tarmac. Pain again thrashed through every nerve of my body. Seconds later, a rescue corpsman from the helicopter dropped into the water and swam next to me.

"Quite a show, Lieutenant! Stay calm, and we'll get you out of this. You doing OK? Do you want the basket or can you make it up in the sling?"

"Thanks, man! Good to see you! The sling will be OK."

At that moment, I did not realize how badly I was hurt. I was more concerned about being able to fly again than acknowledging the extent of my injuries. I was afraid that my aviation career might end if I displayed any weakness. It was like when I was growing up: "Walk it off!" "No pain, no gain!" "Don't let a little pain slow you down!" "What are you – some kind of pussy?" I had worked through pain before and would shrug it off again.

The corpsman cut me out of the tangled parachute cords, released my straps, and swam me in a cross-chest carry to the rescue harness. I almost didn't make it up to the helicopter, however, because my left shoulder was stretching further apart as they winched me higher, and I came close to slipping out of the sling. But I squeezed my arms together tightly and was hauled into the helo by the smiling crew members. I was so exuberant and grateful to see their friendly faces that the pain didn't matter. We landed on the carrier within minutes. They offered to carry me on a stretcher to sickbay, but I insisted that I could walk across the deck and climb down the ladders by myself. The deck crews made a path for me and cheered as I hobbled past them. My back was bent over, and I clutched my left arm to my side, but I let go briefly and waved back gratefully.

Thanks guys! Add that experience to my collection of "Proud Moments" that will be with me forever.

The adrenaline rush lasted until I got on the flight surgeon's examining table, and I began to realize the painful extent of my injuries. I had seen the last of the inside of a cockpit for some time.

If ever there was an accident that could cause PTSD, this was it. It met every conceivable definition of the term. However, I had never heard of PTSD. It never occurred to me that I wouldn't get through my pain. My memories of the accident were generally pushed aside when I was busy. However, some unpredictable event would frequently snap my mind back to re-live this horrific experience, or my mind would drift for a moment and allow some frightful memory to surface unexpectedly. I could brush the images aside for a while, but they would always find a way to interrupt whatever positive progress I was making. I missed whatever connection there might have been between my experience and the problems I had seen in my father.

For the next few weeks, my injuries were so painful that I could barely get out of my bunk, but I gradually became able to stand and walk around. I couldn't bend over or even sit for any length of time without having shooting pains in my back. No one feels someone else's acute pain, however. As I improved, some of my squadron mates thought I was a slacker because I was not able to fly. I received some sour looks – even from Nitro, who never once spoke to me after the accident. I suppose I got the silent treatment from him because he resented that I told the truth about what happened and didn't try to say we were hit by enemy fire. I have no idea what he wrote in his accident report, but from his arrogant behavior I have to suspect that his description of the event did not jibe mine. Official records stated the cause of the accident as "Hit by target debris." Incidentally, Nitro survived without injury and was flying the next day. I became the ready room duty officer, managing schedules and taking phone messages for two months until the end of the cruise.

Homeward Bound
US Navy Photo

We were finally relieved from duty on Yankee Station and headed home. We had seen Vietnam, the Philippines, Hong Kong, Japan, and Hawaii. Our cruise home was uneventful, and we reached the states eight months after we had departed. I could not fly ashore with the squadron because I had not yet been cleared for flight status, so I stayed with the KITTY HAWK as it sailed into San Diego harbor.

Homecoming – 1966
US Navy Photo

War Left Behind, But Memories Followed

OUR HOMECOMING AFTER THE LONG, combat cruise was even more emotional and moving than I could have had imagined. Indeed, all homecomings are special events. A military band played stirring patriotic music. Thousands of families waving flags waited impatiently as tugboats maneuvered the carrier – this massive mountain of a ship – next to the pier. Officers and enlisted men in their dress whites streamed down the gangplanks to meet their wives and families after being apart for many months too long. It was a spectacle – almost electric with emotion and anticipation. There were screams and tears and laughter as couples experienced the thrill of reuniting with each other. Both the accumulated pressures of sea duty and waiting anxiously at home were released at that single moment. Joy and happiness permeated the air for everybody gathered there.

I was one of those happy souls – lifted by the atmosphere and spirits of the crowd. I had spotted Marge and Jeff while I was still standing on the flight deck. She saw me as I made my way down the gangplank, and we waved excitedly to each other through the sea of white uniforms. I reached them and gave Marge a brief hug and a kiss before I turned my attention to Jeff. He was holding a small flag in one hand and a Frisbee in the other. I knelt down in front of him. He was a year old now and certainly didn't remember anything about me. I gave him a little hug and tried to be friendly and casual.

"How you doing, big guy?"

He was so cute in his green shorts with suspenders, an open white shirt, white knee socks, and new shoes held on with leather straps and small brass buckles.

He looked at me awkwardly and fought to get over his shyness.

"Can we play Frisbee, Daddy?"

"Sure Jeff. Anytime you want."

But Marge recognized the lingering extent of my injuries as she watched me painfully stand back up.

45

"Are you OK?"

"Still a little stiff and sore, but I've come a long way."

I always tried hard to be nonchalant about the accident. My behavior didn't match my bluster, however. I had changed from the happy, confident man who had flown away eight months before. We hugged each other like we would never let go again. I kissed her on her neck and buried my face in her hair. She whispered in my ear.

"I have a present for you, but it's at home!"

The smell of her sexy perfume, the touch of her cheek, her lips, her soft neck, the feel of her silky hair, and the immediate press of her body against mine was making my body scream urgently for more.

"How soon can we get there?"

I had 30 days shore leave after our homecoming. Marge, Jeff, and I had a wonderful time relaxing and getting to know each other again. All too soon, however, I had to go back to work. The squadron was now flying out of NAS Miramar while the ship was in the yard. My back and other injuries felt well enough to fly, and I was declared fit for duty. But I soon discovered that my injuries were painfully aggravated every time we pulled extra Gs in a turn, or in a dog fight, or when we recovered from a bombing dive. I also found that I became extremely anxious before and during each flight. That was the worst part. I was even afraid during any mild maneuver that pointed the nose of the aircraft toward the ground – which was a good deal of the time. I was clenching my teeth, grasping my seat, and expecting to die during every landing. I could not purge the angry ghosts from my mind.

The vivid memories, hopelessness, and fears were amplified in my dreams and nightmares. I frequently woke up in the middle of the night having relived the accident in crystal-clear detail. Sometimes, I dreamed that I was in a bombing run and desperately trying to break through the canopy with my fists as I was about to fly into the ground. Or I was trapped in the cockpit while it flooded and rolled over and over and sank into the murky darkness at the bottom of the sea. I would wake up in terror just before the impact of the aircraft or before I drowned. I tried hard, however, to hide the extent of what I was going through physically and psychologically. Marge would be lying peacefully beside me when I woke up, desperately searching for a way back to reality.

When dawn rose over the hills, however, I always went back to being a naval aviator. I became a different person when I put my uniform on. It was a matter of pride, and I was determined not to show any weakness. I believed that these problems would go away with time, and to some extent, they did. I desperately wanted to keep flying, so I kept them to myself. I took over-the-counter medications for my pain and relied on alcohol to find relief from my acute anxieties. Drinking was no longer just for fun – it had become a necessary crutch that allowed me to function. Considering the needs of my family, however, it was certainly a double-edged sword.

Our squadron Executive Officer called me into his office one day. I stood at attention until he looked up from his papers.

"At ease, Blake. I've got some news for you. I think you'll like this. We've worked out a transfer for you. We think you've probably seen enough combat for a while. Your next duty station will be at NAS Oceana in Virginia Beach with VF 102 – the Diamondbacks. How does that sound?"

WOW! I was excited, but tried not to appear that I had hoped for a transfer ever since I had returned from the last cruise. I was thrilled, of course.

"Great Sir! Thank you, Sir."

"Your next cruise will be to the Mediterranean on the USS AMERICA CVA-66. Do think you can manage that?"

He looked at me slyly. I wondered if he, or anyone else, had picked up on the problems I was trying so hard to hide. Was this why I was being transferred? I did not want to learn the answer, so I did not ask the question.

"Sounds pretty tough, Sir, but I'll sure do my best."

He handed me my orders and smiled.

"Goodbye, Ramjet. Good luck."

I gripped the orders, snapped to attention, and gave him a crisp salute. I did an about-face without falling over backwards and marched out the door. What a break! Vietnam was history. Well, it was gone – but hardly forgotten!

•

History judges some wars as necessary and others not. Either way, mankind seems destined to ignore the lessons of previous conflicts and march off to battle – regardless of the immeasurable expense to itself and the ultimate threat to all humanity.

•

Back In The Cockpit Again

MARGE AND I SAID GOODBYE to friends and family in California and packed up a few things for the trip. The Navy shipped our household items, so all that had to be done was cancel the phone, reroute the mail, load the car, and go. I left with a sense of relief and anticipation. Not much time was spent along the way. We needed to save what little money we had for getting settled in Virginia Beach. The trip went well, and I checked in at VF 102 as soon as I got there. It was July, 1966.

Social events were a big part of any squadron's life, and VF 102 was no different. My fellow aviators and I devoted ourselves to enjoying life as much as possible before we "bought the farm" the next day. I don't know how we managed to survive so much fun.

Soon after we arrived, a beach party was planned for the air crews and their families. Someone came up with the brilliant idea that it wouldn't be complete without a lobster roast. Another guy said he had a friend in the lobster business, but he was up in Portland, Maine. Our operations officer scheduled a "training flight" for him and his RIO to pick up 100 lobsters and fly them back. We all pitched in $20 to cover the cost. An external belly tank (called a "blivet") was attached to the F4, and it flew off into the afternoon skies.

The rest of us dug a huge fire pit in the sand, filled it with driftwood, and lit it off. Then we proceeded to hang out, swim, and play volleyball until the plane returned. The sun was setting as the crew made a low pass over the beach and dipped its wings to announce its arrival. A couple of guys left to pick up the cargo. Everybody was waiting anxiously for their return, but it didn't happen as soon as we expected. Was something wrong? We waited some more – and waited even longer. What was the problem? Still no lobsters.

Then the phone rang in the house. Everyone listened expectantly.

"You're sure? – Hell no! – Goddamn!"

Our host hung up slowly and shook his head.

"OK everybody – listen up. It's like this. Our guys got the lobsters – all 100 of them – loaded them in the blivet and packed them with seaweed. Then they took off, climbed to 35,000 feet, flew out over the coast, and hauled ass to get here as soon as possible."

He paused uncomfortably and took a long swig of his beer. We all still wondered what the problem was.

"Unfortunately – I don't know how to break this to y'all – everything arrived frozen solid!"

Nobody had thought that the temperature at that altitude would quick-freeze everything. We all moaned and groaned.

"Yeah, I know. It's so bad that it all froze into one big block of ice! It will take days for them to thaw out."

The flight crew chipped a few away from the rest and brought then to the beach. We threw them on the fire, but they came out tough as shoe leather. This was a major disaster! There was nothing to do except pitch in for hotdogs and hamburgers. We still ended up with a beach party, but damn – it just wasn't the same.

VF-102 had a few months of training before a readiness exercise that was planned in November. It was critical that everything go without a hitch. No element of our mission was left out. Before we went overseas, the entire squadron had to be certified "Battle Ready."

We flew out to the AMERICA, which was off the coast of Norfolk, sailing for an exercise area north of Cuba. We shot rockets and missiles, bombed some derelict hulks anchored out in the ocean, and intercepted incoming threats before they got within the carrier's defenses. We were so damn good that VF 102 won the Atlantic Naval Air Command's Battle "E" Efficiency Award. We were the best of the fleet. That's a really big deal!

Time had come to set off to the Mediterranean. One of our missions on these cruises was to display the flag and flex our muscle in the region. We conducted exercises with allies and put into ports throughout the Med. Accompanying the carrier, as always, was a battle group that could handle almost any challenge to our military might. No one, however, anticipated that we would actually have to use force. We were ready for anything, but from the aviators' point of view, this cruise was expected to be high on pleasure and low on stress. After all, we had signed up to "See the World." What could be better than cruising around the Med at the expense of the Navy?

We sailed through the straits of Gibraltar in January, 1967. Marge had arranged to follow the ship around with Jeff and other friends as it put into ports around southern Europe. Everything was going according to plan. They met the ship in Athens, and we had a great time sightseeing, going to museums, and finding good places to eat. When I could get ashore, we were usually able to find a sitter for Jeff through our hotel staff. Marge and I would go out on the town and become tourists. Every port was different, of course. We were able to make connections in Greece, Turkey, Italy, and Spain.

One of the neat things that I could occasionally do was bring Marge and Jeff aboard the ship for a formal dinner in the officer's mess. I rode the captain's launch (or "gig") ashore to pick them up, and we motored back across the harbor to where the carrier was anchored. Marge wore her best outfit, while I wore my starched dress whites. Jeff loved the boat ride. We would walk around the airplanes on the lower decks and hang out in the big briefing chairs in the ready room. It was a big deal for Jeff to talk with the guys. He was well behaved and liked by the entire crew. After dinner, we caught the gig back to shore.

Every few weeks, the ship would put in at another port. We always found some way to get together. One time, I was able to take leave, and Marge, Jeff, and I took the train from Italy north to Innsbruck, Austria, where we spent a day experiencing the old world atmosphere. We then rode further north through Czechoslovakia to the spectacular Bavarian region of southern Germany. I was advised to wear my Navy uniform in Czechoslovakia because it was then a communist country, and the uniform would prevent us from being harassed at border check points. We got a lot of stares and dirty looks from the military guards, but they did not hassle us. It was a long, overnight ride, and we didn't get off the train until we reached Garmisch, Germany. We were able to relax and enjoy the restful alpine scenery and summer flowers for a few days before we had to return to the ship. It may not sound too exciting, but it meant the world to be able to get away and do this together.

The carrier cruised up the Bosporus to Istanbul and dropped anchor in the middle of the straits. Its immense scale was intimidating compared to any other vessel passing through the narrow channel. As usual, an advance party of Marines was sent ashore to set up a guard shack near a floating pier which would be used by the ship's launches to ferry personnel and supplies back and forth from the carrier.

The Turkish Communist party, however, had different plans. It had gathered a crowd of protesters that loudly objected to the presence of anything American in its waters. The organizers whipped up the anger of the demonstrators to the point that several of them commandeered our guard shack and tossed it into the straits. Our Marines had been ordered not to cause any incidents, so they stood by and watched as the crowd cheered and celebrated its symbolic victory. The protests petered out later that afternoon, and we were able to go ashore normally for the next three days. I enjoyed the sights of the historic city with Marge, although our time together was never long enough. Hell – sometimes we barely had time to rub noses together before I had to return to the ship.

My back and neck injuries had continued to improve, but my apprehensions persisted, despite the fresh start with a different squadron. I had tried hard to convince myself that I no longer had an anxiety problem. I started the cruise flying with any pilot who needed a crew member. That was fine because it was a good way to get to know each other. However, a junior pilot had joined the squadron shortly after the cruise began. A few other back seat drivers had flown with him, but all had said, "No more!" The Navy's policy was that a Radar Intercept Officer could not be forced to fly with any pilot he found unacceptable. Our skipper made a pointed request for a volunteer to fly with the new guy for the rest of the cruise. I was unassigned and convinced that he had to be talking to me. I figured that the pilot couldn't be that bad, so I said I would give him a try. Maybe I could help him improve.

Was I naïve or what? I don't know how this kid had graduated from flight school, but he had no business piloting the F4. It was as though he was always flying twenty feet behind the aircraft. He could not react without thinking about his next move and that instantaneous second of delay could be deadly in a jet fighter.

Frequently, his landings or his setups in the landing "groove" were so bad that we had to be waved off to go around and try again. After three or four passes we would get so low on fuel that we had to "bingo" to the nearest air field on the shore before the engines flamed out, and we dropped into the sea. I had to help with every action he made. Consequently, the experience of my accident was revived during hundreds of bombing runs and dozens of carrier landings that we made together. When he wasn't frightening me out of my sanity in real time, he would trigger my memories which had the same severe impact. My stress level was back as high as it had ever been.

My psychiatrist told me much later that by repeating the events of my accident so many times, I was compounding and reinforcing the effects of PTSD. I have to agree. My heart was racing every time I climbed out of the cockpit, and my flight suit would be soaked with sweat. I became more apprehensive before each launch and nervous during every maneuver. Landings, however, were especially distressing. I had no faith in the man's judgment or abilities. There was no improvement between the first time and the last time that I flew with him. Finally, we had a terrible night trying to land back on the carrier in a soupy fog. We had made four unsuccessful passes. There was no bingo field that was within range, and we had barely enough fuel for one more attempt. It was our final pass before we would have to eject. He made a shaky set-up followed by wild corrections and a desperate dive for the deck. We managed to catch a wire, but he damn near flew us into the fantail doing it. I told the skipper I had taken enough. I drew the line and refused to fly with this dangerous excuse of a fighter pilot again.

Through all this, I did not discuss my problems with anyone, and coped silently with my fears. Most of us were drinking, and I kept up with the best of them. We were taught in preflight that we needed oxygen to keep breathing above 12,000 feet. It also did wonders to clear out cobwebs from partying the night before. Perhaps that was the real reason the Navy put oxygen systems in its aircraft. Anyway, we all got by.

There was a lot of tension building in the Mediterranean during the summer of 1967. Besides unrest in the Balkans, Arab forces were pressing on the borders of Israel. Israel issued several threats of war if certain conditions were not met. All the saber rattling on both sides led our visit to France to be cancelled. Military readiness was increased, and our air patrols took on a greater importance. Planes were flying day and night, armed with air-to-air missiles and bombs in case of any attack. Additional airplanes were loaded, and crews were on standby to launch on a few minutes notice. We had a general quarters drill and remained on a high level of alert. At that point, the battle group was cruising in the Sea of Crete – far from any action in the region.

The Israelis launched preemptive strikes on June 6, 1967 that started the Six-Day War. They hit Egyptian forces massed on the Sinai Peninsula and across the Suez Canal in Egypt itself. They then attacked Jordanian, Syrian, and Iraqi militaries that were pressing on their borders. Israel was pounding the Arab forces.

My pilot and I were suited up on standby in the ready room on the afternoon of June 8th. Sketchy news had just come in that an American ship was under attack off the coast of Sinai some 650 miles away. Planes already flying on patrol were immediately diverted to the ship and ordered to defend it at all costs. Additional planes were launched to join the small attack group. We were given a quick briefing. The USS LIBERTY (an intelligence gathering ship) was being strafed and hit by rockets, bombs, and torpedoes at that very moment. The attackers could be Israeli, but at that point it was uncertain who the actual assailants were. Their identity did not matter though. Our orders were to reach the LIBERTY and fight off any aggressors – whoever they turned out to be.

The problem was, however, that we were loaded to full capacity with ordinance. To fly that distance and return, the aircraft would have only 15 minutes of fuel to stay on station. We would not be able to make it back to the carrier if we engaged in a dogfight or made multiple bombing runs. Because of the hostilities, there were no alternate landing fields that we could use. Refueling aircraft were not available. If we engaged any hostile forces, we were to do whatever was necessary to fend them off. If that meant running out of fuel to defend the LIBERTY, then that was what we had to do. Just eject and wait to be rescued – sometime – hopefully. Effectively, we were being sent on what could turn into a suicide mission.

We rushed up to the flight deck and strapped ourselves into our F4. Both of us understood the implications of the operation, but this was exactly what all of our training was about. We certainly did not have a problem with it and were itching to do our part. If that meant personal sacrifice – so be it. Nobody attacks the United States of America and gets away with it! We fired up the engines and waited expectantly for the signal to launch.

"Ramjet, this is Control. Do you copy, Ramjet?"

"Roger Control. This is Ramjet. Over."

"Ramjet – your mission is scrubbed. Do you copy? Over."

Damn! My adrenaline was pumping, and I wanted to get in on the action. After years of looking back on this incident, I believe I wasn't anxious about the possible consequences because I didn't have time to think about them.

The Israelis were later confirmed as the attackers – but why? If anybody knew, they weren't talking. Apparently, the "miscommunications" between Israel and the United States had been sorted out. All the flights were recalled. The next morning, we had moved closer to the LIBERTY'S position. Helicopters were flying in dead and wounded. I watched over the ready room TV monitor as the victims were carried on stretchers or assisted down to sickbay. Thirty-four of its crew had been killed and over 170 had been wounded. The AMERICA pulled alongside two days after the attack. The LIBERTY was dead in the water and listing heavily. Smoke was still rising from holes in the blackened hull and superstructure. It looked like a ghost ship and was a grim reminder of what military power could do. Thousands of men stood by the rail and gave a spontaneous cheer for the defiant sailors who stood on the deck of their crippled vessel.

Nothing exciting happened to us for the remainder of the cruise. The Six Day War ended. Our routine of visiting ports was re-established. I had a decidedly good time during the Med cruise despite being scared out of my flight boots by that junior pilot.

Subtle changes in my behavior and mental attitude were taking place, however. Chronic back pain was restricting many of the things I used to enjoy – like sports or other strenuous events. I had to hold myself back from physical activities and that limited my interaction with my peers. It was too easy to injure myself and have to deal with a period of more acute pain. I felt myself becoming reserved and insecure. I had been both as a teenager – which I blame mostly from being under the heel of my step-father. I had broken out of those conditions, however, after I joined the Navy, married Marge, and started living my own life. But pain, worry, and anxiety were now causing me to revert into my old shell.

Yes, I was displaying symptoms of PTSD. However, I still did not make the connection between my feelings and the accident which had happened over a year ago. Even if I had figured it out, I probably would not have asked for help. I was too damn determined to show no pain and much too proud to seek any psychiatric therapy. I was also scared of what a psychiatrist might find and what counseling would do to my career.

Ltjg. Blake – 1967 – US Navy Photo

Achievements And Gratification

WE GOT HOME TO VIRGINIA BEACH in the middle of September. The end of my first four-year obligation to the Navy was rapidly approaching. As a reserve officer, I could either get out or "re-up." I struggled with that decision, but didn't have a clue in the world what I would do if I got out. The expense of everything I wanted to do – like go back to school or become an artist – was far beyond my meager resources. I now had a family to support. My next tour would be two years of shore duty, and we soon learned that I would be transferred to the Pacific Missile Range at Pt. Mugu, California. It was a good assignment, and Marge was excited because it would be a homecoming for her. I happily accepted the new orders. We packed up and headed for the West Coast again.

Two very good things happened during this assignment. The first was that I was teamed up with a Marine major, Ken, who was an excellent pilot. The second was that I would now be a Bombardier/Navigator in the A6 Intruder, a sub-sonic aircraft designed for air-to-ground attack missions. The A6 had side-by-side seating and flight controls for the B/N. This was definitely a better way to fly! The controls were there if I needed them, and my anxieties evaporated accordingly.

My specific job was to do test and evaluation work on a new anti-radiation missile that was to be introduced to the fleet (the Standard ARM Missile.) It was designed to hit the radar sites that controlled the SAM Missiles in North Vietnam. My appointment as flight test officer for the program was probably made because I had developed some skills in prep school and college on how to put together sentences and paragraphs. The Ph.D. engineers on the project were good at numbers and electrical layouts, but they were lost when it came to composing a comprehensible test program or report. Ken was not much better than the engineers, so the writing responsibilities came down to me. I submitted program proposals that went to Washington for funding and approval. I wrote test plans, reports, and technical summaries. It was a bit tricky because I had received only a few days of superficial training on this sophisticated program. However, with collaboration from the engineers, we got it done.

All I really had to do was use old reports, change a few numbers, develop new summaries, and resubmit the package. I had to wonder as I reviewed the previous reports – that were so poorly written – if anybody had actually bothered to read them.

•

The brain is half left-brain, half right-brain, and
too frequently all wrong-brain.

•

The missile and its control system needed to be rushed to the fleet as soon as possible. The latest surface-to-air (SAM) missiles which were already deployed by the North Vietnamese presented a deadly threat to our aircraft. There was tremendous pressure from the Pentagon to get a good test. Before I came to the program, the only missile that had been launched had malfunctioned and crashed. Our next firing was scheduled in a few months at White Sands Missile Range in New Mexico.

During my orientation flights, however, I could see that the system was still having problems. The cockpit display was showing a wide range of sideband frequencies for a single radar source, rather than just the main band of the transmitter. The multiple wave lengths allowed the missile receiver to drift off the target and lock onto other transmitters. I maintained that the problem was caused by vibrations because a frequency displayed on the cockpit screen would spread into a fan as engine RPMs were increased, or we pulled Gs that shook the aircraft. It would seem like a simple glitch to solve, but the system relied on about a mile of fragile coax cable and small brass connectors that spliced it all together. The engineers and techs ripped the equipment out of the plane, checked it out on the test bench, replaced all the cables, and reinstalled the entire system. The hardware that worked fine on the bench, however, still had the same vibration problems when the engines came up to speed.

The date for the next firing was imminent. Rather than delaying the launch to fix the problems, the project directors in the Pentagon ordered us to go ahead as scheduled. Delays were unacceptable. They had invested years in development of the system, and their careers were on the line. A remotely-activated destruct charge had been installed in the missile, just in case there was another glitch with the launch. We packed up the equipment and shipped it from California to White Sands. Everything arrived as scheduled, except the super-secret test missile. It was lost somewhere in transit. Two days after it was supposed to be delivered, everybody was rightfully panicked. The commercial freight company could not find the truck that had picked it up. Nobody knew if it was just misplaced, or being analyzed by a cell of foreign spies. Maybe the driver had sold it to an Army/Navy surplus store.

The missing missile became an issue of national security. The FBI and Federal Police got involved and tracked the truck's every movement from the time it was shipped to the time it was last seen. The driver had not checked in since he fueled at a truck stop outside of Tucson. The owner of the trucking outfit was, no doubt, threatened with life in a federal penitentiary – or worse – if he couldn't come up with it. Nobody at my level knew what was going on, so we sat around in the blistering hot hanger and twiddled our thumbs.

Early in the morning of our third day, the project manager in Washington received a phone call. The truck driver had finally surfaced. It turned out that he decided to take time off in El Paso with some hot tamale from across the border and hadn't bothered to tell anyone. He had no idea that the box in his trailer had a critical delivery date of three days before – or so he said. He arrived a few hours later at the hanger, escorted by a convoy of government vehicles with flashing lights and blaring sirens. The cargo was unloaded, and the truck was accompanied off the base by heavily armed guards. The delay had cost the government many thousands of dollars. Our flight crew, engineers, technicians, range staff, and the range itself had been kept idle for all this time.

But we could fret about the shipping difficulties later. I suited up, climbed into the cockpit, and turned the system on. The engines immediately began to create vibrations, and the radar strobes on the display fanned out as though nothing had been done to correct the problems, which I pointed out to the senior test engineer. He was not pleased.

"Just fire the damn thing! Do the best you can."

All I could do was shrug. He was the boss.

"Yes Sir!"

We gave a thumbs-up, closed the canopy, brought the engines up to speed, and lumbered into the air. As the aircraft was climbing to altitude, a range controller vectored us into position for our firing run. My scope now showed multiple frequency fans – each one representing a different radar. Fortunately, the screen was recorded so I wouldn't be blamed if something went wrong unless I messed up. The target was dead ahead about 40 miles downrange. I got a high-pitched buzz in my headphones that confirmed that the receiver had a positive lock on the designated target frequency.

"Ramjet – ready to launch!"

"Roger, Ramjet. Maintain course and speed. Standby – ready – cleared to arm – fire!"

Ken punched the "fire" button. The aircraft lurched when the deadly 2000 pound missile dropped away from its pylon on the wing. The motor ignited with a thunderous roar, and it climbed on its course directly ahead of us. From the cockpit, it felt like the latest Atlas rocket had blasted off beneath us!

All was going according to the test profile. The missile got a few miles in front of us, was tracking on the target, and I began to relax. Then ZAP! My monitor flickered. There was a very strong signal coming from another source at about four o'clock. I looked up and saw the smoke trail curving hard to the right. Sure enough, the system was now locked on to the other transmitter, and the damn missile was homing in on the range control tower!

I immediately started to yell over the radio.

"BLOW IT! – BLOW IT!! – BLOW THE DAMN THING – NOW!!!"

It was seconds away from making a direct hit. Range personnel looked like ants abandoning their hill as they ran from the building as fast as they could and scattered in all directions into the desert. The missile bore down until the last possible moment when it exploded in a huge blast that spread shrapnel over everybody escaping from the building. Somehow, no one was hurt.

I looked at the crusty Major and shook my head in disgust.

"At least we know it can home in on something."

I flew down to San Diego for a debriefing with the project staff. There must have been 20 engineers and technicians in the room. We reviewed all the test results, and I was finally asked my opinion.

"And what do you think the problem is, Lieutenant?"

"Well, we have one of three problems. First – the vibrations may be caused by undersized wiring and their connectors."

About half of the engineers, who had spent countless hours to fix the wiring got up in disgust and left the room.

"Second – somehow, the aircraft vibrations are being picked up in the modem."

The other half of the crowd walked out. They were the ones who had agonized trying to eliminate the vibrations within the computer. The engineers knew very well that these were the issues, but refused to consider that it could be their design or installation that was faulty. We kept coming back to the same problems without making any solid progress to resolve them. We were all justifiably frustrated and upset. The project manager and I were left alone.

"OK, Lieutenant, what's the third problem?"

"Both!"

I stood and left him alone in the room.

The techs tinkered with the systems for months. They were finally able to reduce the interference with the primary frequency. Whatever they did, the system had an easier time tracking on the target transmitter. We conducted more tests and eventually shot a few missiles that actually hit their targets. Hurray!

There was still much improvement that could be made, but I signed off on the program. Actually, the senior program manager – a Navy captain from the Pentagon – stood over me, thrust some papers in my hand, and ordered me to sign them. I would have liked to have worked on the system further, but there was no more time for that. Washington pushed it into production. The Standard ARM Missile was a great success when it got deployed against the North Vietnamese SAM sites in 1969. The later generation systems were much improved. I felt justifiably proud of my significant role in its development.

Those were good times. Marge and I had been busy making babies, and my second son, Matt, was born. He was a very mellow kid – not at all like his brother, Jeff, who was now three years old. Even while we were in Virginia Beach, Jeff had developed an attitude to resist anything in life that ran counter to what he wanted. If I told him not to do something, he was determined to do the opposite. Occasionally, he would hold his breath in protest until he passed out. There was no changing Jeff's mind. Doctors said not to worry – in time he would grow out of it. Matt, however, had an accepting willingness to float with the tide. He considered everybody and everything his friend. I tried to set a good example for both kids, but Jeff began to reject even my gentlest direction. On the other hand, Matt and I got along great.

After completion of the last program, I was assigned to test the Navy's stockpile of air-to-air, radar-controlled Sparrow missiles. They had been stored for years in all kinds of unfriendly climates and conditions. The Navy would select some at random and fire them off to see if that batch still worked. That became my job. To make the evaluations realistic, we would shoot at maneuvering, remote-controlled drones.

The Sparrows had their explosive charges removed, and were programmed to make near misses, so that the targets could be reused in other tests. A successful hit was determined by range radar, which could calculate if the Sparrow actually came close enough to destroy the target. In addition, a smoke charge went off at the collision point to visually prove that the firing mechanism worked. That was the plan, anyway.

The sky was clear over the Pacific Missile Range. We were set up at 25,000 feet, cruising around in a standard race-track pattern. Range Control came up on the air.

"The bogey is inbound – 20,000 feet, 300 knots, 25 miles, heading 080."

We immediately turned in that direction, accelerated, and started to climb. I picked it up on my radar and locked on. I watched the target as it maneuvered to simulate the evasive actions of an enemy aircraft.

"Ramjet locked on."

"Roger, vector in position and make a positive ID."

I gave the pilot turns to bring us behind the drone.

"Positive ID confirmed."

The drone was painted bright red and hard to miss. It was banking back and forth to try to break our radar lock. We settled in a perfect firing position about three miles behind it.

Ken flipped the "Arm" switch and launched the missile.

"Missile away!"

It roared off leaving a twisting trail of smoke behind.

I watched as the target tried to shake our radar lock. At the last moment before impact, it reversed direction and went into a steep dive. The Sparrow made corrections, bored in relentlessly, and hit it perfectly in the middle of its fuselage. The drone exploded, and pieces fluttered down like bright red leaves in an autumn sky.

I could not resist tweaking range control after the hit.

"Oops!"

That was all. I could imagine Range Control trying to figure out what happened by studying its radar. They came back on the air a few minutes later.

"Return to base."

No "nice shot" or anything like that. The Range would now have to come up with another toy to play with. Tough. It could not have been a more perfect test – from our point of view anyway.

Time marched on, and I had only one more launch before the end of my tour. A contractor representative had overheard me talking once about how great the Sparrow missile was. The system was designated only for air-to-air combat because the radar receiver picked up excessive ground interference if it was pointed below the horizon. It was believed that the system would lose its lock on the target when other elements interfered with the signal. I maintained, however, that I could pick out a specific target on the ground and hit it despite the clutter of other ground features. The Rep was skeptical.

"Do you really think you can use the Sparrow against a surface target?"

I was certain I could make it work – almost certain anyway.

"Absolutely – guaranteed!"

My idea became a challenge. The contractor and the Navy designed a test where I would be flying at low altitude over the ocean and have to identify a small boat from the noisy background of waves on the surface. I was to acquire it with my radar and track it to within firing range. If the radar was still locked on, we were to fire the missile and hope that it scored a hit. The remote-controlled target was like an open sled configured to simulate what a North Vietnamese junk or patrol boat would look like on the cockpit screen. If the test was successful it would demonstrate a significant, unused capability of the missile.

The boat was outfitted with dual outboard motors and could be maneuvered like a real high-speed attack ship. The explosive warhead in the missile was again taken out and replaced with a dummy charge. There was still considerable doubt as to whether the guidance radar in the aircraft could maintain its lock on the surface object, so a large reflector was mounted on the boat's deck. It now looked more like a destroyer than a small fishing boat on my radar screen. That was OK, however because the missile should home in on the reflector and not the boat.

On the day of the launch, wind speed was 15 to 25 knots and the seas were choppy. Range Control wanted to scrub the mission until a calmer day, but I objected.

"No way. These conditions are normal and make the test more realistic."

They could not argue with that, so we took off and were vectored by the controller to intercept the boat. The target stood out from the noise from the whitecaps, and I tracked it in from about 20 miles out. As we got closer, the interference indeed got worse because the antenna was looking down at an increased angle. The radar, however, was still holding lock through the ground clutter.

"Ready to launch,"

The missile confirmed the lock with a high-pitched buzz.

"Roger Ramjet. Arm and fire when ready."

Ken flipped the arm switch. The radar continued to track. We could now see the boat plowing through the waves ahead of us. It was attempting to lose our acquisition by making radical turns.

We launched the missile at about two miles out. It dropped from its mounts on the belly of the aircraft and blasted out in front of us. After a few corrections, it flew straight and true – right at the target. So straight and true, in fact, that it made a direct hit on the boat which blew apart and sank immediately – outboard motors, hull, and antenna all disappeared within seconds.

I could not contain myself.

"Bull's Eye!"

We circled the area until the control boat reached the last point they had observed the target on their radar. They saw nothing except a thin slip of gasoline on the waves.

"Dammit, Ramjet. You were supposed to miss! Return to base!"

The controller was definitely not pleased.

But for me it was the perfect culmination to my naval career.

F-4B Phantom II – Low-Level Missile Shot
US Navy Photo

Never Believe That You're Always Right

THE FUN WAS OVER. The time for my next tour had arrived. I was doing very well in the Navy and was promised orders by Personnel in Washington to finish my degree at the Naval Postgraduate School, Monterey, California, which had an undergraduate program at the time. My career path was assured, but the decision presented me with serious dilemmas.

The bad thing about the new assignment was that I would have to sign on for six more years. After two years at Monterey, I was committed to four years of additional sea duty. No doubt that would take me back to Vietnam. And even though I loved the thrill of flying the jets, loved the carriers, and loved the prestige of being a naval aviator, I could not imagine myself surviving the next combat tour. I had the certain expectation that another catastrophic accident would occur. The memories of Vietnam were still haunting me, and fear had become a controlling part of my life. The pain caused by my injuries was not as great as it had been, but I just couldn't sign on again.

If I had discussed my problems with a flight surgeon, my discharge would be delayed, so I remained silent. Every injury and mental problem would have to be analyzed, treated, and become part of my personnel files. I was too proud to allow any diagnosis of mental disorder in my record. And any postponement in my discharge would have meant an indeterminate period of uncertainty. I had already made the decision to leave the Navy and wanted to get on with our lives. I also thought that, if I got away from the service, the pain and memories would fade with time. The Navy X-rayed my back and gave me a clean bill of health. It later became clear that my pain was caused by spinal cord constrictions and muscle inflammations that did not show up on the X-rays, but later did on MRIs.

Other factors affected my decision to get out. I had become increasingly disenchanted with the manner that the Vietnam War was being conducted. We continued to fight with one arm tied behind our backs because of political decisions in Washington. Important facilities like government offices and the presidential palace were still off-limits to our bombs. Our troops were dying because of those policies. It was as if we were fighting, but did want to win the war.

The other major reason was that the private sector offered more opportunity for achieving a higher standard of living – or so I thought. I was impatient with struggling on junior officer's pay and wanted to go on to bigger, better, and more lucrative things.

These rationalizations were valid, but fear was the major element in determining my choice to leave the Navy. I might well have swept the other concerns aside if I was healthy and not so afraid. If I had been the same man that went into the Navy six years before, I think I would have signed on again. The fact is that PTSD was the defining role in this major, life-changing decision.

Marge's family had a prominent history of naval service, and she was the perfect Navy wife. She would have liked nothing better than to have us spend our twenty years in the Navy and be put out to pasture with a nice military pension. Unfortunately, I had even kept the full extent of my pain and fears from her. It was my assumed role as "leader of the household" not to display weakness or uncertainty in any decision I made. Marge was skeptical, however.

"How are we going to survive? It won't be easy with the kids."

"From what I see in the papers, most of the opportunities are in sales. I ought to be able to knock the socks off the competition and make plenty of money. I'll make something work."

My expectations were high, and I was excited. Although she never said it, however, I suspect that Marge was terribly disappointed, anxious, and insecure. Our conversations about this usually ended with a dutiful encouragement that put the decision right back in my lap.

"If that is what you think is right, Dear. I really want you to be happy."

I put on a brave face and declined the Navy's offer in January, 1970. I had just turned 27 when I hung up my uniform. I got lucky when I was mustering out. The personnel officer who had to sign my discharge papers saw that I had been awarded a Purple Heart for my injuries from the accident. He told me to wait a minute while he made copies of the citation, the accident report, and the flight surgeon's log when I was admitted to sickbay. He put the paperwork in an envelope and handed it to me.

"Do not lose these papers, Lieutenant! They have a habit of going AWOL from your records, and you may need them some day."

I did not know how right he was, but I did file the papers away. He had truly done me a tremendous favor.

My back and neck problems became more painful year after year – contrary to what I had anticipated. I made two claims for disability compensation – one in 1978 and again in 1984 – but the claims were denied first because they were not submitted within one year of my separation from the service, and second the injuries had to be proven to be "service related." The only records I could submit were the papers that I luckily had on file. In my opinion these were definitive, but the Veterans Administration review panel somehow determined that I had not proved that my current complications were connected to the accident. Their decision impressed me as being totally without regard to the facts and solely designed to save the government disability money. But the burden of establishing proof has always been on the shoulders of the veteran. If the VA says you need more documentation, you are out of luck unless you can come up with something new. In any event, my silence had come back to bite me.

I was very angry with the VA. I appealed the 1984 decision, but could not come up with documents other than medical reports that I had already submitted. My appeal was denied. I considered it an injustice and resented the VA's unreasonable decision. Bitterness, anger, and depression affected my entire life. PTSD was tightening its subversive grasp over me.

Once I decided to get out of the Navy, I needed to choose what to do, and I had to make up my mind in a hurry. Flying for the airlines was not an option. I would have to start as a navigator in a commercial airliner, which was totally different than a thrill-packed fighter/bomber. After the F4, it would be like driving the back seat of a bus. And I still had a serious problem with the thought of not having control of the aircraft. I was done with putting my life in someone else's hands for my profession. Besides, in the early 70's there were hundreds of pilots getting out of the military, and the airlines were considering mostly multi-engine, subsonic pilots – not jet jockeys. I also rejected the idea of becoming a controller for the FAA because of the amount of stress and responsibility that came with that job.

There was not much of a commercial market for someone who knew only how to shoot missiles and drop bombs. I did not have a technical degree, so working for a military contractor was not an option. My Navy detailer in the Pentagon was a friend and called me several times after I got out. He offered me the same orders and my old rank back. I seriously considered that option, but still could not work around my anxieties. Added to all that, the national economy was sputtering.

My brother, Brian, was a commercial real estate agent in New York. That seemed to me like a manageable career and realistic opportunity. So, I set out to get established in the real estate business. I tried to sell desert properties that nobody wanted and high priced homes that were moving too slowly. Then I got a job as manager for some downtown Los Angeles office buildings. My supervisor soon told me to resign because I wasn't forceful enough with the tenants.

"I can't figure you out, Roger. Either you will do very well or you are going to struggle. In my opinion, you are too nice a guy for real estate."

In my heart I knew he was right, but I buried that thought because I still believed I could make it and had job prospects with other companies. From there, I went on to lease a new office building for a major developer in Hollywood. This was an exciting job. I had an expense account and was expected to use it. No reasonable charge was denied. Many of our prospective tenants came from out of town and wanted to be entertained. Specifically – this was LA, and they wanted to get laid. So, I would take them out for drinks and dinner and then go to a massage parlor. Yes – a few times I was stupid enough to join them. It was nothing more than youthful curiosity. Marge had her flings before we were married, but I had no experience whatsoever. Marge found out about this from credit card statements and was, of course, hurt and madder than hell. I should have learned my lesson, but there was another senseless incident which happened months later. I wished I could take those moments back, but they happened, and the damage was done. I mention this now because a few years later, when Marge had a chance to have an affair, she took it without apology or remorse – and I had no moral authority to tell her to stop.

I soon learned that there were other pitfalls to the job as well. A new prospect came into my office one day and asked to see some space. He said he wanted approximately 3500 square feet, so I showed him several adequate locations that were available. He said that he liked the building, but he wanted a certain corner on a vacant upper floor. I had to tell him that we regretfully couldn't break up the space for his size requirement. The full floor was 19,000 square feet, and we were looking for a tenant that would take at least a quarter of that. A few days later he came back. After our normal pleasantries he got serious.

"Here's where we stand, Roger. I want to be in your building, but we have to have the corner we talked about, and the rate you quoted is just too high. As you know, the market is lousy, and we should be getting a better deal."

"I'm sorry, I've talked with the owner, and we can't make that space available. We would love to have you as a tenant on one of the other floors, and we might be able to negotiate a better deal after we know in detail what your total requirements are. But if you have to have that space, then we need to wait until the floor is broken up. Perhaps your corner will be available then."

The prospect leaned closer to my desk, looked around, and spoke confidentially.

"Well, how about this, then? What I'm going to say is strictly between you and me. OK?"

I had no idea where this was going.

"Sure."

"Good. My company feels it is very important to our corporate image that we get that space and from what I've been told, you will be able to persuade the owner to bend his rules."

I nodded at the compliment, but was beginning to feel awkward with this conversation.

"I really can't guess what the owner will do."

"We want you to try, Roger. Here's the deal – again, strictly between you and me – I'm offering you $10,000 cash if you can get that space for us and negotiate some concessions on the rent. Nobody will know except you and me."

I was taken totally by surprise and could only shake my head in disbelief.

"I don't think so, Sir."

"I realize this may be a tough decision for you, Roger. Take your time, and let's get together in a couple of days. How does that sound?"

"OK."

I did think about it – hard! The money would have made a huge difference in my family's life. I was working on a salary – not commissions, which would have been much more lucrative – and was making barely enough to maintain a moderate life-style. Besides the ethical issues – which were against every moral fiber in my body – the downside of getting caught would have disastrous career consequences. But having that much money staring me in the face was too tempting to ignore.

At our next meeting, the client and I sat across from each other, and he set his brief case on the table. He opened it, pulled out a fat envelope, and pushed it slowly toward me with a friendly smile.

"Well, Roger, are we a go?"

I sighed, looked down, and shook my head.

"No. I'll be glad to present a formal proposal to the owner for you and argue on your behalf. He may agree to the terms, but no, I won't accept your money."

With that, the man put the envelope back in his briefcase, stood, and shook my hand.

"That's OK, Roger."

The next afternoon, at the time I usually left the office, my supervisor came in and sat across from me at my desk. He looked at me with a half-smile before he spoke.

"I dropped by to tell you that the bribe you declined was a setup. The guy you were dealing with was a friend of the owner. There was no company and only paper in the envelope. It was a test of your loyalty and honesty. You passed nicely, and the owner is very pleased."

He left me to collect my thoughts. I realized how easy it might have been for me to cross the line in negotiations. I had come awfully close to crucifying myself and felt an overwhelming sense of relief. The best part of this experience was that it cured me of ever thinking of professional dishonestly again. I took a deep breath and left for the day. Fortunately, I had not told Marge about the offer, so the only recriminations or dashed expectations that I had to deal with were my own. All I could do was show up in the morning and keep on hustling.

While working on this building, I was gathering information on hundreds of businesses. I knew how much space they occupied, when their leases expired, and the names of their executives. I soon developed a better index file of prospects in West Los Angeles than many major brokers. The money was enough, and I was building a good professional reputation. The only problem was that I was too successful. I quickly leased most of the space in the building and found myself out of a job. I had two other job opportunities in very quick succession. I was first hired to lease a magnificent new high-rise office building in Century City. Marge and I were looking forward to this building putting me at the top of my field. I walked in on my first day of work and was immediately fired because the brokerage company that had hired me lost its listing on the property. I hadn't even opened my briefcase. That was a crippling shock! If the position had worked out, my life would have been much different. I had to go home and tell her that it wasn't going to happen. We were both devastated, but there was nothing to do except pick myself up and try again.

The second opportunity was in residential real estate sales. I walked out after listening to the sales manager speak for 15 minutes. He was one of those flaky, high-pressure people whose sales pitch was close to fraudulent. I could not tolerate being in the same room with him.

From Los Angeles, I moved the family to San Diego and went to work leasing some smaller office buildings. However, the economy in 1970 was in a down cycle, and the real estate market in San Diego was also stagnant. And I separated my left shoulder again – this time body surfing off La Jolla Beach. I got tossed by a big wave that dragged me under and tumbled me along the bottom. I hit hard, and my shoulder was thrown out. It was so painful that I didn't care if I ever caught another breath of air again. The only thing that saved me was that my toes touched the bottom, and I reflexively pushed to the surface at the very last moment. My elbow was hanging below my waist. I walked out of the surf grasping my left arm to my side. Within days I had surgery to tie it back in place.

Then the doctors gave me too much morphine to manage the pain from the operation, and for a few months I simply could not function. I eventually received a 10% Veteran's Disability because I had lost some mobility in that shoulder, and the VA accepted that the initial injury happened when I ejected from the F4. I did not have the resources to stick it out in San Diego, however.

"Tumbled me along the bottom" was also a perfect description of how my life had gone since the Navy. We were broke. I had gone through five jobs – not including the two non-starters – and relocated the family twice in the three years since I had gotten out. I borrowed money from my brother, Brian, and moved the family again – this time back to New York where I grew up. I was hoping that, with some relief from our living expenses, I could get a job in the City.

We took off from San Diego with our worldly possessions packed into a U-Haul. I drove the truck. Marge and the kids were in the family station wagon. The Grand Canyon was close to our route, so we took a short detour and camped along the South Rim for the night. It had been a long day of driving across southern California and western Arizona. The kids were especially cranky and needed to run around to work off steam. We were about to set up camp when another sedan and rental truck pulled into the spot next to ours. My eagle-eyed boys immediately homed in on two girls riding in the car. The girls were their age, and the four of them ran off to toss Jeff's Frisbee in a small park.

I noticed their New York license plates. The Dad got out, looked at our station wagon with California plates, and came over to introduce himself. He looked like a successful stock broker type. His wife came over as well. She was a chic, sexy number who had New York City written all over her – tight T-shirt, cropped black hair, baggy fatigues, and combat boots. Of course, Marge was a California gal through and through. She preferred the land of the sun, swaying palm trees, shifting sands, and rolling surf. She was dressed in a sleeveless T-shirt, Bermuda shorts, and sandals. Her casual lifestyle was genetic.

California Light

We chatted for a while, and it turned out that he was being transferred by his firm to San Diego. We all had a good laugh when I told them that we had just left San Diego and were headed for New York City.

The guy's wife was not one to hide her feelings.

"I sure don't want to go to California. I'm going to miss the galleries, the shows, the restaurants – everything about New York."

Marge immediately jumped in with her opinion.

"Well, sure as hell I don't want to go to New York! California is much more fun – much more laid-back."

The other guy and I looked at each other. We were both thinking the same thought, but I piped up first.

"You thinking what I am?"

He did not hesitate.

"Yeah – no question. Let's swap 'em!"

Why the hell not? I pulled out a jug of rot-gut wine, he dug out an expensive bottle of scotch, and we proceeded to get very mellow. We finally decided that the kids would have to stay with their moms. I wanted him to take all the kids, but had to relent. Fair's fair.

It was a great fantasy. The more we drank, the more feasible the swap became. Sparks rose from our blazing campfire into the clear, western sky while we passed the time away. We discussed what characteristics and strengths our perfect mate would have to have. I didn't make out very well in the final tally, and I sure got an earful from Marge about all the job changes, moves, and leaving California.

If I had taken her comments to heart about not wanting to leave California, I might have avoided many problems later. Financially, however, I had run out of options. Changing course was not possible. We all finally called it a night and turned in. I woke up early in the morning with a rotten, bad-wine hangover. I looked over at the other camp site, and our new friends had already packed up and left. I was disappointed. At least I wanted to wish them well. When Marge got up she didn't have much to say to me. The swap idea had hit too close to home.

We made it to my family's house – about 50 miles north of New York City – in one piece, but with only change in my pocket. Welcome to the East Coast. We were all exhausted, and it took a few days to unwind. Mom generously came up with some spending money, and I didn't waste any time getting out and looking for a job. I read the want ads of every newspaper I could get my hands on. When I wasn't in and out of New York City, I was driving around Westchester County interviewing for local opportunities. I applied for a position at the General Mills corporate headquarters in White Plains. Their application was about twenty pages long and took me over an hour to fill out. The last question at the end of the application – after a long list of unnecessary questions – was, "What position do you want to achieve with General Mills?" I wrote in "CEO and Chairman of the Board" and dropped it off on the receptionist's desk. I didn't expect a response and didn't get one. Maybe it gave them a chuckle before they tossed it in the waste basket.

It was summer time, so my kids were home with Marge, Mom, and my step-father. That was not working at all. Reggy was a bed-ridden invalid, but had sexual delusions and was continually propositioning Marge. He even flashed her one day as he lay on the bed in his bathrobe. It was ludicrous, offensive, and totally disgusting. I was as angry and distressed as she was. I tried to talk with him, but he either couldn't or wouldn't understand what I was saying. Marge was at the end of her patience.

"We've got to move out of here – real soon."

"As soon as possible, Honey."

Honestly, however, I couldn't see how that would happen.

I tried a few jobs with small local companies, but it was soon evident that I would not earn enough to support my family. Marge had her hands full getting the kids into school and could not work – at least not until I was settled in some employment. The large companies in the City would not hire anybody who did not have a degree and a successful track record on the East Coast. Selling real estate gave me about as much gratification as selling used cars. I was rapidly reaching a dead end and becoming desperate.

•

Some synonyms of Desperation – Desolation, Despair, Despondency, Dejection, Discouragement, Disheartenment, Defeatism, Disconsolateness, and Distress.

•

Self-Portrait – 1983 – "Used Cars"

The Absence Of Civility Is The Absence Of Humanity

I WAS SITTING AT OUR BREAKFAST TABLE one morning reading want ads in the New York newspapers. It always felt like window shopping at a high-class department store where everything looked fabulous, but nothing was within my reach. Then a large display ad caught my eye. It might as well of had flashing lights around its border just for me. The Federal General Services Administration in San Francisco was requesting applications for a GS-11 Realty Specialist position. Primary responsibilities included leasing of commercial space for federal agencies throughout the western United States.

Perfect! I whooped and hollered around the kitchen. Veterans with a 5% disability, or greater, have priority hiring rights above almost everybody else for federal jobs. I was a veteran with a 10% disability rating. I also had office leasing experience and a current California real estate sales license. My résumé was in an overnight envelope that afternoon bound for San Francisco.

I was soon talking on the phone to Cheryl, the Chief of the Real Estate Acquisition Branch in San Francisco. The interview was more like an interrogation. She was totally no-nonsense and sternly questioned every detail of my experience. She spoke so fast that I had trouble tracking what she was saying – or more accurately – telling me. It took a while, but she finally ran out of breath.

"Since I can't meet with you in person, would you be willing to see my counterpart in New York? Somebody has to get a look at you before you get hired."

"Absolutely."

The meeting was set up in a few days. The personnel office in San Francisco had already verified my service record and signed off on my qualifications. The Chief of the Acquisition Branch in New York and I got along, but one issue had begun to bug me.

"Sir, this is a junior position, so why has GSA found it necessary to spend a lot of money advertising it nationally in *The Wall Street Journal*? Why aren't there local candidates lined up for the job?"

There was an awkward moment of silence before he responded.

"Fair question. Ah – it's a demanding position with a very heavy workload. At times, it will seem impossible. You will be required to become familiar with hundreds of regulations in a very short period of time."

This was all talking around the issue. He hesitated and looked me over as he was trying to make a decision.

"Oh hell, you deserve to know what you're getting into. You should be warned. My counterpart in San Francisco – the woman who you talked with on the phone – is probably the most difficult person I have ever met. Cheryl can be totally unreasonable and demanding. If you do good work, she will say that you should have done better. On the one hand, she is very intelligent and knows the regulations better than anybody. But on the other hand – let's see – how else can I describe her?"

He squirmed and thought for a moment.

"Let me put it this way – she is such an impossible manager that I doubt if anybody local applied for the position! However, maybe you can find a way to get along with her."

I sat back and shook my head. That was not good news. I looked at him and thought for a moment. I should reject any thought of this position. As it was, however, it was the best option available. I was trapped by my family obligations and our need for steady income. I made up my mind to take the job and do everything I could to make it work.

"Thanks for the heads up, Sir, but I'll contact her tomorrow. I think I'll give it a shot."

"Very good, Mr. Blake. I'll let Cheryl know to expect your call."

That evening, I discussed the whole situation with Marge. She was concerned about a clash of personalities, but her apprehension was trumped by the need to get back on track economically and away from New York and Reggy. And San Francisco would be great – any place other than here! Her parents had moved to Oakland and that would make the transition back to the Bay Area easier. The situation in New York was absolutely hopeless as far as we both were concerned. The other problem was that we had no money to go back there and get set up. The Government only pays for moves if you are already employed and get transferred by the Government. Mom came up with the travel money this time. The papers were signed, sent, and returned. I was to report to San Francisco in a few weeks. The new job might

77

be hell, but I had already been there and made it out alive. We packed up another U-Haul and off we went again – leaving New York and the East Coast in our rear view mirrors. We arrived in California with a sense of promise and hope for a better future. The family moved in with Marge's parents until we were able to buy a house further east in Concord.

Whatever hopes I had been able to muster lasted for maybe ten seconds after I walked into my new office. I knocked and stepped into the receptionist's cubicle. It was eight o'clock Monday morning, and I could hear someone already being loudly berated in the Chief's office. Cheryl had some poor guy nervously standing at her desk. Insults were scattered indiscriminately throughout her tirade. She was not in any way helpful, tactful, or reserved in expressing her displeasure. She would ask an insinuating question and then beat him down with an accusation before he had a chance to answer. Everybody on the floor could hear every offensive word that came from her office. I had suffered with some bad supervisors in the Navy, but they were nothing like Cheryl. I had been warned, however. I was nevertheless amazed because the Federal Government has reams of regulations that are supposed to prevent this degree of abusive management. The nagging thought kept urging me to run for the exit and find another job.

The receptionist, Leslie, stopped typing and studied me for a moment. She seemed to be reading my mind. I think she was actually waiting to see if I did leave. But I looked at her, told her who I was, and asked to see the Chief. I was probably grimacing the whole time. She gave me a tight-lipped smile and asked me to sit for a few minutes. She picked up the phone to let Cheryl know I was there.

"Have him wait!"

I didn't need the speaker phone to hear it. Then the Chief chewed into her victim for a few more minutes. Leslie was fussing with some papers when I quietly interrupted.

"Is it always like this?"

"Oh, yes. You'd best get used to it."

She lowered her head and returned to her typing. Thoughts raced through my mind. Why not leave? No – I can do that anytime. I need this job. Marge would never forgive me. Take the job and look for a better one. Make the best of it – you have to! The guy hadn't even been able to utter an explanation before the Chief dismissed him and marched around the partition to welcome me into her lair. I noticed she had a limp. She gave me her officious "now you're mine" smile and shook my hand firmly.

"Glad you made it. Come on back."

I sat in Cheryl's office while she looked me over.

"I like your résumé. I need someone in the office with your commercial leasing background. Most of these people have no idea how to negotiate a lease."

She waved her arm around to implicate everybody in the office.

"That's one thing I do well."

"Fine – we'll see."

She tried to stare me down, but I just relaxed, crossed my leg over my knee, and waited. I was not about to let her intimidate me with her overbearing crap.

"Well, there are a few things you need to understand. First, we have a huge workload and are severely understaffed. I'm not running a popularity contest around here. All the procedures have to be followed meticulously. The Ts have to be crossed and the Is dotted. Your work has to be perfect or we all get in trouble. There is no margin for error. Understood?"

"Yes, Ma'am."

So she's a perfectionist – or a rabid fanatic – I thought. I sat still and waited for more. She studied me for a moment, and then we got down to real business.

"OK. I'm assigning you a difficult territory. You will be responsible for Nevada and Northern California, except San Francisco – I take care of San Francisco myself. How does that sound?"

"Great!"

I meant it. At least I would get to travel away from the office.

"Good. Let me show you your work station."

She was up and half way around the corner before I could even stand. I followed her as she jumped/ran with her stiff-legged limp towards a cubical against a back corner. People glanced up as I walked by, but nobody said hello. Their silence spoke volumes.

"OK. This is it."

It was only a small desk, side chair, and desk chair – all stacked high with files. There was no view, but at least it had some privacy and was as far away from her office as I could get.

"All the regulations you will need to read are in the file cabinets over there against the wall. Get with personnel downstairs and then come back up. Leslie will introduce you around. Start studying the case files. They have been neglected for far too long. You will find some leases that are close to expiring, so work on those first. Any questions?"

"I'm sure I'll have some later."

"And – oh, I almost forgot – normally you would have a supervisor to oversee and review your work, but he found another job. Until I can recruit another one, you will report directly to me. Understood?"

"Of course."

She was obviously not pleased that someone had escaped from her control.

"OK. You've already met Leslie, so get started."

With that she turned and raced/limped back to her office. I was left frowning and trying to get a grasp of the situation.

"Goddamn!"

I grabbed the files that were on my chair and dropped them on the floor. I sat to check out the comfort of the seat cushion. It was hard as a rock.

A fellow across the aisle looked up and grinned from under a head of long, bushy hair. He wore faded jeans, a tie-dye T-shirt, and sandals over his bare feet – obviously a San Francisco hippie that they didn't let out of the office. I was wearing a conservative business suit and tie. But he was the first friendly soul that I had met in the office.

"Welcome to the fun house. That chair keeps moving around the office. There are others to choose from that might be better. Just look for one gathering dust and exchange it when Cheryl's off the floor."

"Thanks. I better get down to Personnel, but I'll see you later."

After a year or so, he was working for me and doing a fine job.

Personnel took a while. When we got through with all the explanations, photos, and forms, I needed my morning jolt of caffeine.

"Where do I find some coffee, please?"

"Sixth floor cafeteria, Sir."

I got off the elevator with my cup and bumped into Cheryl, who was lugging a stack of files in her arms. She frowned and glanced at her watch.

"Break's not for another fifteen minutes."

She disappeared behind the closing elevator doors, but at least I knew that she was off the floor. I left my coffee at my desk and went in search of another chair. I found a more comfortable one and switched them out before Cheryl got back. My day felt complete, and it was only 10:15. I sat down at my desk and flipped through a few of the files. They were all very orderly and easy to understand, but some leases I looked at were indeed on the verge of expiring. The Federal Government – like every other tenant – has no right to occupy space in which it doesn't have a signed lease, unless it takes the extreme measure of condemning it in the public interest. I couldn't wait to talk to some of the property owners to see what kind of renewal problems I would have. The lessors could demand any exorbitant rent they wanted, or kick the agency out onto the street. Some of the spaces were small recruiting offices, but even their locations were important.

There were larger offices as well that the government had invested substantial amounts of money in for improvements. Having to find other acceptable space and move would take many months – and cost the government money that hadn't been budgeted. Sometimes there would be no alternative space available. I was way behind the eight ball before I even got started.

"Oh well. The damn files can wait a few minutes longer."

That being my first executive decision, I met with Leslie. She looked over the rims of her glasses and handed me a tall stack of phone messages with an amused smile.

"Your lessors."

Then we were off to be introduced to everybody. I was always welcomed as another lamb ready for slaughter. A few were amused and questioned directly how long I planned to stay. Everyone was friendly enough, but this was the most sarcastic, negative, brow-beaten collection of people I had ever met in my life.

I learned that Cheryl's limp was left over from a broken leg she got when she crashed her Harley-Davidson into a bus or something. It probably wouldn't get out of her way! I also learned that the only reason she still had her job was that she was the favorite of her supervisor, the Director of the Real Estate Division. He let her have free reign over the office. A few hinted strongly that they were having an affair. I found that hard to believe, but I supposed that it was not impossible.

I was told that there had been several complaints filed against Cheryl, and that the Director had quashed them all. She could do no wrong as far as he was concerned. Another grievance was in process against her though. This one was by a Realty Specialist – a black man who was suing her for racial discrimination. He had lawyers involved, and the issue was beyond the Director's control. Apparently, the suit presented a good case, and everybody was impatiently waiting to see how it would be resolved.

A strong undercurrent of angry displeasure always flowed around the office. It became clear that Cheryl would cut a break for a female Realty Specialist, while always coming down hardest on her male workers. Everyone assumed that she hated men – except for the Director, of course. But I worked hard and kept my head down as much as possible. I managed to negotiate extensions, which allowed time for new negotiations. After a year, I was then promoted to Realty Supervisor, with a larger territory that included Hawaii and Arizona. That was great. However, Hawaii was my responsibility in name only. Whenever an assignment required a trip there, Cheryl gave that action to herself. She always made the excuse that she knew the real estate market and the lessors on the Islands better than anyone. The rest of us were left with the more mundane negotiations.

I soon became bothered by the commute on the Bay Area Rapid Transit (BART) to and from downtown to my home in Concord. It was a one hour ride each way that went under San Francisco Bay, past Oakland, and through the Berkeley tunnels. I was uncomfortable in that enclosed space, pushed together tight as sardines with so many other commuters. I would get to one end of the car and study the faces for any signs of a threat or some evil purpose. But going under the bay was the worst. I was tense and nervous thinking of what might happen if there was an earthquake. We frequently stopped in the tunnel for several minutes. Sometimes we were told what the delay was and many times not. My anxiety level would peak and images of the car collapsing and flooding with water exploded in my head. I actually became quite paranoid. My apprehensions followed me even after I got off the train. I could not figure out why I was unable to leave them behind. All these symptoms can be identified with PTSD. As usual, however, I didn't discuss my problems with anyone, and alcohol was my preferred form of escape therapy.

Through my years with GSA, I was going downhill – physically and emotionally. I was out of shape and gaining weight. Sometimes I would have several drinks after work and stumble home in an ugly mood. I could not get the office out of my mind. I brought all the negative pressures and tensions home with me. Marge knew I wasn't happy, and our relationship was becoming more strained than it ever had been.

Cheryl had been on her best behavior for the few times that Marge had met her. My opinions of the job were confirmed, however, by other acquaintances from the office that Marge was able to meet. I told her that I couldn't take the job much longer, and she rightfully became anxious. She took on a job as a bank teller, which helped our finances, however I felt that Jeff and Matt were beginning to drift away. Marge and I both did our best, but our increasing absence from their lives made them more independent and created time for them to explore destructive ways to entertain themselves.

I tried to bring something positive into my life by taking art courses at night school. Painting was something I had been interested in since high school and college. The classes were a welcome diversion for me, but I got home late on those nights. It meant even less time spent with the family.

Marge declared one evening that she was having an affair with a guy named Tom, who we had both met at a party. I knew I had been less than exciting lately, but her announcement hurt me deeply. Besides the issue of the relationship, I found Tom's personality to be appallingly artificial and couldn't believe that Marge found him attractive – and I told her so. Part of the deal was that I was to have a relationship with Tom's wife. I gave it a try, but found her and the whole arrangement grossly unsatisfactory. It was a mistake, and all I really wanted was to have Marge back. I started thinking of divorce, and I assume Marge did too, but we didn't talk about it seriously.

Nevertheless, the void that had been growing between us for some time was getting deeper. I had to get her to stop seeing this guy.

"Marge, this is not working. You are becoming too close to Tom – it's much more serious than a casual fling."

"I can't help it, Dear. I really love Tom – not like between you and me – but I'm really attached to him."

I kept trying, but nothing changed. She went on like this for a few months, and the same conversation repeated itself many times. Marge would come home to me and say how much she loved me. I did not want to get a divorce, but our marriage was getting to a point where it was an emotional pit.

Nothing changed at work. The scene in the Chief's office when I had first walked in was repeated many times each day – every day. The work flow was overwhelming. It was always, "Do more with less – and do it faster!" The stress level can only be described as "nuclear." Cheryl's abusive management style never changed. She acted like she owned each of us because we just happened to work in her office. I came to seriously resent being taken for granted by such an outrageous excuse for a supervisor.

One night late after the family had gone to bed, I sat at my drawing table trying to complete something for art school. It was a "free study" course, so I could make anything I wanted. I was dead tired from yet another strenuous day at the office, but I thought I could at least get something started. I considered painting a dreamy seascape or mountain scene. Those ideas did not excite me that night, however. I was always trying to create something different.

My job was uppermost in my mind, so I set out to paint an image of what it was like. The idea was definitely a challenge. Thoughts of bodies, wreckage, and carnage passed through my mind. I started sketching a tangled prison of steel beams and barbed wire fences. That was enough to begin painting. Other ideas would usually flow once I got something on paper.

I brushed in a few broad areas of color and then had to wait for the paint to dry. I dozed off with my head resting on my arms at the table. That is all I remember until morning. I woke up at sunrise with my head still lying on the table and a very stiff neck. Sometime during the night, I had finished the painting, but I have no memory of doing that. None. I must have acted in some kind of subconscious trance. In one way or another, the images in my mind had flowed onto the paper. I looked down and saw an illustration of all the pressures, tensions, and frustrations Marge and I were going through. I was dumbfounded. It was perfect!

There is more to this story. Painting was becoming an obsession, so I rented a small studio/gallery and tried to sell some of my art. A friend who I had worked with at GSA came by and related entirely to the picture. He had to have it. I wouldn't have considered selling it if I didn't need the money so desperately. I told myself that I could paint another one whenever I wanted. But after several tries, I admitted to myself that duplicating it would be impossible. The original was built with complex layers of watercolor and gouache paints. The lines were put down by tiny brush strokes and pallet knife edges that I could not come close to replicating. That was in 1975. I had stopped by my friend's house twice over the ensuing years to visit the painting and offered to buy it back each time. He and his wife would not consider selling it.

Trapped – 1975

36 years later, I thought again of this painting as I was writing this book. It was indeed an illustration of those dire times with GSA. Even more significant, however, was that the painting expressed all the symptoms of PTSD that have affected me subconsciously since the Navy. I cannot conceive a more definitive picture of my mental state – then or now!

I had to have the painting back. Besides the book, I needed it for myself. I hadn't talked with my friend for 15 years. I tracked down his current phone number on the internet, screwed up my courage, and gave him a call. He still did not want to sell it. I explained all my problems and how lost I was without it. I pleaded, wouldn't he please – PLEASE! – sell the painting back to me now? I was quite distressed. He said he would talk it over with his wife and be in touch.

He called back the next day. He was sponsoring a lady who was working on a project in South America. If I would pay his asking price, he would send the money to her and sell the painting back to me. He was asking a lot, but he gave me a little off his price when I balked. An opportunity to correct a mistake sometimes only presents itself once in life. I gritted my teeth and accepted his offer. The painting arrived in my hands a week later. I still feel strongly that this image expresses PTSD – the anger, fear, depression, paranoia, and hopelessness – better than any representation I can imagine!

After two and a half years, I could not take working at GSA any longer. The Chief and I were arguing about a trip that I had planned to Phoenix to conduct a survey for a new office location. Cheryl objected.

"Your time is more valuable spent here in the office. Get someone else to go."

"I've already contacted owners and realtors – all the appointments are set. My people are busy, and I've got this handled. It's my territory, and there's no reason I shouldn't go."

"I'll tell you when and where to go. Assign the trip to someone else."

It was not that big of a deal, but it was the last straw – one of too many last straws that I had put up with. I was fed up with her bullying and tossed the orders on her desk.

"Assign it your-damn-self then. I resign."

I stormed out of her office and went down to personnel. Along with my resignation I wrote an angry statement for my reasons for leaving being:

"1. Basic, substantive incompatibility between me and the Chief of the Acquisition Branch due to her management practices.

"2. Management's evaluation of workload is unrealistic. There is no possible way that I can effectively supervise leasing in 3 states with only two technicians and act as a technician in one of them myself."

The personnel officer advised me not to submit this because it would just be disregarded by Cheryl and not be made part of her personnel records. Besides, a resignation like that in my file might damage my chances of ever getting another position with the government. I didn't care. I could not imagine myself wanting another federal job. Even the term "federal job" had a derogatory connotation. I left the language in. I was right to walk away, but as with my previous periods of unemployment, I had to find something else to do quickly.

A few days later, another supervisor quit, and a week after that a third. Taken together, to have three seasoned supervisors resign made quite a statement, but no damage appeared to be done to the Chief's career.

I was seriously questioning the profession I had chosen. Commercial real estate had attracted me initially because it appeared to be a professional, lucrative, and challenging career. The people I had come to know in the business were rewarded with success and comfortable lifestyles. But that was far from the reality that confronted me. I had only managed to barely keep afloat. I kept asking myself, "Why?" or "What's wrong with me?" Answers to those questions remained beyond me. But when I asked "Am I cut out for this?" the answer was an unambiguous, "No!" The logical questions that followed were "Why not?" and "What do you want to do?"

As I wrestled with these dilemmas, I was struck by the difference between the person I was in prep-school and college, and the person I had now become. In my teenage years I had been deeply interested in international events, our fragile environment, America's declining international image, powerful trends that were changing our country, and the injustice of prejudice and racism in our society. I had thought seriously of joining the Peace Corps. My strongest urge, however, had been to be an artist. I was in love with the beauty of everything around me and wanted to recreate it on canvas. Creators of fine art were my heroes.

What had become of those worthy goals? In those days I saw myself as a diplomat, an environmentalist, a journalist, or an artist. I was a Red-Blooded Son of the Good Ol' U.S. of A and capable of doing anything I set my mind to. What had become of those dreams? Was it too late to change my career? The dilemma was tough because the person I was to become had to bring in an income that could support the needs of the household. Anything less would be an instant failure. The unfortunate reality was that a career change would put me in an entry-level position that I could not afford. My dreams had to be brushed under the carpet. This was a hard truth for me to accept. Here I was – unemployed again. I had an opportunity to change everything about me from what I did for a living to what my priorities would be. But I could not figure out who that new person could be. I was trapped. I had come to dislike having to deal with bosses, developers, attorneys, and real estate agents – any high-pressure people with whom I would not normally associate, and arrogant people who did not know how to say "Please," "Thank you," or, "I'm sorry." I found the thought of selling anything to anybody distasteful. If someone didn't like a product I was selling, my reaction was, "That's fine. Just go buy what you want." The merchandise had to sell itself.

Art school and my gallery had opened windows to my creative nature, which had been closed since I went into the Navy. The courses had even led to a few artistically interesting pieces. I was spending most of my days painting, and was very content except that the gallery was costing me money. I sold a few paintings, including the one I already mentioned, but it was not enough. The one occupation I enjoyed was proving to be self-destructive.

The gallery couldn't last. I realized what was happening, however I felt helpless to stop the slide. Marge was still carrying on with her boyfriend. What could I possibly do that would keep my family together? My mind felt numb. I could not find solutions for my problems. As I looked back over the years since I had left the Navy, I could not identify anything positive that had happened. I still maintained the romantic notion that life was supposed to be a path toward greater comfort and happiness. Mine had been a roller coaster ride, with every success followed by professional disappointment and financial failure. My family was struggling, and I was coming apart at the seams.

I was close to waving a white flag and saying, "To hell with everything! I surrender!" I wanted to escape. To drop out and be a truck driver, bartender, waiter, or garbage man were very attractive alternatives. I was afraid of shooting for success because I was certain my efforts would again end in failure. Nothing in my life made sense.

Self-Portrait – 1987 – "Fractured"

Climbing Ladders To Futility

FOR NOW, MY BEST OPPORTUNITIES were in commercial real estate, but even that field appeared hopeless. I had started mailing out résumés about one year before I had resigned from GSA, but had not received even one response. It became clear that my experience as a Realty Specialist for the federal government did not carry much weight in commercial industry. About two months after I left, however, I received a strange phone call from someone asking if I was still interested in a position in Salem, Oregon. I replied that I might be interested, but I didn't remember inquiring about a job there. It turned out that the company was a Seattle-based developer who had an office building in Salem that needed to be leased. Someone else had been hired initially, but he had not worked out and the building was still mostly vacant.

I was flown to Seattle and given the red carpet treatment. I met the owner, who impressed me as a sharp businessman and spent time with the manager who would be my boss. My interviews went well, and I was thoroughly impressed. I was to have three years to fill the building. The employment package included perks like an allowance for moving expenses, housing in a new condo in Salem at a reduced rate, membership in the local country club, and a base salary against commissions. I then flew down to Salem to look the building over. It was a decent "spec" project that I thought should be fairly easy to lease. The rental rates were optimistic, but that had never slowed me down before. I had been an agent for several owners and frequently had more problems selling a proposal to them than I did to a tenant. I accepted their offer and was optimistic again.

I hoped the move from the Bay Area would get the kids away from the drug culture that was beginning to infest the public schools. But Marge was not so sure she wanted to leave her boyfriend behind. I was fed up, however, with the entire scene. It had gone on much too long.

"I'm leaving. You can stay if you want, but I'm not going to put up with any more of this crap between you and Tom. It's either him or me – make your choice."

Marge struggled with her decision, but she finally came along. We packed up again and this time headed north. The trip was better for me than for Marge and the kids. She was withdrawn, and the boys had trouble leaving their friends at school. Things began to brighten up once we got to Salem, however. The condo was comfortable, there was not much pressure with the job, the boys easily made new friends, and Marge enjoyed the country club and other social activities. I soon became part of the Salem business community, was sponsored for membership in Rotary, and appointed to the Salem Downtown Development Board.

I made a conscious effort to get healthy again. I wasn't drinking as much as I used to put down in the Navy, but it was still a lot. I started running and playing golf, which I had never done before. I wasn't very good at either sport, but I did OK and enjoyed the exercise. Running was also a solitary activity which suited me well. I enjoyed the challenge of longer distances and soon moved up to 10K's and half-marathons. Running made my back ache, but not enough to make me quit. Golf, however, was making my shoulder hurt more and more. The pain got so bad that I could not follow through with my swing. When the joint separated as I rolled over in bed, I knew I had to have it fixed again. The surgeon put in a screw to replace the old staple that had come loose and stitched everything together. The procedure was a success, and much of my pain was relieved.

Marge was unhappy, however, and decided that she had to go back to visit her boyfriend in California.

"I can't stop thinking of Tom. I've got to get him out of my system."

"Fine, but this is the last time. If you can't leave him behind – don't bother coming back."

I was coaching one of my boys' soccer teams when the time came for her to take off. She showed up and said goodbye to Jeff and Matt, but just gave me a look and drove away. I didn't care if I ever saw her again. After ten days or so, however, she reappeared at the door. We sat in our kitchen silently for a minute or so. I tapped the eraser of a pencil absently on the table top and studied her closely. She was looking down at her hands apprehensively. All I could think of was how much I wanted her back – how much I wished that this mess had never happened.

"Is it over?"

"Yes. It was tough saying goodbye – but it's over."

I had a lot more questions, but she had answered the important one. That was good enough for now. Marge was hurting emotionally, and her decision had been truly difficult. I did not push. Time would hopefully fill in the gaps and heal the hurt. I probably would not want to hear the truth anyway.

"OK."

I sighed, stood up, and returned to whatever work I had been doing. We were awkward and cool with each other for a spell, but eventually we got through it – which is entirely different than getting over it, however.

Jeff was growing up all too fast. He was always doing things his own way, and ignoring whatever advice or guidance Marge or I had to offer. He would try everything else – including my patience. One summer we enrolled him in an Outward Bound Wilderness Program, hoping that the challenges might teach him some lessons in team work, personal limits, and humility. The program would have been a success if it had only mellowed him out. He came back totally blasé about the experience, however.

"What did you think, Jeff? Was it worthwhile?"

"Everything was pretty easy – not nearly as tough as I thought it would be."

"It wasn't difficult for you?"

He shook his head and shrugged.

"Nah – each event was designed so that even if you failed there weren't any consequences. They watched us pretty carefully."

"How about the survival exercise?"

He had been given a bare minimum of food and was supposed to ration it over three days.

"I ate it all the first afternoon – didn't want to be thinking of food all the time."

"Weren't you hungry when you didn't have anything to eat?"

He shrugged again dismissively.

"It wasn't so bad."

As usual, Jeff had obstinately made his own rules and learned nothing from the program. The positive changes in his attitude that we had hoped for did not happen.

We couldn't have been more successful in Salem in most other respects. We made wonderful friends and were involved in many aspects of the community. I had developed a skill for sketching space layouts for prospective tenants as part of my sales package. I could figure out – in minutes – how many square feet the tenant would need, how the space could be laid out, and what the costs would be. Many companies would have had to hire a space planner or architect to determine information that I could develop while we were sitting across the table from each other. I removed much of the expense and uncertainty from the negotiations.

Again, however, I leased myself out of employment with the developer in a year and a half. Oops again! That meant that we would have to move out of the condo, pay for the country club membership, and I would have to find other work to do. I had some good commissions that were still coming in, so I wasn't too concerned. I had a solid reputation in the community and had made many business contacts.

The problem, however, was that Salem did not have any other large projects for me to work on. It only had a population of around 50,000. The principal employers were the Oregon government, Willamette University, and timber companies. I tried driving every day to Portland and back – over one hour each way – and worked with an established Portland real estate company which had several buildings I could represent. That did not work out, however. Portland's market was overbuilt, and businesses were cutting back rather than expanding their office space. I hardly earned enough in commissions to pay for gas money.

•

To waste your time, energy, and talent on jobs
that don't stimulate the best in you is to allow your life to drain away
while you watch and let it happen.

•

Career Path

Chapter *16*

1982 – Age 39

Being Out On A Limb Is For The Birds

I MOVED THE FAMILY out of the condo and dumped our country club and other memberships to cut down on expenses. That didn't bother me, but Marge responded with grim resignation. I then tried working with an industrial developer who I knew in Salem. The economy nationwide was turning sour, however, and the flood of high-tech California companies moving to Oregon was dwindling to a trickle.

Despite the down market, I felt that a significant number of Salem's real estate investors were not being professionally served. It was frustrating because I firmly believed there was room for a commercial brokerage in Salem, but I didn't have the money to get one started. Another friend – an accountant – pulled me aside at a party one evening and said he would be willing to finance a new real estate venture. We would be equal partners – I would be in charge of all real estate matters, and he would control the finances. We were off and running. I soon hired a secretary and was training three young salesmen to work on commercial/investment properties. I was energized. We were listing properties all over the greater Salem area and beginning to put together a few deals.

I was also seriously training for a marathon. The harder I trained, the more energy I had for the business. In addition, I set up a drafting table in our basement, so that I could continue to draw and paint. The downside of these solitary pursuits was that they isolated me further from the family.

Nevertheless, I did make time for outdoor activities that we all could enjoy. We went canoeing and fishing down the many rivers in the Willamette Valley. We explored the Oregon coast and climbed peaks in the Cascade Range. Our winter recreation was skiing. Most of our trips were to our favorite ski area – Mt. Bachelor in Eastern Oregon. Jeff and Matt were fearless. They would race down the slopes, skip over moguls, and go soaring off jumps. Jeff was aggressive, and Matt would do the same runs with more control and finesse. They were both athletic, and it was wonderful to watch them develop and become confident with their abilities. Skiing was a time when they felt free – unfettered from all their parental pressures and the dutiful requirements of growing up. Marge and I also enjoyed skiing together, and we usually took a four day weekend to make a mini-vacation out of the trip. Although it was a stretch financially, these times gave me some of my best memories of the boys – and of our marriage. The good times

95

became overshadowed, however, by both boys' problems with drugs. We began to realize that the schools in Salem were far from substance free. Jeff, now 17 years old, began to have serious difficulties. We tried to talk with him, but he would angrily dismiss our concerns. His grades were terrible, so we arranged a special conference with his homeroom teacher. She refused to admit that there was a drug problem in the school because that would "create a liability for the district." So it was the school district's policy to turn its head the other way while pot, cocaine, and every new drug-of-the-month flowed freely throughout the campus.

Jeff's behavior sank from awful to terribly worse. He went up to a concert in Portland one weekend and got tossed in jail for disorderly conduct. The police called and wanted me to pick him up.

"Fine. I'll come get him in the morning."

He was still strung out when I got there. He cursed out security at the concert, the police, and everybody other than his generation. We were "too old" to understand. I finally had to tell him to shut up or walk home. He quieted down and pouted the rest of the way without saying a word.

Marge and I enrolled him in a tough alcohol/drug rehabilitation program that had the reputation of being the best in the area. He was supposed to detox and get therapy for his addictions. $5000 and two weeks later, he said he could get more pot and cocaine in the rehab center than he could at school. Some patients had found ways to sneak drugs in and share them with the others. We saw no improvement whatsoever.

Matt began having his own troubles at school. He was a tall, well-built kid and had been a first-string goalie for his soccer team in previous years. This season, however, he didn't even make the cut. His grades were also going downhill. After Jeff's problems, we knew it had to be drugs. We talked with Matt seriously, and tried to make the point that working hard and doing well in school were critical to his life and future happiness. He would agree, but could not change his behavior – or did not want to.

One day, Matt popped a question that we hadn't yet heard from either boy.

"What do you think I could do after I get out of school, Dad?"

I thought seriously for a moment. He was not showing any interest in anything academic and was not college material, so I enthusiastically fell back on sports.

"You would be a natural place kicker in the NFL. I've seen you boot a soccer ball halfway down the field. You have exceptionally long and powerful legs. Really. You could also be a soccer star – either as a goalie or a fullback. You have the potential to be very good, Matt!"

He nodded his head thoughtfully.

"I don't know."

"Well, you certainly aren't going to have to make that decision now. But I'll get a football, and maybe we can do some practice kicking. What do you say?"

"Sure. That sounds good, Dad. Thanks."

We tried kicking extra points and field goals on the next couple of weekends. He was deadly accurate at close range and was getting better at longer distances after just a few practices. At 15 years old, Matt showed the natural talent to be a pro. Then I suggested he try out for his high school football team that fall. He looked at me and shook his head.

"I don't think so, Dad."

He didn't give a reason and just walked away. He wouldn't pick up the football or talk about it again. Many years later, Matt told me that he knew he wouldn't pass the NFL drug tests, so why bother? He was already convinced that addictions would be part of his life.

One night, Jeff and some friends drove my Chevy Suburban into a culvert and smashed up the front end. He was able to back out and make it part of the way home, only to drive it into another ditch. The front wheels had been spread askew. I got called by the police again to come and pick him up. It was easy to see that he was stoned. I lost my cool and was yelling in his face.

"Damn it, Jeff. Look at yourself! You're fucking blind! You've wrecked our car, for chrissake!"

He screamed back.

"I got forced off the road. It's not my fault,"

I looked at the pavement and did not see any skid marks.

"That's a bunch of crap, Jeff, and you know it. At least you could take responsibility for your goddamn actions!"

"I told you it was not my fault, Dad. You always blame me for everything!"

I was beside myself with anger. Drugs had defeated all my efforts to teach him anything – even about honesty and responsibility.

"OK Jeff, have it your way. But it's the last goddamn time you'll ever drive one of my cars!"

We got the Suburban towed home, and Jeff rode sullenly with me. He slept through most of the next day. Much more extensive damage to the car was visible in the daylight. At dinner he became so disrespectful and obnoxious that I ordered him back to his room. He wouldn't go. I couldn't take his insolent attitude for another minute. I wanted to knock his head off, but instead slammed my fist on the table, stomped out the front door, and drove off in my other car. I cruised around until I cooled down and then spent the evening at my favorite bar. I was still fuming when I made it home late that night.

I had probably scared Marge more than Jeff when I hit the table. She approached me delicately.

"I was worried about you."

"I'm sorry, Honey. I couldn't stand any more of Jeff's crap. Did he even say he was sorry or anything?"

"No – what are we going to do?"

I think we both realized something had to change. I just couldn't tolerate his behavior anymore.

"He has to go."

The next day, Jeff packed up, and Marge moved him out of the house while I was at work. Maybe tough love and being on his own would set him straight. I felt relieved to not have to continually fight his belligerence. In my mind, he had chosen the course his life was on, but that did not mean that I had to let him control mine. He was happy to get out from under my authority and went to live with a friend – who, of course, was one of his druggie pals. All this happy domestic life was going on while I was trying to put together the many pieces of the new business.

After the startup period, the income started to grow, and it looked like our enterprise might succeed. Then, my partner quit his accounting job and decided to work in our office. He would arrive at the office late in the mornings so hung over that he looked like walking death. He was embarrassing to have around, but he had a right to be there. I couldn't do anything about it.

During the time that we had the business, I had bought some rental apartments that weren't much, but at least they had a small, positive cash flow. I planned to eventually fix them up and to moderately increase the rents. That was in the early 80's when the nation's interest rates soared above 20%. Investment properties could not be financed at those rates, and buyers who could buy without a mortgage were staying out of the market. Our fledgling real estate business was not going to make it.

My partner then stated that he wasn't going to put up the money anymore. That was the last straw. We sold the business to one of our competitors and basically broke even. He got all the depreciation because I had received more income, and I got a large tax bill that I couldn't pay.

Another killer was that because there was no housing market, there was also no demand for timber. My apartment rentals were occupied mostly by loggers, mill workers, and their families. A majority of them disappeared almost overnight. Sometimes, they gave me notice – more frequently they just vanished. I learned that nearly all of them went to Texas to get jobs in the oil fields. That left me with no tenants, no income, and several large mortgages that I couldn't handle. Another crisis was about to crush us.

Marge and I were sitting at home having a serious discussion about our financial situation. I brought her up-to-date on what was going on, what our liabilities were, and what commission income we could expect to still come in. Marge was getting the picture that we were in serious trouble.

"What should we do?"

"Unfortunately, we don't have a choice. We bought the apartments on real estate contracts, and the sellers still have title to the properties. With the vacancies we have, there is no way we can make the mortgage payments. The first thing we have to do is give the properties back to the sellers. Then we need to protect whatever assets we still have left. We need to declare bankruptcy."

She sat and coldly studied me for a moment. She then stared with disgust and very real hate in her eyes.

99

"That's it. If you file for bankruptcy, I'm filing for divorce!"

I was caught by surprise. Yes, we would lose all the money we put down on the properties and mortgage payments that we had made. Yes, I had dragged her to too many places and disappointed her too many times. Yes, our finances had been close to falling off a cliff for too many years. Yes, all of the risks I had taken to improve our situation had not worked out. But I had always done my best. And I had worked hard to build our real estate business and buy the properties. I felt that I was the victim of the economy, politics, and bad timing. I did not feel that our problems were entirely my fault, but for Marge it was only the last of many failures. She was not going to put up with it again.

I looked at her grimly.

"Well, I'm sorry, Dear, but I don't see that we have a choice."

Her look got even harder and became a sneer.

"I should have dumped you in San Diego before you dragged me to New York!"

She stood up abruptly and stomped out of the room. Marge might as well have hit me in my gut with a sledge hammer. I was breathless and couldn't say anything, even if I could have thought of how to respond. Had she been thinking that all these years? Yes, she had. I was devastated. Then, a little light blinked on inside my head. Marge had been waiting for an excuse to get rid of me, and this was it. I sat there alone feeling sorry for myself. I had thought our marriage was doing OK despite these tough times, but I had been blind!

Then, another little light flashed on. I realized that this was also a moment that I too had been waiting for. I had wanted my freedom for a long time. For all the years after I had been out of the Navy, I had sacrificed my dreams for my family. I had accepted those responsibilities – as I should have – but the truth was that I was only striving to make money to support them. I could have cared less about real estate except for the money. Even if I had been successful, I never would have felt happy or fulfilled.

"I wish you had left me in San Diego too."

It took a few months to declare bankruptcy and wrap everything up. The boys would stay with her. Jeff had quit school and was already out doing his thing – whatever that was. Matt was old enough to understand what was going on between Marge and me, and I took him aside one day to talk about it.

"You shouldn't blame any of this on yourself, Matt."

"I don't feel that way, Dad. I'm just sad that the family is breaking up."

"I feel the same, Matt. Mom and I won't be together, but please know I'll be there whenever you need me. Call anytime. OK?"

He nodded and withdrew into his thoughts. I wished that I had found more to say, but the words did not come. We both understood that we would be apart from now on, except when we might find some way to get together after things had settled down for me. I also did not check with him as much as I should after I left simply because I didn't want to deal with Marge. There were many things I should have done better for both boys, and communication would have been a good start.

Marge kept all the household stuff and the car. I promised to pay an unreasonable amount of alimony and child support. Where the money was going to come from – I had no idea. I would work that out later. I got the old Chevy Suburban and bought a small used trailer that I could live in as I traveled around trying to find something else to do. There was no way I could stay in Salem and live with the embarrassment of business failure, bankruptcy, and divorce.

•

When your life hits a wall – hit the road.

•

... And Left Yesterday

Freedom Is Good, But It Can Hurt

THE BEASTS that had pursued me all these years had broken through my defenses. Marge did not try to contain her emotions and was happy to see this day come. It was I who was bummed out. Despite our problems, I still loved her and part of me felt that we should try again. But it was time to say goodbye. I hugged Matt and Marge and drove away. I was to catch up with Jeff in Eastern Oregon on my way out of the state.

Self-Portrait with the Wolves - 1984

I spent my first night in a campground along the Santiam River. Drenching rain hit the aluminum roof of the camper as if I had parked under a waterfall. I lay in the bunk and let my mind run through, once again, the history of the last 14 years after my departure from the Navy. What always hit me were the patterns that I had established. I jumped from job to job only to fail and have to jump again. I naively trusted people to act with the same values that I had and was frequently burned in the process. My judgment was regularly incorrect. My optimism, persistence, and hard work had never proved to be enough. I could find many reasons for my failures, but I could only blame myself for allowing them to happen.

I was sad and seriously depressed. Between the rain and the roar of the swollen river next to my trailer, I almost hoped that I would be washed away and caught beneath a snag – never to be seen or heard from again. No one would care and that would have been fine. The river would be doing me a favor.

I woke up to the sounds of water dripping off the pines. My depression persisted like a hangover from the night before, but I kept moving. The weather had cleared, and I headed further east. I met with Jeff briefly. He was working at a landscaping job for a large manufacturing company. At least that was something positive. When I drove up he was mowing a large lawn in front of the plant. Jeff had let his hair grow down to his shoulders, and his clothes were ragged. He knew about the divorce, but we had not talked about it. Jeff's attitude toward me was still tense. His whole bearing displayed the large chip he carried on his shoulder and an unwillingness to have a meaningful conversation. I tried to ignore the barrier that he had built between us.

"Good to see you, Jeff. It's been a while. You doing OK?"

"Yeah."

"Well, I'm heading out – just wanted to say goodbye."

He looked down as though he had something to say, but was uncomfortable saying it. He looked back up and pressed his lips together in a frown.

"Well, Dad – good luck. Seeya' later."

"Thanks. Take care, Jeff."

I wanted to give him a hug, but he was too distant. We just shook hands before I drove away.

I called Marge twice while I was still in the area to try and change her mind about the divorce. I told her I thought that it was a big mistake and pleaded for her to give us another chance. She would have none of it, however. There was no way I could turn it around, so I finally stopped calling. I realized eventually that I was in love with who Marge used to be – not the bitter person she had become – and I no longer knew who that woman was.

At least I was free now to go wherever and do whatever I pleased. I swore to myself that I would never do real estate or sales again. I had no interest in anything competitive. I had always wanted to be an artist, so my destination became Taos, New Mexico, which had a thriving art community that I had read about. I took my time, sketched some of the scenery, and painted some small landscapes as I meandered my way south. I stopped by Reno and checked on openings for whatever job I could find in the casinos. They told me brusquely that there were no possibilities if I didn't have a dealer's or a bartender's license – just forget it. So I forgot it.

The Suburban was using way too much gas towing the heavy trailer and costing me money that I didn't have. I downsized them for a 1970 VW bus and some cash, bought some additional camping gear, crammed everything in to the VW, and started off again. The wheels on the rear transaxle were splayed way out from the weight. After Reno, I took a detour up to Lake Tahoe to look around and then puttered south over Monitor Pass at an elevation of 8314 feet. I expected the bus to putt its last putt and roll over "wheels-up" at any moment, but it didn't skip a beat. The scenery of the high Rocky Mountains was spectacular, and I couldn't resist pulling over at wide spots in the road to spend a few hours sketching or painting. Art was getting into my head. I camped out all the way, and the VW and I became great friends by the end of the trip.

A week or so later, I pulled into Taos covered with dust and encrusted with bugs. The VW fit in with all the other artist heaps driving the streets. The town felt very comfortable with its scenic setting, the old-world atmosphere of its rambling adobes, and all the art galleries, cafés, and shops. I found the diverse mix of cultures refreshing. The Native Americans, the invading Hispanics, and the conquering Anglos all maintained their separate identities, but functioned reasonably well as a community. That was on the surface anyway. I later saw that there was a lot of friction between them racially, politically, and economically, but they still managed to prosper together. I arrived in the middle of June at the height of the tourist season. Most of the vacationers were Oklahomans and Texans who drove to the high mountains of New Mexico to escape their brutal summer heat and humidity in the flatlands.

I found a cheap bed-in-a-closet to rent for a few days and started to look for work, but soon discovered that it would not be easy. The good jobs had been taken before the summer season even began, and openings came up only when someone left or there was a change in a business for some reason. I considered seeking a more challenging position such as a gallery manager, or even a real estate salesman, but rejected the idea. I wanted nothing to do with the pressure of sales or any type of supervisory responsibility. If scraping bottom was all I was good for – then so be it.

After a day of asking around, I was given a tip that an owner of a local restaurant in Taos had just bought another one in Red River – an old mining town high in the mountains about 35 miles north of there. Maybe he would be hiring new people. I looked him up and, sure enough, he needed a waiter. I didn't have any experience, but he needed someone immediately and could I start this weekend? Sure! The salary was next to nothing, but I would primarily be working for tips, which should be pretty good. The only problem was that the restaurant had a western motif. I looked about as "western" as a New York greenhorn at a dude ranch.

"No problem. I'll buy a pair of boots, get a cowboy hat, and fit right in!"

The owner got a laugh out of that, and I was hired. The outfit worked, despite the blisters I got from the cheap boots.

I drove up to Red River the next morning to have a look around. It was bustling with tourists and their families, and the restaurant looked promising – worth a try anyway. I needed a place to stay, but all the cheap apartments had already been taken. On the way up, I had passed the small village of Questa which was close enough to Red River, so I drove back down the mountain to try to look around. I found a notice on the bulletin board in a local café offering a two room adobe "casita" for rent at $175 a month, including utilities. Perfect! I got hold of the owner and met him at the cottage. The elderly Hispanic gentleman – easily in his 90's – said it had just become available. I looked around and was skeptical because of the amount of dust on everything. Hell, I knew how to dust, so I dismissed that issue. I asked about the packed earth floor, and he responded, "No problem. Very easy to clean." The casita sat at the edge of a pasture, with a big cottonwood shading the front yard, and a small creek running behind it. It was quiet and picturesque. I gave him the cash and moved right in. I had been traveling light and needed a bed frame for my thin mattress. I told myself that the frame could wait and tossed the mattress on the floor.

Great luck – until the sun went down and the cockroaches came out to play. I've never seen bigger ones and hope I never will. They emerged from under the kitchen cabinets, from a hole behind the toilet, and from cracks in the plastered adobe walls. Hundreds – no thousands – of them. When I stepped on a few, many more would fill their place and start eating the ones that I had stepped on. I had a broom and started to sweep them out of the bathroom into the bedroom. I had to be quick because they would try to scurry back, but I stayed ahead of them. Then I closed the door, stuffed a sheet under the bottom, and brushed away at the bedroom floor. It was like shoveling snow in a blizzard. Any place that I swept was soon covered by more roaches, and they just kept coming. I swept and yelled and swept and shouted till I finally got most of them corralled in the kitchen. I couldn't stand their skinny little legs, jittery antennas, and dirty little feet!

I pushed them from the kitchen and sealed the bottom of the outside door with T-shirts. Now, maybe I could get some sleep. I went back into the bedroom and saw several dozen roaches scurry into the cracks and under the mattress. I lifted it and shook out a bunch more. I wanted to exterminate the place by burning it down.

This was not going to work. I gave up the fight, carried the mattress out to the VW, and slept there for the night. The next evening, I was ready for the nasty little buggers. Before work, I bought about a dozen cans of "crawling insect spray." I squirted all the cracks, seams, and openings inside and around the outside foundation with a layer of industrial-strength roach exterminator. I saved a few cans just in case. I had to spray on a regular basis to keep their relatives and offspring from coming in and taking the place back over. It was a chore, but I held the creepy-crawlies at bay for the rest of the summer.

I arrived at the restaurant late Friday afternoon – ready for work in my new western duds – feeling only a little bit ridiculous. I cleaned and set up tables, memorized the menu as best I could, and waited for the customers to drift in. I was the oldest guy on the staff at 41 and instantly became known as "The Old Man." There was nothing to do except grin and bear it. I decided I would be as aware, personable, and humorous as possible. Nothing bothered me more in restaurants than waiters or waitresses who were arrogant, perfunctory, aloof, or disinterested. The customers were there to have a positive experience, and I intended to give it to them. I asked them where they were from and what they were planning to do on their visit. I tried to engage the kids in conversations, which usually created some laughs and surprises. Anything to draw a smile out of the tired travelers. It was easy. I enjoyed myself and got good tips for my efforts.

The specialty of the house was a two pound chicken-fried steak covered in gravy, with a large helping of mashed potatoes, a scoop of green beans, a dinner salad, and bread. One night, an enormous guy – easily 6'5" and a rock-hard 300 pounds – walked in with his wife and two kids and took a seat at one of my tables.

"How you doin', folks?"

The big guy grunted, glanced at the menu, and firmly placed it down on the table.

"Fine. Tell me – is that two pound chicken-fried steak really two pounds?"

"That's what they tell me."

I noticed that the owner was watching me closely.

"But you don't know?"

The guy was playing with me, but I strung along for the ride.

"Well Sir, I don't weigh them myself, but it looks pretty big to me."

"I don't want to buy it if it's not two pounds. How do I know that it's two pounds?"

I caught him cracking a bit of a smile.

"I'll tell you what, Sir. If you're still hungry after you finish the steak and everything else on the main course, I'll buy you dessert! How's that?"

"Hmm."

His cute little wife chirped up,

"It sounds like a good deal to me, Honey. They don't know how much you can eat!"

He looked at me with a grin.

"OK, Bud. You're on!"

I took the other orders, went out to the chef, and asked him to fry up "The biggest, damn, chicken-fried steak you can find and don't hold back on the potatoes and gravy!"

I served up a heaping dinner salad and a basket of bread for starters. The kids ordered hamburgers and fries and his wife got a grilled chicken breast salad. The guy's dinner plate was as big as a bar tray.

"What else can I get for you, Sir?"

He had already started to dig in but managed to speak through a mouthful.

"Looks good. Ah – I'll be needin' more butter for that bread!"

I brought out a dish of butter and watched from a distance as he tackled everything before him. It looked like I would be buying dessert.

"Can I get you more bread? Need anything else?"

"Nope."

He took his time and finished everything. He looked up at me with a Texas-sized smile and patted his lips daintily with his napkin. I was sure I had lost the bet.

"OK Sir. You win. What can I bring for your dessert?"

He sat there, thought for a moment, and shook his head. His wife could not believe it.

"Come on, Honey. You've never passed up dessert before."

The guy just looked at the table and leaned back in his chair.

"Nope, you win, Buddy. I can't stuff in another bite! Damn fine meal though. You can just bring the check, please."

He got up without seeming any worse for wear and paid the bill with a generous tip. He swaggered out the door with his wife and kids bringing up the rear. The oldest was giggling and imitating his bowlegged swagger, and the old wood floor sagged and creaked as he walked out. The owner had observed the whole thing and gave me a pleased grin and even an extra tip.

After work on that first night, the fumes had cleared in my casita, and I looked around each room with a flashlight. There was an army of dead roaches lying around, which I swept out, but the hordes that I had met in battle the night before had been conquered. I sprayed around the cracks and holes again and set up a cot I had bought that morning. I moved my mattress back into the bedroom, made the bed, and collapsed dead tired. I lay there looking at the ceiling of the moonlit room and wondered to myself, "What the hell am I doing here?" It was the same question I had asked myself many times since my first night in the pre-flight barracks in Pensacola. An easy answer still escaped me, and I soon drifted off to sleep.

The next morning, I was awakened by a loud crash as my bedroom window swung open on its hinges and hit the wall. I shook my head to clear my cobwebs away and sat up as the massive head of a white horse pushed its way inside. The horse looked at me and shook its head as if to say, "Hi Pal!" It opened its mouth, whinnied, and showed its teeth. It didn't take me long to understand that it was looking for a handout. What can you do? I stumbled into the kitchen and found an apple. He took it, nodded a few times, and retreated back to the meadow. Welcome to New Mexico! My landlord told me that the previous tenant had fed him carrots. There was no option other than to leave the window open and stock up on horse treats. He was always there as the sun came up. The good news was that I never needed an alarm clock.

That was how my summer went. I was out to have a good time, and the customers responded. It was fun. I took on another daytime job as a jeep tour driver driving vacationers back to some of the old gold mines higher in the mountains. On my days off, I drove my VW up these same 4-wheel drive roads and camped out. Its high axles made it a pretty good off-road vehicle if I took it easy over the bumps and boulders. I took my art supplies along and spent many relaxing hours dabbling with my paints and brushes. Nothing I liked came out of it, although it was a delightful way to spend my time. I had a great summer, but the tourist season ended abruptly with the passing of Labor Day.

Somehow, the rocky trails of the gold mining territories high in the Sangre de Christo Mountains felt vaguely familiar. I learned later that my father had used the backdrop of this rugged country in his books. A favorite storyline throughout his writings was the independence and toughness of the men who explored the west before the settlers came. He wrote about fur trappers, mountain men, and the last drivers of wild horses. When I gazed over the same magnificent landscapes as my father, I wished, as I supposed he had, that I had been the first to enter this unspoiled wilderness. His characters reflected his deep desire to be one of them and to conquer the daunting challenges that they had to face in their everyday lives. I shared his romantic empathy for these independent pioneers and his love for this spectacular frontier. It was now time, however, for me to set those thoughts aside and find a way to stay afloat.

I then went to a bartending school and worked for a few hotels in Santa Fe. Bartending was OK, but I hated dealing with the drunks. I got fired from one place because I refused to give one of its local boozers another drink. I had to quit another job because the band was so loud it rattled my brain. I had similar reactions to loud or violent movies, concerts, or athletic events. Noise overwhelmed me.

The season soon ended in Santa Fe with the beautiful turn and fall of the aspen leaves in the high country. It was time to find something else to do. Marge was on my case about getting behind in her alimony payments, and the IRS was threatening to attach everything I had – including my income. But I didn't have any assets or income for the IRS to bother about, and whatever money I sent to Marge was never enough. I would not, however, be able to let things slide much longer.

One of my biggest regrets was not doing more to get into the art scene. I had become familiar with most of the local galleries and museums and seen a lot of art. However, I was not able to balance my time between work and painting. I had to spend too many hours and too much energy earning enough income for basic expenses and to send what I could to Marge. When I found a few hours to paint, I was always too tired to feel creative. The predictable result was that I didn't end up with anything that I was pleased with.

"Maybe next time, sigh!"

I knew that there were hundreds of artists that made New Mexico home. I found myself talking with a well-known painter at a reception one evening and couldn't resist asking a question.

"How many artists do you think there are in Santa Fe?"

He thought for a moment.

"Maybe three or four."

Perhaps that was a standard joke in Santa Fe, but I instantly identified myself with all the other struggling artists who were working hard to paint good pictures and build a reputation for themselves. I wanted to be one of the "three or four," but realized that I wasn't even close to being there. He was absolutely right – fine artists were rare indeed.

The last of the summer tourists left Santa Fe, and the skiers would not start arriving in earnest until the Christmas holidays. I sold the VW – which was finally falling apart – and used the money to fly to Hawaii. I figured with all the resorts there, I could easily get a bartending job. Maybe that would lead to something better. But when I landed in Maui, I was seriously sick with some kind of flu. I checked into a cheap motel, paid for a week's rent, and told them I didn't want to be disturbed. I lay down on the bed exhausted, feverish, and disoriented. All that I remember of the next five days was the trade winds blowing constantly, and the windows rattling in their aluminum frames. I had been basically unconscious all that time. If I had gone to the bathroom or got something to eat, I couldn't recall it. When I woke up, I couldn't remember where I was until I heard the glass shaking and the unremitting gusts still howling outside.

I was pale and weak, and the cost of the motel had used up most of the money I expected to spend while I looked for a job. Nevertheless, I spent a few days going around to see what might be available. It soon became clear, however, that I wouldn't be successful because I wasn't an Islander and didn't have a great tan or big boobs like the local wahinis. Besides, I was too old. There must be bartenders in Hawaii older than 25, but I missed them.

With my tail between my legs, I caught a flight to San Diego and hopped on a bus to New York. It was time to get a "regular" job and catch up with my payments to Marge and the IRS. I had a lot of time to think during that trip. Familiar questions kept running through my mind, "What the hell am I doing here?" "Why can't I get a good job that sticks?" "What's wrong with me?" I still couldn't come up with any answers. Working hard had never been enough. Some problem would always hit me that I couldn't deal with – like my two and a half years with GSA. I had to quit with nothing to show for my time and energy – except more problems and a head full of mental bruises. After my leasing position in Salem, each new dead-end job turned out to be a step down from what I had before. I didn't have any lower to slide.

•

The bad news about hitting bottom is that life really is bad down there.
The good news is that the only way out is up.

•

Out Of The Fire – Into The Future

I DON'T RECOMMEND spending three non-stop days on a bus as it makes its way across country. Despite the romantic advertisements, buses make it impossible to enjoy the scenery. The best thing about a bus trip is when it ends. Besides eventually getting me to New York, the only thing that the trip did was to leave me exhausted, anxious, and down in the dumps. The buses were filled with a constant stream of drunks, cranky kids, and disturbed and downright dangerous individuals. I always took a seat in the back, but I couldn't sleep for fear of being whacked on the head and robbed of the few dollars I still had in my pocket. But that didn't happen. I arrived safely in New York – although utterly depleted from the ordeal.

I slept for the better part of the first two days at my old family home. My step-father had died several years earlier. It was sad that a man with such a proud history was gone, but the bitter knowledge that he had done so much damage to me personally was more than I could let go. I will grant that his intentions were good, however his total denial of my creative nature left me without a foundation on which to build my life. I am the first one to acknowledge that we must accept the consequences of our decisions. In the case of Reggy, however, he made these decisions for me when I was a teenager – despite my objections. I wish I had found the force of will to overcome his dominance, however I sadly did not have it in me. As far as I was personally concerned, his inexcusable episodes with Marge were a sad ending to my sad story with him.

Mom had become a severe alcoholic after Reggy died. She had stashed bottles all over the house and would get stumbling drunk at any time of the day or night. I took her aside at more sober moments and explained that I was dreadfully concerned for her. I pleaded with Mom to quit or to get counseling, but my worries did not change anything. The time had come for me to pull my own life together. I started to commute daily into New York City and search for jobs.

I interviewed with employment agencies, talked with art gallery owners, and even dropped in on real estate offices. Nothing clicked. I avoided talking to the federal government. There was no way that I would ever work for GSA again – under any circumstances! If GSA allowed such a bad supervisor to stay in her job, that indicated an agency-wide problem that I refused to expose myself to again. My attitude may not have been reasonable, but that's the way I felt. There were other agencies that hired Realty Specialists, however. I broke down to reconsider working for the Government again because it was the only employer where I might get a position quickly with some decent pay.

Another reason I was still interested in the Feds was that I could add my time spent in the Navy with my time in GSA to go against my retirement. That would be a good deal if I could somehow last another 11 years with the government. The other large agency employing Realty Specialists was the Army Corps of Engineers (CoE). It was responsible for a broad range of civilian and military projects that required real estate expertise. Any job with the Government had to be better than my experience with GSA, so I resolved to check the Corps out.

I went downtown to the Federal Building and walked into the CoE Personnel Office. The specialist I talked to was non-committal about any openings, but said he would order my records from the main office in Washington, DC. A week later the Chief of Personnel called me at home and asked if I could come in for an interview. The next afternoon I was waiting outside his office. He came out, handed me my file and asked if I would go upstairs to meet the Chief of Real Estate. That's moving things along, I thought.

The Real Estate Division was buzzing, people were working hard, and the office atmosphere had a totally different quality from GSA. That would not have been difficult. Unfortunately, however, specialists were stacked in tight rows with no partitions. Anti-smoking regulations had not been thought of yet, and a thick nicotine haze hung over the entire work space. It was like a sweat shop, and I would have trouble dealing with that. I did notice the same tall stacks of files and assumed that the workload here was as bad as at GSA. At least I would be kept busy.

The Chief came out, introduced himself, and invited me into his office. He was a trim, middle-aged, well-dressed man with a nervous intensity that revealed the extreme pressure of his position. The first thing he did was to pour himself a cup of coffee from a coffee maker on top of his file cabinet and ask if I wanted one. I thought that was cool.

"Sure. Just black, please."

He brought it over, sat down, and spent some time flipping through my file. He mumbled something under his breath that I couldn't understand.

"Hmmm."

He looked up and asked about my time flying in Vietnam. I told him a few colorful stories and brushed lightly over the accident that "got me out of the war." I could have talked a lot longer, but we moved on with the interview.

"Your experience in GSA certainly relates directly to our needs. The Chief of Personnel tells me that we can give you the same pay grade level that you had with GSA."

He offered me a cigarette, but I declined, thank you. I was a non-smoker. He lit one up for himself and flipped another page.

"Hmmm."

He looked up at me with a totally serious face. Then he looked back down and read some more. I could not see what he was reading, but he uttered some expletive to himself and then looked up again.

"Well! Ahmmm – that's quite a statement you wrote when you resigned from GSA!"

I was crestfallen. I had totally forgotten about that letter. All I could do was shake my head, smile, and tell it as it was.

"Yeah – and every word of it was true!"

He shook his head and broke out in a broad grin.

"I believe it."

He slapped his free hand on my résumé and took a drag on his cigarette.

"I had to deal with that – 'woman' – a number of times, and you are absolutely right! I respect you for quitting and writing those comments. Not many people act on principle, even if they get hurt in the process. I respect that."

I couldn't hold back a laugh. I raised my cup in salute to him.

"God, she was awful! I appreciate the compliment, Sir."

"You're welcome. Did you ever hear what happened to her?"

I shook my head.

"No. I never bothered to find out."

He puffed away on his cigarette for a moment.

"Well, here's what I understand. She – or actually the Government – lost the discrimination suit against her. You probably knew about the lawsuit. That cost us taxpayers a lot of money, but it was not what did her in. She missed a deadline to renew a major lease in downtown San Francisco. I was told that she had tried to get a lower rent than the rate specified, but the landlord wouldn't accept her proposal. She dickered right through the date that the option expired, and the landlord then hit her with a new rent which was at current market rates."

I was enjoying every bit of this information.

"That sounds just like her! So, what happened then?"

"She had to accept the owner's proposal, and the government was obligated for an additional million dollars over the term of the lease!"

"Wow! Did she try to take that out of petty cash?"

"Well, she sure had a lot of egg on her face. Everybody in real estate with the feds heard about it. The extra rent was bad enough, but that slip-up probably would still not have cost her the job. You know – we all make mistakes. What was worse was that she and the Director tried to cover it up. They got caught and both got fired by Central Office in Washington."

"Hoo-Ray! And good riddance! A very good riddance to them both!"

The Chief agreed and we both had a good chuckle.

"OK, Roger, here's where we're at. You caught us at a good time. We do have some positions that are currently being reviewed for approval by Personnel. I would like to try to hire you for one of them without going through the normal advertising and review period. I think – no, I don't know – but I'm hopeful that with your background and disability rating that we can get approval to hire you as soon as possible. How does that sound?"

"Super! Really, that would be great. Is there anything I can do to speed things along?"

He crushed his cigarette in an ashtray.

"I'll call the Chief of Personnel and let him know what we are trying to do. Why don't you go down and try to get in to see him? Here's your file to take with you."

"Very good! Many thanks for meeting with me – and for the coffee. Hearing about Cheryl made my day – no, made my last ten years! I hope we'll be talking soon."

I left believing that he was hedging his bets. He wouldn't have said what he did if he wasn't confident that he could make this happen. The receptionist at Personnel said that the Chief was busy, but that he had briefed one of his senior specialists and told her what was going on. She came out of her cubicle, and I handed her my file. She was one of those invaluable, grey-haired employees who had been there forever, knew how to work through regulations, and could maneuver through all the shortcuts to move things along in a minimum amount of time. She looked at me with a sly smile.

"I can't wait to see that letter."

News gets around fast in government agencies. My reputation was established even before I got there. It took only a week before I was offered the job. I was hired on a Friday and reported for work on Monday.

After completing the initial paperwork with Personnel, I was introduced to everybody, and then taken around to review their file systems and project flow-charts. The Assistant Chief initially assigned me a desk that was between two chain smokers. I tried to grin and bear it, but my eyes soon started to water and my throat was getting sore. I went back and told him my problem. He looked at me sourly and puffed on his own cigarette.

"Nobody has complained of that before. You should learn to live with it."

"Sorry, Sir. If I can't get another work station, I'll have to leave. I can't deal with it."

I was beyond taking any crap from any supervisor! He muttered something nasty about prima donnas and thought for a moment.

"OK. Let's go see if there is another desk available."

There wasn't, but one specialist in the front row was a smoker, and he agreed to move to the desk that I had been assigned. That was fine. I moved over to his position and enjoyed slightly cleaner air. The Assistant Chief never got over that, however. I was on his shit-list, but he got a promotion at another district and the problem went away.

117

Then there was an organizational briefing. The Corps of Engineers had to service civilian projects – such as beach erosion protection, flood control, and environmental (Super-Fund) clean-up sites. Our military responsibilities included acquisition of real estate for communications and radar antenna sites, recruiting office leases, flight easements for military airbases, negotiations with developers to build on-base military housing, the sale of base closure properties, and much more. New York District had responsibility for all these functions in New Jersey, New York, and the six New England states. We also had a dual set of supervisors – one military and the other civilian. It was a cumbersome system designed to be dysfunctional. Consequently, the workload created a constant flow of overdue problems and crises.

At my level, however, the management problems didn't involve me very much. Above me – to wrestle with all those issues – was a Realty Supervisor, the Assistant Chief of Real Estate, and the Chief of Real Estate. I was very well insulated from the top. All I had to do was take care of the assignments that came down to me. Nevertheless, we were constantly under pressure to meet deadlines, negotiate the best prices possible, and avoid costly mistakes.

I could deal with the workload well enough if my supervisors left me alone to get it done. I was not a good team player. It took them a while to realize that I was a loner and not to micro-manage me. All they had to do was explain what the action required and leave me alone to get it done. I soon found that I could use the same technique that I had used in the Navy. I took old agreements, changed the numbers, replaced the property description and summary of the negotiations, and submitted the package for approval. When I ran into a problem, I wasn't shy about asking for help.

I was working so hard that my first year with the Corps of Engineers blew past before I knew it. I had become familiar with our territory, and how to work with the players who had a piece of the action. I had handled some good-sized projects and wrestled the problems to the ground. The pace was brutal, but I was up to the challenge and nobody messed with me. I received several Letters of Commendation and an end-of-year bonus. I was happy and did not have time to dwell on the past.

I had parked myself in a small railroad apartment in Hoboken, New Jersey. It was on the third floor, high enough not to be bothered by street noise. The neat thing about Hoboken is that it's one of the terminals for the ferry system that hauls commuters back and forth from lower Manhattan. I could walk to the ferry, enjoy a beautiful view of the New York skyline, land at the Financial Center, and walk through the World Trade Center to my office in the Federal Building. It was a pleasant, relaxing commute, and only cost two dollars each way. In the evening, I would sit outside at the Financial Plaza and have a relaxing drink while I watched the peaceful sun setting across the Hudson River.

One evening after I got home, my telephone rang. It was my youngest son, Matt, on the line.

"Hi Dad. How ya' doing?"

"And a big HELLO to you, Matt. What a surprise! I'm doing fine. What are you up to?"

"Nothing special, Dad. Still wrestling with school."

"It's difficult, son. But education is the only way to get ahead in life. Stick with it."

"Sure thing. Did you hear about Jeff?"

"No, I haven't heard a thing. Jeff and I don't talk to each other. I hope that will change someday, but I'm not holding my breath."

"Well, you'll like this, Dad. Jeff cleaned up his act and signed up for the Marines. He just left for San Diego to start basic training."

"WOW! That is absolutely the last thing I would have expected. I'm surprised, but it's exciting!"

"Yeah, Dad. We were all surprised."

"So how's Mom?"

I tried to be nonchalant when talking about his mother. He had snapped at me once saying that she was still his mother, even if I didn't like her anymore.

"Mom's been seeing Jerry. You know that guy that owns the gravel business. He used to live next to us. They seem to be happy together."

"Good."

I had expected Marge to go after her friend in California, but what did I know? Jerry could provide her with the security that I had been unable to achieve. If she was happy, that relieved me of some of the guilt I felt because of our failed marriage.

"Anyone new in your life? Any girl friends?"

"No girls, Dad. You remember Tad? I'm spending a lot of time with him."

"Sure, I remember."

Tad was not one of my favorite kids. I thought he was responsible for supplying Jeff and Matt with most of their drugs.

"Please be careful, Matt. Tad got you and Jeff into a lot of trouble. I wish you would find a different crowd to hang out with."

"Tad's OK. He's slowed down a lot. So have I. Disregard all this growing up bullshit, and he's a smart guy. He's my best friend now."

"OK, Matt. It's your call. Just be careful, please."

"Yeah, Dad. I hear you."

Matt paused for a moment. This had been a touchy conversation.

"Well, Dad, that's about all. I can't think of anything else to report."

"I'm really glad you called, Matt. Keep in touch more often. Bye for now."

"Great talking with you too, Dad. Bye."

Back in the office, there was talk of establishing a new field office at Ft. Devens, Massachusetts, close to Boston. The Corps of Engineers was expecting a large increase in the work load in New England because of the Base Closure Bill that was working its way through the Department of Defense and Congress. If that happened, New York District would have to appoint a chief for that field office. I was too buried in work to pay much attention.

•

Take care of business before business takes care of you.

•

120

Sometimes Progress Overtakes You

RUMORS PERSISTED about the new field office. I became mildly interested, but had to wrestle with the idea of being a supervisor again and subjecting myself to new responsibilities. I would be able to hire my own staff, however, and be out from under the direct thumb of district supervision. Living expenses would be lower in Massachusetts, and I could relocate easily. Bottom line was that I was nervous about taking this on, but I pressed ahead because the benefits far outweighed the negatives. When approval for the field office came down from Washington, I was first in line to apply for the position.

There were applicants from other districts, however I had the inside track. My 10% disability again eliminated everyone else. I got the appointment and was sent to Ft. Devens to establish a work space for the operation and to advertise for our staff. I was authorized to hire two Realty Specialists, an appraiser, and a secretary. Our office was on the lower floor of an old WWII barracks with about 2000 square feet. I had a reasonable budget to get the space renovated, so I was off and running. I placed "Help Wanted" ads in the Boston Globe, had telephones installed, and designed a space plan for how I wanted the office to be laid out. We contracted for the renovations and responses to my ads came in.

I selected a secretary who turned out to be fabulous. Carolyn was an experienced clerical worker, but had no expectations of moving into higher positions. After two years, however, she knew as much about real estate as anyone in the office. I encouraged her to get a sales license and to apply for the next position that came up. She was selected and did terrific work as a Realty Specialist for the office.

Then I hired two realty specialists. One of them, Helen, was a transfer from a GSA office. She was already familiar with most of the regulations and hard work didn't bother her. She was like a work horse, and kept a steady pace as she plowed through her heavy load of assignments.

The other specialist, Glen, did not turn out well, however. Maybe I missed something in our short interview, but I did not get any indication of a problem until later. The man seemed personable, professional, and confident. He had a real estate sales license, had worked the area, and

Bad Feng Shui

seemed like a good choice. But once he got into the office, he could not keep his mouth shut. His endless conversation with himself became an annoying distraction for everybody.

Finally, I came to the selection of an appraiser. I expected this position to be the most difficult to fill because any appraiser worth his or her salt would not consider this low paying job. My chances of getting anybody with quality credentials were slim. In fact, the only prospects I had to interview were two old men who wanted to come out of retirement, and a gal without appraisal experience who had just gotten her Massachusetts Appraiser License. I had to eliminate these three before I could re-advertise for more applicants. One of the guys declined the position when he learned how little he would earn. The second man was unacceptable because he wanted to work from his home and come into the office only once a week. He also did not want to travel. How can anyone appraise something without seeing it – for chrissake?

Then I asked the third applicant – the gal – to come in. Her name was Melissa. Oh – my – gawd! She was drop-dead gorgeous! Was I in deep trouble or what?! She was about ten years younger and a few inches shorter than me – she was carrying a letter-size, alligator-skin, attaché case – she had on elegant, Italian leather shoes with tall, spiked heels – her business outfit was made of thin, expensive, pastel-colored fabrics that draped smoothly over her slender body – her calves were bare and tightly toned – she obviously worked out and spent time in a tanning booth – her pixie-style hair was naturally blonde – more perfect than any bleached blonde I had ever seen – if she wore a bra it wasn't obvious because her full breasts jiggled seductively when she moved – her nipples pushed out though her blouse and even through her thin suit jacket – the edges of her panties showed through her superbly fitted skirt as they came up around her tight, little butt – her looks were natural, sexy, confident, and intelligent all at the same time – she had a mole on her cheek exactly like Marilyn Monroe – and her subtle perfume almost blew business entirely out of my mind.

WOW! I swear I wasn't staring and had observed all this in my very first glance. I had to keep this interview on a strictly professional level – of course – but my mind was dizzy with questions, and my poor little heart was going flutter, flutter. Melissa was a shock to my system after I had buried myself in my work for the last year. It was like the sun had suddenly popped up after hiding on the other side of some dark clouds all this time. We shook hands and introduced ourselves. Her grip was tight and strong. She smiled sweetly and studied me with her aqua blue eyes. I felt like I was melting.

"Please have a seat, Melissa."

Her arm brushed mine as she passed close to me in the tight space.

"Let me take a minute to review your application, please."

I really needed time to collect myself.

"Oh, I've updated the résumé I sent you. Please use this."

Melissa half-stood and leaned over the desk to hand it to me. There was damn little left for me to imagine – or admire.

"Ah, what's different other than this mauve paper and the photograph?"

The photo was a professional publicity shot. The paper was a heavy bond with a smooth, rich finish.

"Oh, just the address has changed. Now I will be closer to this office – if I get hired, of course."

"Yes, of course."

I had to pause and take a deep breath. My expectations were getting out of control.

"OK. I see that you just got your Appraiser's License a few months ago. What other business experience do you have that would be relevant to this position?"

"Well – not much, but I did work with a large developer once who was subdividing property. I learned a lot from him. He really got me interested in real estate. I also have a good feel for values in this area. I've lived here all my life."

I bet you did learn a lot from that developer, I thought silently. I had to force myself to snap back to reality.

"I see here on your résumé that you've been a freelance photographer for the last seven years. Please, tell me about that."

"Yes – well, I worked for a lot of magazines – rock magazines, actually."

She studied me to make sure that I was going to comprehend all this. She continued matter-of-factly.

"I took gigs to photograph rock bands while they were performing in concert. You know – U2, ZZ Top, The Rolling Stones, The Grateful Dead – a lot of the big names."

"OK, Melissa. Uhmmm – let me be frank here. Why do you want to take this job? It's entry level, doesn't pay much, and you'll be working your butt off. Frankly, I think it would be a big let-down after working around rock stars."

She tilted her head and looked at me with a smug little grin.

"Does my butt really need working off?"

She had broken the ice. I had to chuckle.

"Ah – no. Your butt looks just fine."

I could have kicked myself for saying that, but it was true.

"Now please tell me, why do you want to work for the Government? Your photography jobs must pay you well and be very exciting."

"Yeah."

She gave me a cute, sideways look and then lowered her eyes thoughtfully for a moment. She shook her head and looked back up.

"It's like this, Roger. Oh, I'm sorry. Can I call you Roger?" I nodded. "I hope what I'm going to say doesn't kill my chances here. Please try to understand."

"OK."

I looked at her attentively and waited.

"I need this job to get back into the real world! Yes, I made a bunch of money. Yes, I've had an exciting and fast life – more than I can take really. Frankly Roger, I need an obligation – a responsibility that will keep my feet on the ground."

Then she looked down and rubbed her hands in her lap. She sighed again. Melissa's eyes got watery, and I noticed the beginning of a tear falling down her cheek before she brushed it away. She hesitated a moment and then continued haltingly.

"Sorry. Yes, much too fast. Actually – I've GOT to get away from the drugs and everything crazy that is part of that life. I need to anchor myself again. All I really am is a very simple country girl. Like – I've inherited my grandparents' old farm in Maine. I dream of getting back there and fixing up the place. Can you understand all that?"

I nodded and thought for a moment. She was begging me for a new life. I smiled to myself. We all need second chances, I thought.

"I do understand, Melissa, but you have to realize that I'm not running a rehab center here."

"Oh no. I don't need that. I'm not addicted to anything. Yeah, I enjoy some of that stuff, but I'm not addicted. I just need a quieter life style. It will never be a problem. I'll never let you down – I promise!"

She let out a big sigh.

"Please, Roger."

Again, she seemed close to tears. I waited for a moment as she struggled to collect herself.

"OK. How about the money? How can you be happy working hard and earning peanuts compared to what you can be making?"

"After you have enough, more money doesn't matter – to me anyway. And between you and me – I shouldn't say this – I'll probably still take a gig from time to time."

"How would that work, Melissa?"

I was curious. This woman was fascinating as well as beautiful. She was back to her captivating self again.

"I'll just do it on weekends, Roger. Sometimes I might have to ask for an extra day or two. Like if I have to go to LA or London or Paris or somewhere."

"You would have to take leave to do that. I just can't cover for you whenever you want to take time off. And wouldn't London or Paris take longer than a couple of days? I don't see how you could manage it."

"Right. I understand totally about the leave – I'll have to earn the time first. And if I have to go overseas, they'll fly me over on the Concorde. I'll just go Friday night, do the show on Saturday and be back for work on Monday. Zip, zip – no problem."

She made it sound like it was the most ordinary thing in the world. I couldn't help laughing.

"Well, Melissa. You live in an entirely different world from me. Let me think about all of this for a few days. OK?"

"Sure, but do you think I'm qualified?"

"Well, you have your license – that's a plus. And your knowledge of the area is in your favor. This is just an entry level position, so the qualifications are pretty minimal ..."

I tried to act serious and thoughtful.

"... And there's no drug test for this position. That's also to your advantage."

Melissa squirmed and gave me a dirty look.

"I do have one concern, Melissa. How good a negotiator are you? There will be lots of times when you will have to justify your appraisal to difficult property owners and to the government agency that's paying the bill. It isn't easy to arrive at a price and then get it accepted by everybody. Do you think you can do that?"

Melissa's face turned strong and confident.

"I've negotiated contracts with the toughest lawyers in the business. Believe me, I can negotiate."

I watched her and had to smile. She had the ability to change her look from sexy, to tough, to vulnerable, to whatever – whenever she wanted. I was intrigued.

"OK, I believe you. Just give me a few days to think this through. I'll get back to you as soon as I can."

She stood and reached across the desk to shake hands. She held my hand and looked me in the eye.

"Thank you, Roger. I know we will work well together! I'm looking forward to hearing from you real soon."

All I could think of was smothering myself in that beautiful cleavage. I would die a happy man! Melissa released me with a smile and a little jiggle of her titties just for my benefit. She turned and wafted out the door like a breath of fresh, spring air. I collapsed in my chair. I simply couldn't believe it. Here I was, wrestling with one of the toughest jobs I've ever had and in walks the most beautiful, most seductive woman I have ever met – with brains even – and she wants to work for me. I must be dreaming! On paper, she met the requirements of the position. I needed an appraiser – I couldn't do my job without one – and I could not reject her just because she had good looks. I would just have to hire her. Shucks!

I did let one day pass before I gave her a call. I became worried that she simply did not fit the mold of other government employees. How would she present herself when she had to go to our District Office in New York? We would frequently have to travel together on many of our projects. How would that work out? She would certainly be a distraction for me. Would she be a loose cannon, or would she be an asset to the office? These were questions that would have to be resolved over time, however. I felt sure that she would be trouble for me personally, but I found myself excited to discover how much pleasure that trouble would bring.

Faxes had barely been invented in 1985 and hadn't reached Corps of Engineers offices yet. I stuck Melissa's résumé in overnight mail to Personnel. No, I did not include her photo. I needed Personnel's seal of approval before I could step out and do anything. They responded later on the following morning that she would be OK. That overcame what little resistance I still had, and I gave her a call the next day.

"Hi, Melissa. This is Roger Blake from the Corps of Engineers."

"Yes, of course, Roger. How are we doing?"

"Good. If you're still interested, I would like to offer you the job."

"Super! I accept. Now what happens?"

She sounded genuinely excited.

"Let's see. This is Wednesday, so let's wait till next week. It's the start of a new pay period, and Monday will be easier for Accounting."

"Gosh – That's great, Roger! Is there anything I should be doing in the meantime?"

"No, just enjoy your freedom for now and get lots of rest. You're going to need it."

"I'm really excited, Roger! I don't think I'll get much rest. I appreciate you pushing this through so fast. Were there any problems?"

"No. No problems. Well – the only real problem was me. I was having difficulty imagining how you would fit into the office. I hope you understand – this is not meant to be criticism in any way. I would just ask that you – hmmm – dress appropriately and keep a low profile. I'm trying to be delicate, but I hope you know what I'm saying."

"Yes, of course. I've run into this before. I understand that my appearance can be – ah, disruptive. I'll just work hard and be professional. No one will notice that I'm even there."

"I doubt that, Melissa. The only other thing is to plan for a trip to New York on the following week. I have to introduce you and the other new people to the folks down at the District Office. You will frequently be dealing directly with them, and I've arranged for some orientation lectures. We want to get everybody off to a good start."

"OK. I'll see you Monday then. Uhm – thank you so much, Roger."

"You're welcome. I'm sure this will work out well for both of us. Be seeing you."

I kicked myself as soon as the words were out of my mouth. I did not mean to imply any double meaning. What I meant to say was that I thought she would be a damn good appraiser. And if she manipulated clients as well as she handled me, she would simply knock them dead!

"Well, goodbye till Monday."

"Bye – Roger."

She said "Roger" like it was the sexiest name on the planet.

I hung up. I was sweating through my damn collar! Was it just me, or was her seductive tone really there? Yes, it was, alright. How could she make "Roger" sound so – so – sensual? Wow. My expectations were climbing off the scale. It had been a long time since a woman had turned me on like this.

•

Romance was the first game of chance and,
of course, the first contact sport.

•

Forward Is Not Always The Right Direction

I SPENT MY TIME THAT WEEK looking for an apartment that was affordable and finally found a one room studio in an old house. It had polished oak floors, a new kitchenette unit, and freshly painted white walls and ceiling. It was clean and OK for now. I moved in on Friday afternoon and was tired after a long day. I put water on to boil for noodles and some spaghetti sauce to heat up in a new pan that I had bought that morning. The lid was a little bent and tight when I placed it on the pot, but I guessed that was why it had been on sale.

Then the phone rang, and it was Matt again.

"Hi, Dad. How's it going in Massachusetts?"

"Pretty good, Matt."

I was thinking of Melissa.

"I'll have to tell you about it sometime."

"Glad to hear it. Um – did you hear from Jeff?"

From the dejected tone of his voice, I could tell this was not going to be good.

"No. What's going on, Matt?"

"Well, he gave me a call a little while ago. He said he went AWOL."

"That's freaking stupid! What the hell happened?"

I was disgusted, angry, and deeply disappointed.

"He said he finished boot camp OK and then volunteered for RECON – you know, like Special Forces. He was going through more training, but got pissed about the bullshit they were putting him through – like jumping up and down on his stomach after he had just run five miles with a full pack on.

The sergeant kept yelling over and over, 'You've got to be tough, Blake!' That's what Jeff said, anyway."

"Damn! He could have just washed out of the program. That would have been the normal thing to do, and he could have still stayed in the Marines."

"It gets worse, Dad. He wanted to make a statement – you know how stubborn Jeff is. So, on his next day off, he went out and got stoned on cocaine. He didn't return for a few days. They did a blood test when he checked back in and, of course, he came up positive. They wrote him up and tossed him in the brig. They were going to give him a 'Less than Honorable Discharge,' but when they let him out of detention again, he went off-base and kept on going."

"How in the hell could he be so damn dumb? AWOL! Now he's a fugitive. This is serious shit."

"I'm sorry I had to be the one to tell you, Dad. Anyway, I asked what he was going to do. He said he might hitchhike across country and come see you. I'm just trying to give you a heads-up."

"Matt, I'm sorry. I'm angry with Jeff – not you. I appreciate you letting me know, but this is really sad news."

I knew how difficult it must have been for Matt to make the call.

"Yeah Dad. Well, that's it. I'll let you go. I hope it turns out OK."

"I hope so too, Matt. Thanks again – 'bye."

I collapsed on the couch and sat there thinking. I couldn't understand how Jeff could go so wrong. I blamed myself for not being closer to him. At least I should have made him feel comfortable enough to call me for advice when he needed it. However, he certainly wouldn't have taken any from me. But that didn't matter. Somehow, I should have found a way to become a better father. Maybe I should not blame myself for everything, but that was the way I felt. I just sat on the couch and stared miserably at the floor.

I was still wringing my hands and shaking my head, when – KABOOM!!! A bomb could have exploded in the room. I dove under the kitchen table, but not until after I had been sprayed by something red and hot. I started to shake uncontrollably. I cowered with my hands over my ears and my eyes clinched shut. The cover of the pan had been a bit sticky when I had set it on the pot. It must have expanded in the heat and stuck tight until the pressure inside had become too much, and the whole mess of spaghetti sauce exploded. The lid had banged against the ceiling and crashed down on the other side of the room. My heart was thumping in my chest, and my pulse was running wild! I finally collected my nerves and peeked out from under the table. It took a few minutes, however, before I could calm myself down and think straight.

In PTSD, my response would be called, "... reacting to stimuli related to a previous trauma."

I had recoiled at loud, unexpected noises before, but this time was the worst. All I could think about were the bombs exploding beneath my F4. For a moment I was back there, trying to hang on for dear life. Why couldn't I leave all that crap behind?

The entire apartment was covered in gooey-red sauce – ceiling, walls, floors, rug, furniture – everything! Covered. Even the new bedspread I had bought the day before. Groan! I had never had to deal with tomato stains before. I went right after the walls, but it was already too late. I borrowed a ladder and wiped down the ceiling, the lights, the high walls, and then everything else in the apartment. I was cleaning like mad and cussing Jeff out at the same time. That took me past midnight. The rest of my weekend, and a few more evenings the next week, were spent cleaning, doing laundry, and painting everything – including the doors, cabinets, trim, and window sills. Even with all that, the burnt sauce smell never left the apartment. And I couldn't get Jeff out of my mind. Welcome to Massachusetts!

I was grateful when Monday came, and I could go to work. I got there about ten minutes early, and Melissa was already at the entrance waiting to be let in. I tried to appear cheerful.

"Hi. How was your weekend?"

I kept fumbling with the keys for some reason.

"Fun! My new place is on a small lake, so my boyfriend and I went waterskiing, sat around, and had a barbeque. How was yours?"

"Not so hot."

I don't know why I had not expected to hear there was a boyfriend in the picture. At least she hadn't said, "My husband."

"Anyway, you're the first one here, so take the desk that you want."

She walked up and down the row considering all the location factors.

"This is yours?"

She pointed to the only private office on the floor.

"Right."

"Then I like this one."

She started to put her stuff down. It was the only desk I could see from mine.

"Uhmmm – why don't you move to the one up front, please? Getting work done will be tough enough without having to look at you all day."

Melissa smiled sweetly and looked very pleased with herself. She went up to the first desk in the row and plopped her stuff down.

"Is this OK?"

Melissa looked at me with a smirk. She took her coat off and was wearing a fuzzy, peach-colored sweater with a wide turtle-neck collar that lay on her bare shoulders, a pair of trim-fitting jeans, and a different set of spiked heels.

"Fine. Just fine."

The others were coming in. We all gathered, and I introduced everybody. I showed Carolyn to her secretarial work station and put Helen and Glen behind Melissa.

"All our files should be arriving from New York in about half an hour. Getting the cases organized will be our first priority, but I'll get into that later. In the meantime, come into my office after you get your stuff put away. I've got stacks of regulations for each of you to start reading. I'll get some coffee started."

 I had bought a new coffee maker and a bunch of mugs for the office. Melissa came into the storage room and helped me unpack it all.

"So what was 'not so hot' about your weekend?"

"I had a spaghetti disaster."

I told her the sad tale of losing the battle against the pot with the tight lid, diving under the table, the weekend spent cleaning and painting – etc. etc. She gave me a funny look and then burst out laughing. Everybody was gathering around to find out what she found so funny. I wasn't cracking a smile. She finally stopped laughing and proceeded to tell the story to the others.

"You won't believe this, everybody!"

She was a lot more animated than I had been, and my crew was laughing along with her. Glen sniffed the air, came over, and took a whiff of my jacket.

"I thought I smelled something funny!"

Everybody was getting a good laugh out of the story at my expense.

"OK, everybody shut up before I have to hand out demerits."

I dug in my pocket and gave office keys to everyone. Melissa got hers and held it thoughtfully.

"Do we have flex hours, or do we have to come in at a specific time?"

"Good question. I don't care what time you come in, so long as it's set with me as a regular schedule. You have to put in a nine hour day. That includes a one hour lunch break, but you can come in at 6 a.m. if you want."

Melissa approved.

"Great! That will give me time for a work out in the afternoon!"

I should have expected as much.

"Carolyn, can you get this coffee going? Three heaping tablespoons to a full pot – strong. OK?"

"Cream and sugar?"

"Black, please."

"No problem – coming right up, boss!"

Geez. I wasn't getting any respect from anybody. But this was great. I wanted to build this kind of spirit – to get everybody comfortable working together as a team. We would have to do a lot of covering of each other's backs when times got busy. I smiled, nodded, and went into my office. In a few minutes they all gathered around the folders on my desk, and Carolyn brought in my cup of coffee. She also carried a dictation pad and a sharpened pencil. Most of the time, I never saw her without them.

"OK, folks. Here we go. Melissa, this pile is appraisal regulations. These two stacks are for you Realty Specialists. You don't need to memorize each regulation, but you do have to become familiar with them, so that you can find whatever you need. Eventually, I expect you to get to know them pretty well. Next week, we will be getting work flow charts that will help you plan each step that you have to take.

"And don't assume that the Government does things the logical way, or the same way you may be used to. In fact, if something could be made more difficult, the government lawyers have found it and written a law to make you do it. These may be 'Regulations,' but they have the force and effect of law, so don't mess around with 'Regulations!' Any questions? – No? Everybody understands perfectly? Good. Take these off to your desks and get started. Carolyn, you and I will unpack your equipment."

This was 1985. Carolyn's equipment amounted to an IBM Selectric, a large copy machine, a calculator, a stapler, and a 3-hole punch. Computers would not arrive at the Corps of Engineers for another two years. There was a place on base where we could get office supplies like paper, carbon paper, pencils, erasers, and most importantly – white out. When we were done, Carolyn took off to do shopping for all of us. We were up and running.

Our files arrived that afternoon – only six hours late. There were about a dozen boxes full with hundreds of case folders. We had to generate extensive summaries with pertinent information on each file, and then get approval from New York District for the actions that needed to be done. Our work was cut out for us. The process was time consuming and tedious, but by the end of the week everyone had a handle on what needed to be done. We made several copies of the spreadsheets and took them with us to New York.

•

Life is full of opportunities and pitfalls that sometimes appear very much alike.
The trick is to tell the difference.

•

You Never Know Your Luck

MONDAY ARRIVED and we all met at Boston's Logan Airport to catch our flight to LaGuardia, which was packed with other business commuters. We crammed ourselves in with the rest of the bodies, briefcases, and carry-on bags. My group got scattered around the cabin and, as usual, I took a window seat as far to the rear as I could get. I hated everything about flying – the noise, vibrations, people, waiting, and most of all, not being in the cockpit. The engines revved up, and the airplane strained against the brakes. The plane was released, we rolled down the runway, and lifted off into the skies over Boston.

As the city was falling away beneath us, I looked out the window and noticed that a section of aluminum skin on the wing was being peeled up by the flap when it was raised to the stowed position. The piece of metal was thrashing around wildly in the wind. I had watched my wings come apart once before in the Navy and was not happy. I expected the wing to fall off at any moment. I pushed the button for the stewardess. She made her way back to me, and I pointed out the problem. The hole had gotten bigger.

"Oh, I'm sure the pilot knows about it."

"Well, I'm sure he doesn't, or we wouldn't be flying right now."

"I'll bring it to his attention when I'm not so busy, Sir."

She might as well have flipped me off. She was attractive, but I doubted that she had been hired for her problem recognition abilities. Anyway, she made me really angry.

"Goddamn it, Miss! Tell him now or I'll go up the aisle telling everybody to look out at the fucking hole in our wing!"

That grabbed her attention. She got on the cockpit phone and told them about the problem, giving me dirty looks the whole time. The piece of aluminum had fallen off and probably hit some unfortunate bastard when it landed. Pretty soon, the co-pilot came back, and I pointed out the hole, which was now about two foot square and really should not have been there.

"Well, Sir, I'll certainly tell the pilot. Thanks for pointing it out."

He must have been the stewardess' brother.

"Aren't you going to do something – like land?"

"That is not my decision, but we'll keep our eyes on it. Thanks for pointing it out, Sir. I don't think it looks too dangerous for now. Please relax and enjoy the flight."

"For now! Jesus."

My only consolation was that if we went down, the crew would hit the ground first. The stewardess came back to my seat and acted as if nothing had happened.

"May I get you a drink, Sir?"

"Whiskey?"

"No Sir. I was thinking of coffee or a soda."

She rolled her eyes while she was still smiling at me. That's quite a trick, I thought. I didn't know that anybody could do that. Must have been part of her training.

"Well, get me a Coke with a slice of lemon. I'll make believe there's some rum in it."

I went back to nervously watching the wing to see if it really was going to fall off. The only good thing about that flight was that it was short. We landed at LaGuardia without any further problem. Our group met at the baggage claim area. We all had small overnight bags – except for Melissa who had a hot-pink suitcase with a matching suit bag and cosmetic case. I had to laugh as she set the cosmetic case on top of her suitcase that had rollers and was struggling to lift the suit bag over her shoulder. My chivalrous nature had a perfect opportunity to shine.

"Hey. Let me carry that for you."

She gave me a grateful smile.

"I can manage."

"Maybe, but you don't look good in bags."

I had to try twice to swing it over my shoulder. It was really heavy.

"What the hell do you have in here?"

"Oh, it must be the ankle weights on the bottom. I'm afraid I don't know how to travel light."

I noticed she was stuffing a business card into her purse – probably some guy she would meet later, I thought.

"Goddamn! You must have brought the whole gym with you!"

We found a rack of carts, paid our 50 cents, and wheeled everything out to the line of waiting taxis. The dispatcher wanted us to use two cabs, but I insisted that we all squeeze into one. We had business to discuss on the way downtown. The first three cabs wouldn't take the whole group. I offered the driver of the fourth an extra $10 tip if he would drive us all. That was fine. We loaded the baggage into the trunk and piled in. I took a window seat in the back. Melissa slipped in beside me, and Glen sat on her other side. Carolyn and Helen squirmed into the front.

It was a hot day, and the cab's air conditioning wasn't working. We had to put the windows down and got the soot from the diesel exhausts and traffic noise all the way into town. We couldn't hear each other, so I just looked out the window and let my hair blow in the wind.

I felt Melissa's leg press against mine a couple of times. I tried to ignore her, but it wasn't possible. I thought of discouraging her, but she tried a little harder the third time. I pressed back while I still looked out the window. She had her suit jacket over her knees, so I shifted my shin over next to hers and rubbed a little. We fortunately pulled up to the Federal Building before I got too excited. There was no security check in those years. We just walked in and took the elevator up to Real Estate. I was still hefting Melissa's pink bag over my shoulder.

The office was just as smoky and frantic as when I had left. I couldn't help but notice how pale and stressed everyone looked compared to the people in our office. I hoped I still didn't look like that. A few folks nodded and said "Hi" as we passed by, but just about everyone was focused on Melissa as she ambled across the floor. We walked up to the Chief's secretary, whom I had known well from before I went to Massachusetts.

"We're here."

"Nice bag, Roger!"

"It's Mr. Blake to you, dammit!"

She snickered and went in to tell the Chief. He came out and introduced himself to everyone.

"Why don't you leave your luggage here? The first thing you have to do is to go down to Personnel – get your ID's and paperwork done. That will probably take you the rest of the morning. Be back here at 1 p.m. after lunch, and we'll start the orientation."

The Chief grabbed my arm as the others started to walk away.

"Where did you find her?"

"She found me. Life is hard!"

"Good work!"

He shook his head and watched as I followed the others back to the elevators.

Personnel sent us straight down to the Security Office where we got in line to have our pictures taken and get our ID card. When it was Melissa's turn, she gave the camera a dazzling smile that left the photographer weak-kneed and choking on his cigarette.

"Sorry, I missed it. Would you mind doing that again?"

Melissa was glad to oblige. She posed like a movie star on the red carpet at the Academy Awards.

I took everybody over to my favorite buffet for lunch. We loaded up with whatever we wanted and went to the cashier. Melissa had only taken two slices of carrots, a piece of celery, and a little cottage cheese. When she got up to the checkout, the burly, unshaven guy behind the cash register glanced at her plate and looked up at her. He grinned and gave her a long, loud, appreciative wolf-whistle.

"No charge for you, Baby Doll. That's on the house. Come back anytime!"

She gave him a warm smile and walked over to our table. I was beginning to expect Melissa to create a scene wherever she went. Most of the time, she

139

wasn't even trying to draw attention to herself. Melissa obviously enjoyed it, however. But Glen feigned being hurt because he wasn't getting the same attention.

"Gee, I didn't get a free lunch."

Carolyn jumped in.

"Well, you're not a natural blonde ..."

She looked around and leaned over confidentially.

"... and ya' don't have great boobs, stupid!"

We all howled! That was totally out of character for Carolyn – our reserved, soft-spoken New Englander with her thick downeast accent. The restaurant, which was noisy with luncheon conversations, became quiet while everybody turned to wonder what this loud group of out-of-towners found so funny. Melissa was blushing bright red, but laughed nervously along with the rest of us. She looked at me and gave a little shrug.

"It's not my fault, dammit!"

That afternoon, we listened to three, stifling hours of orientation lectures while trying to swallow back yawns. When the Chief was finished with his introduction we pulled out our spread sheets to show him. He studied each one for a while and asked a few questions.

"We could sure use something like these down here, folks. Our tickler files are continually missing some important action. We always have to drop what we're doing to put out the damn fire. Planning is a helluva lot smarter than reacting!"

He shook his head and rolled up the spreadsheets to take with him. Then, there were the heads of the Acquisition, Management & Disposal, Planning & Control, and Legal Departments. When they were finished, we hit each one with a spread sheet tailored just for their requirements. Finally, our Army colonel came down and impressed us with the seriousness of our military mission.

I was very pleased with the way the afternoon had gone. When he left, I turned and smiled to our group.

'Great job, folks!"

•

Data management doesn't get anything done,
but nothing gets done without data management.

•

It was finally time to quit for the day. We were all staying at the same crummy hotel. We picked up our bags, caught a couple of cabs, and headed uptown. We each had separate rooms, of course, but Melissa's and mine happened to be on the same floor. I was still carrying her suit bag and my own while she was struggling to hold onto her other two and her purse. We got into the same elevator, and I followed Melissa down to her room to drop off her gear.

"Thanks, Roger."

"You're welcome."

"What room are you in?"

I glanced at my key.

"Down the hall – 1412."

She gave me an unexpected peck on my cheek and whispered in my ear.

"See you, then."

I was stunned, but before I could say anything dumb like "I'm too tired," Melissa disappeared behind her door. I had planned to grab a bite somewhere and crash early. Tomorrow promised to be another busy day. I just shook my head and went to my room which turned out to be tiny – not much bigger than a damn walk-in closet. The furnishings were cheap and shoddy. My bed was a sliver of what a single should be. This was the government's idea of saving a buck, but oh well – I was too tired to care. Outside, the street noise of Manhattan blended into a muted roar punctuated by horns and sirens that drifted through the dirty, single-pane windows. I set my bag down, threw off my clothes, stretched out naked on the bed, and fell asleep.

I was dreaming of drifting on soft, billowy clouds over the mountains of New Mexico when I heard through the mist something like thunder. It took me a moment to figure out that the boom – boom – boom was someone pounding on my door. I noticed that it was getting dark outside, but I felt that I couldn't have slept for more than a few minutes. I stepped into my pants and looked through the peephole. I half expected it and sure enough – it was Melissa.

I opened the door. She carried a bucket of ice under one arm and held a bottle of vodka in her other hand. Her white fleece bathrobe, matching slippers, and towel wrapped around her head were nothing less than inviting. Her eyes seemed to sparkle with anticipation.

"Wanna' drink, Roger? You lugged this around all day so you might as well take a hit!"

I had a fleeting moment of professional doubt that quickly passed as "what the hell?" How could I refuse such a beautiful lady? I ran my fingers through my hair and shook my head to chase the sleep away.

"Sure – come on in."

We stood and looked at each other for a moment. She put her stuff down and tossed out her hair. I could smell the wet fragrance of her shampoo – a delightful mixture of citrus. She lifted the bottle and took a swig. A charming little burp escaped her smile as she passed the bottle to me. I tilted it up and took a swallow. The heat from the liquor jolted me awake and warmed every nerve of my body down to the tips of my toes.

Melissa reached over and undid the button on top of my trousers – letting her fingers linger for a moment on my stomach. My pants dropped to the floor. She opened up her robe and spread it to give me a view of her naked, sumptuous body. I was mesmerized as she made a little twist that slipped her robe off her bare shoulders. It fell down to her hips and then through her graceful fingers that let it float softly to the floor. She cupped her breasts with both hands and massaged them gently. The fingers of one hand slowly ran down through her cleavage and went lower. She was breathing deeply and becoming more aroused as she touched herself lower and lower – all the while never loosing eye contact with me.

I stepped out of my pants and took a step towards her. The thought flashed through my mind again that I really should say "No," but the more I looked at her the more hopeless that thought became. We stepped closer, kissed, and pressed lightly together. I caressed her breasts, and let my hands wander down below her tummy. Melissa threw her head back, moaned deeply, and pressed her leg into my crotch. We fell on the bed and desperately gave all of ourselves to each other until there was nothing left to give.

I wasn't thinking about how beautiful it was as I lay there wasted. I wasn't thinking at all. My mind was swimming in warmth – as if I had landed back in some soft, caressing womb. I dozed blissfully for a few minutes with her body draped comfortably over mine. Her breathing softly caressed my neck. Melissa finally rolled off and tapped me on my shoulder.

"Hey, big guy, wake up. Want another drink?"

"I think I need one."

My eyes were still closed, and I didn't want to stop the flow of intimate feelings that still possessed me. I struggled to come out of my trance. Melissa leaned over and massaged the back of my neck gently until I woke up. It took me a few moments, but I finally sat up and rubbed my tired eyes.

"Gawd – I hope you know how good you are!"

She smiled and handed me the bottle.

"I need to mix it with something."

"How about a dirty martini? I brought olives – we could use some of the juice."

Melissa continued to amaze me. She knew what she wanted and had no problem going for it.

"Fine – with just a splash and on the rocks, please."

She dug a small bottle of olives out of her bathrobe pocket and walked naked over to the bathroom. I could only shake my head and watch her every sensuous move. She came out, put ice in some cups, and mixed a pair of martinis. She kissed me lightly on my forehead and handed one of the cups to me. We sat naked on the bed, leaned against each other, and sipped our drinks. After a few minutes, I decided that I was getting hungry.

"I need something to eat."

"Me too."

Melissa fished her fingers around in her drink and caught the olive. She licked it a few times and sucked it in slowly between her lips. Then she put her fingers in her mouth, pulled them out slowly, raised her martini, tipped her head back, and downed it in one gulp. She was truly magnificent!

143

"I'm ready. Let's go."

She squirmed a bit as the liquor hit her body. I pulled on my shirt and trousers and stepped into my shoes. We walked together down to her room with her bathrobe pulled over her shoulders. I watched as she slipped into her jeans, sweater, and heels and grabbed her purse. We walked out, holding hands, and looked for a place that was still open. On our section of Seventh Avenue there were small, all-night cafés on almost every block. We dove into the first one we found. Melissa pointed to a table by the window. I sat with my back to the wall, and she sat in the chair across from me. An overhead light shone brightly down on us.

Our young waitress had deep circles under her eyes, and a tired posture that showed she had been on her feet most of the day and night. She was dressed in a stained, restaurant uniform that fit her poorly. What little money she was making was obviously not being spent on her work clothes. I had been there and identified with whatever struggles the poor girl was going through. She managed a weak smile, put our menus on the table, and asked if we wanted coffee. "Yes, please," we replied in unison.

She brought over cups, poured the coffee, and asked for our orders.

"A grilled cheese sandwich with a side of tomato slices, if you can, please."

No wonder Melissa had such a fine figure.

"The breakfast plate for me, please – scrambled, whole wheat toast, bacon, and hash browns."

"No problem, folks."

The waitress left and handed our order to the cook who got off his stool at the counter and walked around to the grill. She took his seat, lit a cigarette, and sipped coffee while she studied a page of want ads.

I imagined us as the customers in Edward Hopper's melancholy painting, "Nighthawks." Melissa stood out in the gloomy night like a jewel – a beacon that attracted the down-and-out souls who wandered the streets at that time of night. They would walk up to the window and stare, wondering who she was, and where they had seen this beautiful celebrity before. Melissa didn't mind. She occasionally smiled at her audience and would then turn her attention back to me.

However, one disheveled guy in a rumpled business suit, with vomit encrusted on his shirt and jacket, staggered up unsteadily. He put his face close to the window and tapped to get Melissa's attention. He then reached into his pocket and pulled out a wad of hundred dollar bills. She gave him a disgusted stare and flipped him off.

"Mother fucker!"

A clock on the wall clicked as the hands passed midnight. Our waitress delivered our orders and set them on the table.

"You're getting lots of attention."

"I'm used to it."

"I bet."

The waitress filled our cups with coffee and gave us a tired smile.

"Can I bring you anything else?"

"Just keep the coffee coming, please."

The servings were simple, but perfect for the moment. We ate our meals slowly and started asking each other questions about our many past lives and what dreams we had for the future. Our waitress kept coming around with coffee, and the place was quiet, except for an occasional customer who drifted in. Melissa talked about herself matter-of-factly – not with any regret or wish that anything had turned out differently. She knew how unique she was. Instead of pride, she was amused at herself and the events that shaped her life. She listened closely as I went through my story. I was careful to tell her all the inconvenient truths along with the good parts of my life.

"What changes would you make in your life if you could, Roger?"

I thought for a moment and then answered frankly.

"Just about everything! Even the stuff I've done well hasn't amounted to anything."

We were silent for a few moments while we ate our meal.

"So my dear. When did you decide that you wanted to seduce me?"

She studied me for a moment.

"I was interested in you when we first met, but it was when we were in the taxi. You looked like some lost sailor, adrift in a storm with your hair blowing out the window like that. Yeah. 'Lost' is the word. Maybe like a stray puppy. Your thoughts were a million miles away. I wanted to help you find your way home, or maybe help you heal or something. Is that all right?"

"Perfect."

I drank my coffee quietly. I wanted to take her in my arms and hold her tight – forever.

"So, how about you, Melissa? Tell me about yourself."

Melissa had grown up in a household dominated by an abusive father. Her mother had died years ago, but her father was still around, always criticizing her, and making her life difficult at every opportunity. She believed that her mom died because of her Dad's unmerciful harassment. Melissa escaped the house when she turned sixteen. She simply ran away to an older man with only the few things that she could carry. It was 1969, the year of Woodstock. She was there – one of the girls who were passed around on the raised hands of the crowd. That's when she was introduced to drugs, and when she lost her virginity – many times that day and the days that followed.

I rubbed my forehead and imagined her and the amazing gathering of free-loving spirits. I was still in the Navy at that time. The military and the war had kept me from participating in the movement of a whole damn generation! As much as I enjoyed my marriage and the years in the Navy, I had always felt that I missed something important. If I had been part of that scene, however, I probably would have trashed my brain and been worthless the rest of my life. Oh well.

Melissa was really an American icon – a classic symbol of a decade in our country's history. She dug into her purse, found a pink leather case and pulled out a cigarette. I opened the matchbook that had been lying in the ash tray, lit the match, and she cupped our hands as she leaned over to get the light. She took a deep drag and blew the smoke away from the table.

"Sorry. I know it's aggravating, but sometimes I just need a smoke."

I was not surprised and shook my head.

"Doesn't matter."

She continued to talk. From Woodstock on, she loved sex and men. Her body opened many doors for her. Like the well-known photographer – the man who took her under his wing. He instructed her on the fine points of photography and introduced her to executives in the rock-and-roll industry. He also taught her all about how to treat and handle men and how to enjoy her own sexuality.

Melissa told me how she would get on stage with the bands while they were warming up the crowd. She wore a tight tank top without a bra, her signature spiked heels, and an almost non-existent pair of cutoff, split, and tattered jeans that barely covered her ass. She didn't wear panties on stage. She would bend over to take a photo and stick her butt out at the audience. Her ample, blonde bush would escape from around the edges, and everybody would hoot, cheer, and go absolutely out-of-their-minds crazy!

She was part of the entertainment, and producers would pay her good money, regardless of how well the photographs came out. That was never a problem, however. Her photography had a contemporary, rock-and-roll quality that was sought after by the magazines. One secret of her success was that she never copyrighted her work. She just sold all her negatives, and the publishers could do anything they wanted with them. She didn't care about recognition, or even about having a personal set of prints. All she wanted was to be there, to be part of the action, and to take home the money.

She was proud of her work, though. A couple of times, I saw her looking through magazines that had published her images. She knew which shots were hers, even though she did not receive credit for them. "That's damn good!" she would say.

I asked her about the parties, the drugs, and all the famous rockers. Oh yes, she had done it all and had sex with a lot of the guys in the bands. The whole scene had been fun and good recreation for a while. There was no attachment on either side. The only requirement was that she do it and look really good with the guy afterward. Now it had become something else.

"That's what I need to get away from, Roger. I've had too much of everything. I feel like – like one of their fucking couches – literally – goddamn it. I was along to be bounced on – any freakin' time they wanted!"

"I'm sorry."

I shook my head and tried not to imagine all the drunken orgies she had been through. I couldn't help remarking about how she drank.

147

"You can sure put a drink down."

"Yeah."

She shook her head and rolled her coffee cup back and forth in her hands.

"Sorry – I lied a little in our interview. When I'm drinking, I want to get a quick buzz. It's not a party without a good head going. I love parties, so I suppose that's the same as loving booze. But a little doesn't affect me at all, and I rarely get a hangover. Yes, I drink a lot, but I have a hollow leg, I guess. Alcohol has never been a problem."

Melissa had a distracting way of unconsciously putting her hand down her sweater and caressing her cleavage while she spoke.

I changed the subject to her boyfriend. His name was John. He was a carpet installer who was also trying to get a band started. John was the drummer. He loved her tenderly, and Melissa couldn't imagine being apart from him.

"Doesn't he mind you going out with other men?"

"No, he lets me go my own way. He has to. I wouldn't keep him around if he didn't. Nobody will ever tie me down!"

That was going to be my challenge, and our future time together came under an entirely different light. I had naively assumed that I could capture Melissa's exclusive love and devotion. Now, I was much less sure. But I brushed that thought aside and complimented her on her amazing good looks.

"Yeah – yeah. I didn't have anything to do with it. You want to know something cool?"

"Sure."

"I'm sure you noticed my mole? Marilyn had one in exactly the same spot. Not only that, she and I have the same birthdays. We're both Gemini's – sign of the twins!"

"No kidding! I've always loved Marilyn! You two do look amazingly alike. But your hair is natural, she was a peroxide blonde. The strange thing is that you both have the same presence – like, um, you're a star wherever you go. And you can turn yourself on and off like a light bulb whenever you want to. You are unique – very special, my dear!"

"And I love to show off – just like Marilyn. Actually, it's deeper than that. We're both exhibitionists. She loved to expose her body, and so do I."

That thought made me laugh.

"That is certainly true of you and good for me!"

"Glad you like it, Roger."

"I still can't believe you want to work for the Corps of Engineers. What are your plans for the future?"

"Nothing more than to be who I am. I don't want to change anything – just be happy and have fun. How about you?"

"All I want to be is an artist. Someone totally creative. That's what I was meant to be. Somehow, however, I keep doing everything other than pursuing that dream."

I paused and thought for a moment.

"And this job doesn't cut it."

She smiled appreciatively, took my hand, and rubbed it thoughtfully. I looked at the clock. It was past 2 a.m.

"I could talk with you all night, Melissa, but we have a long day tomorrow. I need to get some sleep."

Our check had been sitting on the table for hours. I stood up and went over to the waitress. She had cleaned our table a long time ago and had kept our coffee cups full. She was dozing with her head propped up on her hands with her arms resting on the counter.

"Excuse me. We're finally going to leave you."

The check came to less than $15. I had folded up two twenties and put them in her hand.

"Thanks, you take care now."

She looked at the money and then to me quizzically.

"You sure?"

"Of course. You're great. Have a good life – OK?"

The poor gal nodded.

"Thanks, mister."

From that evening on, whenever I met a hard working individual who was trying his or her best to serve me well, I would leave that person a generous tip. If I didn't have much with me at the time, I would give them half of what money I had in my pocket. I could always make more. I walked away feeling wonderful.

I took Melissa by the arm. We strolled the empty street back to the hotel – neither of us talking. Like the couple in "Nighthawks" we were one with the millions of other tired souls who were the beat and heart of the "City that Never Sleeps."

I walked Melissa to her room. We held each other tight and had a long, tender kiss. I was still wondering how I was so fortunate to have Melissa – if only for that one night.

"Thanks for a special evening."

"Likewise, Roger. We'll get together again soon."

I went back to my room and lay on my bed with my eyes closed, but sleep wouldn't come. Our evening kept rolling and replaying through my mind. Indeed, the evening had been special. It marked the end of the lonely isolation after leaving Marge. I had broken out of many of my inhibitions that had been building up after my divorce, and the future looked much brighter now.

I only caught a few hours sleep when my alarm went off at 6 a.m. I went through the motions of getting up, went out to our café from the evening before, and sat at the same table. A new waitress came over to take my order.

"Good morning. May I help you?"

"Coffee and a toasted bagel with cream cheese, please. What time did you come on?"

"Six o'clock – much too early."

"So, you replaced the gal who had been here all night?"

"Right – Peggy. She worked two shifts yesterday and was half dead when I came on. If I had been late, we would have had to haul the poor girl out in an ambulance!"

"Yeah, I was here for a couple of hours – until around 2 a.m. She was having problems staying awake."

My waitress frowned.

"Working graveyard is brutal – long hours, and the tips are lousy."

"I'm sure."

I smiled. She brought over the coffee. The bagel came a few minutes later.

"Sounds like you had a long night too, Sir."

"Right, but a very good, long night."

She grinned and went off to serve the other customers. I ate and drank my coffee reflectively. Outside, the street was busy again with traffic and people bustling off to work. Strange, I thought. Only a few hours earlier, I had felt the loneliness of the city. Now, with all the people trudging off to work shoulder-to-shoulder, I felt even lonelier – totally invisible.

The spring morning was pleasantly cool. I made my way through the bustling crowds back to the hotel and knocked on Melissa's door. She opened it, still in her bathrobe. She gave me a brief kiss and a smile.

I was feeling smug and satisfied, but I had to ask.

"How was your night, my dear?"

"I met this neat guy."

"Hmm. I did pretty well myself. We should leave in half an hour. I'll drop by and help you with your bags."

"Thanks. I'll be ready."

Melissa looked much more refreshed than I did when I looked at myself in the mirror. This would be a difficult day to get through. Already, my eyes desperately wanted to close and doze through all the meetings. We all gathered at the office and went to the conference room. Since I was familiar

151

with all the information, I sat in the rear and let my mind wander. I was pleased about how well everything at the office was going. I felt more positive than I had felt in a long time. And it sure didn't hurt to have some romance to make life interesting.

The division managers presented talks on how work flowed through their departments. It was more information than anyone could absorb in one brief sitting, but it gave my people a good outline of how their assignments had to be handled. The real understanding would come as they worked through the cases. The presentations were done at noon. I was exhausted emotionally and drained physically. I tried to nap during our flight home, but, as usual, I had to monitor everything that was going on. We landed at Boston without incident and made our separate ways back home.

I threw my bag on the floor, poured myself a glass of wine, and took a long swallow. Then, I remembered that I needed to walk outside and check the mail. There were a few ads and one official looking letter. I went back inside, tossed the ads away, sat down with my wine, and looked at the envelope. It was from the Oregon Department of Human Services (DHS) and had trouble written all over it.

I sighed and ripped it open. It was a collection demand for past due payments to Marge of approximately $5400. What a damn crock! I was keeping up with my payments, but had not been able to make a dent in the past-due amount. They must think that I have a gold mine in my backyard. I tossed the letter aside and replenished my glass of wine. I lived paycheck-to-paycheck and was lucky to have a dollar in my pocket when the next deposit hit my meager account. The IRS was taking almost $250 out before I even saw the money. I was steaming.

I threw together a sandwich, had another glass of wine, and crashed on my bed. My mood crashed also. How in the hell could I get out of this? The IRS is after me and now this. Too many people want a chunk of me. All I wanted to do was escape and disappear!

I called DHS the next day and was told that the bill included both alimony and child support. They did not differentiate between the two for collection purposes, so the amount that I owed was correct. I got to the office late and started by giving everyone specific instructions about getting their first assignments underway. They needed to make plans for travel, contact owners, schedule Melissa to make appraisals, etc. Melissa stayed after the others had left.

"OK, Roger. What's the matter?"

"Damn! Do I look that bad? I didn't know it showed."

"It shows. Now, what's wrong? I hope it's not me."

She sat down in a visitor's chair across from me. I shook my head.

"Hell no. You're the best thing that has happened to me in a very long time! Marge has the State of Oregon after me …"

I gloomily explained about the collection letter and the IRS.

"I don't know what I can do."

"I've never understood alimony. When a woman wants a divorce, she should be on her own – unless her husband is abusive or something."

"You and I agree, but that's not what matters."

I tried to perk up a little bit.

"Did you know some lady attacked and raped me the other night?"

"Yeah. It was on the evening news! When do I get to see Spaghetti Grotto?"

"Not much to see, but how about tomorrow after work?"

"Sound's good. I'll come by after exercise. Keep the ice cold."

She left me to my thoughts in the office. Carolyn brought in a cup of coffee, which I took gratefully. For some strange reason, I was less than interested in real estate assignments and started to fantasize about tomorrow night.

The office was buzzing along, except that Glen was revealing his compulsive need to jabber. Actually, I had noticed signs of trouble last week. I caught Carolyn and Helen rolling their eyes a few times when he wasn't watching. Melissa had even gone up to him and complained about it.

"Uh – Glen, do you think you might keep the chatter down – please?"

Helen's desk was directly in front of Glen's. She kept turning around to give him dirty looks. She asked him once to quiet down, but that only lasted until he took his next breath. He was distracting everybody. Until now, Helen had been the quiet, motherly type, but she marched into my office and sharply closed the door.

"What are you going to do about Glen? He's driving me nuts!"

I had seen this one coming.

"I'll talk with him."

"Better hit him on the head with a goddamn brick!"

"Wow, you've been holding back on me, Helen."

"You don't want to see me when I get really pissed!"

She turned with a flourish and stomped out.

There was another work station behind Glen. I judged that we could turn his desk sideways so that he would be perpendicular to the other desks. I asked him to come into my office.

"Glen, we have a problem."

I went into how disruptive he had become, and that the only talking he should be doing had to be related to business.

"I understand. No problem – I'll take care of it."

He went back to his desk. Within an hour, however, he had turned the jabbering back on. I didn't wait for someone to complain this time. I went out and told him we were changing his work station to the last one in the row, and we were going to turn his desk around. That way, we agreed, he would be talking to the wall and not bothering anybody. We manhandled the desk and file cabinet around. He was contrite and got back to work.

Glen stayed quiet until after lunch when he started chattering again. He was very happy talking to himself even without anyone else around to listen – as if he had to have a radio or TV on in the background to get any work done. But the move worked, and his noise did not carry through the rest of the office. It turned out, however, that his work product was mediocre as well. I would have been better off if I had not hired anybody for that position.

The whole process with Glen took up too much of my day. I had reserved some difficult actions for myself and started to work on them. The staff was in and out of my office with questions, and Carolyn came in to take shorthand for a letter I needed to send to the New York Office. She tried hard, but it had been a long time since she had to use shorthand. It wasn't part of her job description, so I just drafted my letters in long hand and told the others to do the same. That was OK because she was very good at everything else – and kept calling me "Boss."

Melissa came into my office right after lunch. She wanted to discuss a complicated appraisal assignment. As she was running through her questions, she casually put her hand down her blouse and started to rub her breast. Her rubbing went on until I couldn't take it anymore.

I leaned over the desk and motioned for her to come closer.

"Damn it, Melissa, stop that – stop caressing your damn boobs!"

She immediately removed her hand and giggled.

"It's subconscious. Sorry, Roger – I don't even know I'm doing it."

Her hand was back where it left off in less than a minute. I guessed that I would just have to live with some distractions.

She came over the next evening after her workout. I had stocked up on vodka, vermouth, and olives. She brought a bottle of wine. She didn't say anything about my sad, small, low-class apartment. It didn't matter to her. We were well into our second round when the phone rang.

"Hi, Dad. It's Jeff."

"Well Jeff! I've been worried about you. How are you doing?"

Melissa threw me a frown.

"I'm doing good, Dad. I guess Matt told you about the Marines."

"Right. That's really too bad – so, what are your plans?"

"Right now, I'm AWOL. I'm staying with a gal I met hitchhiking. We're at her place in Trenton, New Jersey. I was hoping I could come up and spend some time with you."

I thought for a moment. I hated to say no, but I had to.

"I'm sorry, Jeff. That's not possible. You are wanted by the Federal Government, and I'm an employee of the Feds. If you got caught staying with

155

me, I would be harboring a fugitive and could lose my job. I can't afford to have that happen."

"Gosh, Dad. I was looking forward to seeing you."

"I've got to say no, Jeff. I'm sorry – not until you get this AWOL stuff straightened out. If you want my advice – turn yourself in and let the Marines do what they want with you. You'll probably have to spend some time in the brig. When they let you out, you'll be a free man and can do whatever you want. Even come here. I'd love to see you then."

Melissa raised an eyebrow after hearing that. I rolled my eyes. She went over to the counter and noisily threw ice cubes in our glasses for another round. Jeff couldn't help hearing what was going on.

"I hear someone mixing drinks. Are you with someone?"

"Yeah, Jeff. Sometimes even your old man gets lucky."

I frowned at Melissa.

"Good deal. Look, I really don't want to hitchhike all the way back to California."

"You don't have to, Jeff. Just find the nearest recruiting office. Tell them who you are and that you are turning yourself in. They'll inform you what to do from there."

"OK. I'll think about it. Thanks, Dad."

"Good luck, Son. Give me a call after you get this straightened out. Bye for now."

It was my turn to throw down a drink. Melissa took my glass and mixed another.

"You handled that well, Roger."

"I hope so. I'm surprised he wants to come see me though. But if he has grown up, I would like to see him too."

She gave me a kiss and rubbed the back of my neck. I winced.

"Does that hurt?"

For some reason my neck was very sore.

"Just not too hard. It's been hurting for the last few days."

"Maybe from carrying my bag?"

"Nah, that's not it."

She was right, but I didn't want to lay the blame on her. I tried to twist my head around to make my neck loosen up, but it continued to hurt. A thought popped into my head.

"Gosh! Jeff's 20 years old now! How did that happen?"

"He'll start calling you 'My old Man' and feeding you oatmeal."

I laughed and shook myself out of my funk.

"I like oatmeal, dammit! Now, how about some lobster? Maybe then we can christen the apartment."

"Sounds like a plan."

I truly wanted the affection. Again, I was the lost puppy that needed help from some kind soul. Melissa fulfilled her role just fine.

The days passed, we managed our heavy workloads, and our supervisors in New York stayed off our backs. I was pleased that they were happy with our work and passed that thought onto my staff whenever I had the chance. Melissa and I behaved ourselves in the office, but on-the-road was another matter. When I got involved with a complex project, Melissa would usually have to join me to appraise the property. It happened so frequently, that each time I put in for travel orders, Carolyn would smugly ask if I wanted Melissa to join me a day or so later. I could only smile and nod innocently.

"Of course!"

We stayed in motels from upstate New York, to Cape Cod, to the northern-most tip of Maine – and everywhere in between. We ended up in a hot tub in Portland, went scrambling up Mt. Katahdin – the highest mountain in Maine, hung out in a rustic lodge in the Adirondack Mountains, and revisited our "favorite" hotel in New York. I suggested that they put a plaque in the lobby commemorating our first night together. We made a rule for ourselves that work always came first, and then we could play later. We had a terrific time and completed everything that needed to be done.

Melissa turned out to be a superb negotiator. I was with her a few times when she would flounce into some stuffy guy's office, or a conference room filled with belligerent attorneys. She would show as much cleavage as possible and act like some bimbo looking for action. After she got them wrapped around her little pinky, she would then skewer them on their own fantasies.

"OK, fellows, this is the way it's going to be. I've determined that the price is such-and-such. Please sign here so we can get your money to you."

There was usually a few questions, but they would invariably sign and ask when she would be back again. Even when she wasn't using her body, she was fearless – better than the rest of us, including me. I was pleased to assign the toughest negotiations to her.

One of the most outrageous things about Melissa was that she truly was an exhibitionist. Besides her skimpy clothes, she was always looking for an opportunity to go topless or even totally naked. We went canoeing a few times, and her clothes came off. When we went hiking up some mountain, she would go topless. If we found a soft patch of moss in the sun, she would lie down naked – spread eagle – and take a snooze. We went up to her grandparents' old farm one time, and she spent the whole weekend in slippers and an open bathrobe. She simply liked being naked.

On one trip, we were staying in a motel outside of Portland. We checked in after dark, had a couple of drinks, and went to bed. She got up in the morning – stark naked as usual, and stretched her stiff body until she got the kinks out. Then – as was her habit – she went to the window and flung open the drapes. Much to her surprise, she was facing the motel's restaurant and all its astonished customers. She stood there for a moment, said "OOPS!" and pulled the drapes closed again. She was blushing, but it actually made her day. Her morning routine did not change, except now she usually checked the scene outside the window the night before.

One evening, around the middle of August, the phone rang, and it was Jeff again.

"Hi, Dad, guess what?"

"Well, since you're calling, I guess you're out of the Marines. So, how are you?"

"I'm doing OK. I turned myself in as you suggested. It took me longer than I expected to get out, but I'm free now. That's all behind me."

"That's great, Son. You did the right thing. So, what are your plans?"

"I'd like to come see you, Dad, if I could. Actually, if it's OK, I was hoping I could spend some time there and find a job."

I thought of Melissa. It might put a crimp in our relationship, but we could handle it. Jeff came first, and I wanted to help him if I could.

"Absolutely! We won't be living in the Ritz, however. And it can't be for a real long time, but we can sure get you started. I see lots of 'Help Wanted' signs, so you shouldn't have a problem."

"Gee. That's great, Dad. I appreciate it."

"No problem. Where are you now, Jeff? How do you plan to get here?"

"I'm still on the West Coast. I'll start hitchhiking tomorrow. It may take a while – especially if I meet someone interesting – if you know what I mean."

"Sure. Well, give me a call when you get around the Boston area, and I'll come pick you up. I'll give you my office number also. I might be off on a trip, so you can leave a message with my secretary."

He sounded upbeat and excited. I had my reservations, but was optimistic that we might be able to start off on a new footing. I was looking forward to seeing him again.

•

"Outrageous" suits some people as naturally as their skin.

•

Not Your Mother's Yellow Brick Road

Chapter **22** 1985 – Autumn

Too Many Guests At The Table

I SAT DOWN WITH MY DRINK, stirred the ice cubes slowly with a finger, and stared at the swirls reflectively. I was having trouble juggling all my responsibilities at one time. There was the IRS, the State of Oregon, my job, and now Jeff. I was always putting out one fire at work only to be faced with another. The IRS was taking its bite out of my income before I even saw the money. I still had not been able to do anything about Marge's back payments. As delightful as Melissa was, even she made my life more complicated. Depression was settling in again. This time, however, I also had an uncomfortable sense of being overwhelmed – like I was coming apart at the seams.

My usual set of questions revolved through my mind. They were becoming a constant dialogue that I was having with myself. This time, however, the questions resulted in very different answers. Keep the job. It's good for now. Just relax, do the best you can and enjoy it. That's number one, so stay the course and work through the problems.

Depression clouded everything, however, and was strangling those good intentions. But there were two other positive ways I had been passing my free time – other than romancing Melissa. The first was going to art museums and galleries. I had been to the Worcester Art Museum, the Boston Museum of Fine Art, and spent a weekend checking out the galleries on Cape Cod. Those excursions had been thoroughly enjoyable. There were other museums scattered around New England that I had read about and wanted to see. If I still enjoyed art so much, why not try painting again?

Antiquing had recently caught my interest as well. I had been browsing through antique malls and catching some of the many shows throughout the area on weekends. Old furniture and objects – particularly folk art – connected with my sense of history and design. I was on a treasure hunt without knowing what I was looking for. I was not able to buy much, but just the process of looking was informative and exciting.

I recognized that I could wean myself from depression by occupying myself with positive activities that I enjoyed. My travels provided ample opportunity to see other regional museums and galleries. I became excited

161

about painting again and spent much of my time in the evenings in front of my easel instead of sitting around with a drink and getting depressed. I told myself that by changing my lifestyle, maybe I could actually work my way out of this.

I also needed to find a larger apartment before Jeff arrived. Right now, if I wanted to paint, everything in the kitchen had to be pushed aside. All my paints and canvases would spill into the living space. When Jeff showed up, he would have to sleep on the couch. So, I made a determined search through the area to find something bigger that would be closer to the office and still be at an affordable rent.

After much time and frustration, I got a tip about a loft that used to be the top floor of an old railroad depot that was in the process of being converted into a two bedroom apartment. It had cathedral ceilings, old timbers for beams, hardwood floors, and a new kitchenette. The larger bedroom was great for me, and the spare room would work for Jeff. The other end of the loft was wonderful space for a studio, and it was only 15 minutes away from my office. I met with the owner and signed a lease. It took him a few weeks to finish the renovations before I moved my stuff in. There was much more space than I had furniture for. I bought a used bed, a dresser, and a few chairs at a thrift store for Jeff. I decided to make it a long term project to find old, rustic furnishings that would be comfortable and go with the rest of the space.

The loft had two main problems, however, which was why the rent was low. I had known about the first one before I moved in, but did not realize how bad it would be. The railroad tracks that ran next to the depot were still in use. Any time of the day or night, a freight or passenger train would rumble through and blow its whistle at the crossing about 50 yards away. If I was sleeping, I would be awake after the train passed down the tracks. It wasn't so bad between 1 and 6 a.m. or on weekends because the commuter trains were not operating. Freight trains, however, had a habit of stopping, dropping off cars, reconnecting to others parked on an adjacent siding, and then pulling out again. Of course, every time one went through the crossing, it would have to blow its damn whistle just to make sure I was paying attention. I hoped that Jeff would be able to deal with the noise.

The second problem was that when the depot rattled and shook as the trains went by, 100 years of dust would find its way off the beams and fall through every seam in the ceiling. If I cleaned in the morning, the loft would be covered with dust by the time I got home that evening. I tried draping covers over everything, but all the dust flew up again when I removed them. It was a never-ending, losing battle. I grew somewhat adjusted to the noise. The dust, however, was a constant aggravation. The thought frequently crossed my mind that my father and I gravitated towards similar, unconventional, living spaces.

I found some art stores in the area where I could pick up painting supplies. Getting started again was frustrating, and I felt that my finished products were seldom worth keeping. With each drawing and painting, however, I saw parts that I liked. Although the final results may not have been acceptable, they gave me enough encouragement to keep trying.

Antiques, art, and painting pulled me out of my ugly moods. It had been a long time since I had felt that I was accomplishing more than just surviving in a job.

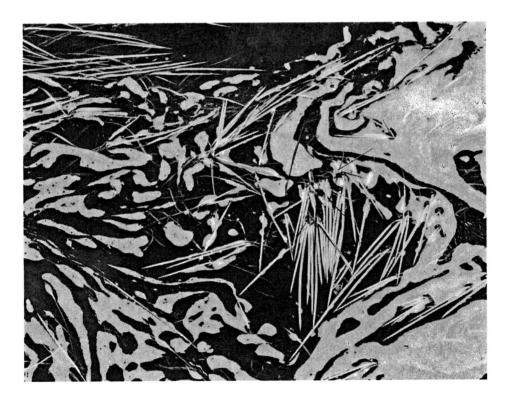

Eddies

A Star Just Short Of Shining

OVER THREE WEEKS HAD PASSED since Jeff had called from the West Coast. He checked in, however, about the time that I was becoming concerned. He had been staying with his lady-friend in Trenton again and had done some odd jobs to earn a little money. He was ready to buy a train ticket and make his way to Massachusetts. We arranged a schedule, and I was to meet him at the station in the nearby town of Acton.

The setting sun radiated colors through the stately maple and oak trees, adding a soft warmth to the evening. Only a few others waited on the platform. The train came around a bend and blew its whistle as it rattled over a railroad crossing and rolled to a halt with a loud hiss of escaping air and screeching of brakes. I had the definite feeling that a new chapter of my life had just arrived at the station.

Jeff stepped down from the last car. He looked trim and fit and his hair still had its military cut. He was wearing combat boots, a clean pair of jeans, and a T-shirt with "Carlsbad Beach" printed on the front. All of his sloppiness was gone. He slung a duffel bag over his shoulder and walked towards me with a broad grin. He dropped his bag when we got close and gave me a warm hug. Damn – this greeting was too long in coming, but welcome progress indeed!

"Good to see you, Jeff. You're looking great!"

"You too, Dad. I'm excited to be here!"

The train blew its whistle as it pulled away, like it was adding a cheerful punctuation to Jeff's genuine enthusiasm.

"We're only a few minutes from the loft. Let's get out of here."

We threw his duffel in the back of my old, rusty Mustang and off we went. Jeff was checking out the industrial parks and warehouses as we made the short trip.

"Gosh, there looks like tons of places I can talk to about a job."

"This is a prime manufacturing area – you shouldn't have a problem finding work."

"Wow, and Boston sure looked neat. I'm going to have fun cruising downtown."

We pulled up to the loft with all its cast off clutter from its active days as a depot. Jeff was excited about everything. It must have been an adventure for him to be the first of the family to discover the lifestyle that I was living since the divorce. I thought of tracking my father down, and wondered if it was as strange for Jeff to discover how I lived as it had been for me to find Forrester. The loft was certainly different from anything he knew when we were together as a family. We climbed the long flight of stairs to the second floor. I unlocked the door and held it open as Jeff went in. He spent a minute just staring around and getting a feel for the space.

"Wow! This is nothing like what I imagined, Dad. This is neat!"

"That's the way I feel too. Your room is over there. The bathroom is down the hall. Why don't you drop off your bag? It's about dinner time, and I'd like to take you out. I imagine you're pretty hungry after being on the train all day."

"You bet! Let me clean up, and I'll be right with you."

I couldn't get over the difference in the Jeff now from the Jeff that used to hate my guts. I was exceedingly relieved and grateful.

We went out to one of my favorite taverns. The old, weathered building looked like it had been around during the Revolution. The chimney was built from field stones, probably plowed up in some farmer's pasture close by. Inside, the log walls, pegged beams, and hand-hewn flooring put me back in a much earlier time. The tops of the old tavern tables were smoothed by the hands of countless people who had shared each other's company and conversation there. Flashing beer signs provided cheerful warmth to the room.

A waitress offered us a booth, and Jeff ordered a beer. I asked for bourbon, with a splash of water and a twist, please. We chatted about his trip while we waited for the drinks to come. Jeff told me that his friend in New Jersey was very special, but he didn't give any significant details except that she was well off and a lot of fun. Maybe he would get back together with her again someday. The drinks came and Jeff grinned.

"They didn't card me. That's great!"

I had totally forgotten that he was only 20 and the drinking age in the state was 21. Nevertheless, we both raised our drinks and clinked them together.

"Here's to you, Son – and to much success!"

"To you too, Dad."

He took a long swallow. He was enthusiastic about everything – the exact opposite of what he used to be.

"Hell, here's to both of us!"

He then asked if he could taste a sip of my drink.

"I want to get familiar with the different tastes of booze."

After going through basic training in the Marines, I was sure he deserved to drink anything he wanted, but I was uncomfortable with the way he was putting it down. No doubt he had done much worse.

"Watch out for hard liquor, Jeff. You can't drink it like beer."

"No problem."

"Gosh, how long has it been? A little over two years since I saw you in Oregon. You sure have changed."

"Yeah. I decided it was about time to get my act together."

"Good! So – what happened in the Marines? If you don't want to talk about it, that's OK."

I wanted to get the Marines out of the way and behind us first. He took a swig of his beer and struggled with how to tell me.

"Dad – they pushed me too damn far. I just snapped. I couldn't take any more of their bullshit!"

He paused and took another swig.

"This one sergeant – he made it his business to tear me apart any way he could."

"Matt told me about someone jumping on your stomach? Was that the guy?"

Jeff frowned from the bitter memory and paused reflectively.

"Yeah, same guy. There was a helluva lot more, but let's not go there. They wanted to break me, and they did. But I'd be damned if I would take any more of it!"

"That's what they try to do. Basic training is all about pushing a guy to his limits. I had Marine drill sergeants in the Navy, but nothing like you must have gone through."

"Well, I'm out now, so it doesn't matter anymore. All I want to do is get on with my life."

"What discharge did they give you?"

I hoped that Jeff would open up and tell me.

"Less Than Honorable, Dad."

He nervously spun his coaster around like a top. Then he reached into his shirt pocket for a pack of cigarettes.

"Mind if I smoke?"

He lifted a cigarette out of the pack and tapped it on the table.

"Just not in the apartment, please."

He nodded. I was relieved that at least his discharge wasn't "Dishonorable." There wasn't any use criticizing Jeff's decision to go AWOL – it wouldn't change a thing. He would find out as time went on how damaging that decision would be to his future. I downed what was left of my drink and signaled to the waitress to bring us another round.

"OK. You're about as stubborn as I am."

There was a pause in our conversation while we both considered what we should say next. I drank my whiskey and decided to suggest something that had been on my mind since he told me he was going to come see me.

"I'm not going to be critical or judgmental, but I would ask one thing."

167

Jeff did not look up. He did not want to get a lecture.

"What's that, Dad?"

"While we're together – or any time after if you want – if something is bothering you please tell me about it. Let me give you whatever comments I can offer. I will never tell you that you have to take my advice, but please listen. You're old enough now to make your own decisions. However, it never hurts to consider a second opinion."

Jeff looked up and smiled. He was a handsome young man without that chip on his shoulder.

"You know, I'd like that, Dad. A year ago, I wouldn't listen to anybody – yeah, and especially not you. Now, however, you don't seem so much like the angry dad that I knew back then."

The second round of drinks came. I took my time to think about my response to that. Was he so blind that he didn't realize that he had been my problem?

"Well, Jeff, I have to say that I really was angry. You were screwing up royally, and I couldn't get you off the drugs or whatever else you were doing. You were making my life miserable."

He nodded and sipped his beer.

"I'm sorry, Dad."

The waitress came over and asked if we wanted to order.

"The 'Tavern Burger' is good, Jeff."

"OK, I'd like that."

"Make it two."

"Anyway, that crap is all behind us now. That was another time and place. You're here now. All I want to do is help you to get started. Do you have any special plans?"

"Nothing special. I'll do almost anything. I need to get some transportation, and I want to get out on my own as soon as I can. Wherever that leads me will be fine. Do you have any ideas?"

"We've only got my old Mustang for transportation. It's about ready to die on us, though. The engine's burning oil and smoking like crazy. Anyway, Helen, one of the ladies in my office, drives by here on her way to work. I'll call her tomorrow, and ask if I can hitch a ride with her for a while. Then you can take the car around to look for work. The closer to the loft you can find a job, the better. You might even find something you can walk to or ride to on a bike."

"Sounds good, Dad."

The burgers came, and we talked about a lot of things – signing up for the Marines, Jeff's problems in school, my job and what I was doing, and how Jeff dreamed of someday being able to buy and do anything he wanted. The evening passed pleasantly. It was dark when we left. We drove back to the depot, and the rest of the evening was spent getting Jeff settled. I was tired and said good night, but he stayed up and watched TV. It was a real shame that all those years were wasted between us, and I was looking forward to the fresh start. The TV was still on when I fell asleep, so I had no idea how late he stayed up. In the morning, however, he didn't surface until after 10:00.

It was Sunday. I had coffee going and cooked up breakfast. Jeff mixed his half a cup of sugar with some coffee and cream.

"Helps me get going."

We ate our bacon and eggs quietly. Jeff looked like he still needed time to wake up, so I continued to read the Sunday paper and drink my coffee. I pushed the want ads over to him. He just shook his head.

"I wouldn't know what I'm looking at. I've got to get to know the area first."

"OK. Why don't I drive you around today? You can get a feel of what's going on locally, and maybe you will see something that will interest you."

"Good deal."

He poured himself another cup of sugar/coffee.

"Give me time to take a shower, and then we can take off."

We set out on our tour. I handed Jeff a map and showed him where we were located. I had also brought along a note pad and pen, so that he could take down information about places that might interest him. We drove through some industrial parks that were close by, and he was taking notes about each warehouse that had a "Help Wanted" sign posted in front of the building. I glanced over and saw mostly scribbles that I doubted even he could read. He seemed to be excited though, so we kept driving. We stopped for a late lunch at a mom-and-pop burger joint whose specialty was old-fashioned milkshakes that were the best I had found anywhere. In addition, it had an old Wurlitzer juke box that was always pumping out 1960s hits. My kind of place.

"So, what do you think of what we saw, Jeff?"

He was sucking on the straw of his milkshake like he had never had one before. He finished it as our sever set the burgers on our table.

"That was good! Mind if I have another, Dad?"

If I drank that much sugar, I would be bouncing off the ceiling. I shrugged and nodded the waitress. Then I recalled all the sugar he had put in his coffee that morning. I wondered if that might indicate some problem.

"All these places look good. I just won't know until after I go around and talk to them."

"There's lots more to look at. We only hit the south side this morning. After we finish this, we can go around to some of the places north of here."

Jeff shook his head.

"I already can't remember everything we saw today. Maybe I should wait until I can check those out myself."

I looked at him questioningly.

"We've got the car, and I don't always have time that I can spend with you like this."

"You said I might be able to have the car tomorrow. I would rather do that."

"OK – your call."

We finished up and went back to the loft. Jeff turned on a football game and sat down. I went into my studio to work on some drawings. When I came back to heat up some coffee, Jeff was sound asleep in the easy chair. OK. Something was wrong here. I was suspicious that all his sleeping and the sugar were warning signs. His hand writing – or lack of it – might be related to the same problem. A few years ago, I had read some material about addictions. There were lots of studies that indicate that cocaine, caffeine, alcohol, and sugar give the same kind of high and are all related chemically. You can also add marijuana and nicotine to that list. So if he's doing cocaine, but that isn't available, sugar can be an easy substitute. Actually, sugar was said to be one of the worst of the addictive chemicals. There might well have been a connection to his sleeping so much. On the other hand, I could just be over-reacting.

I poured myself some coffee, went into my bedroom, and closed the door. I first called Helen and asked if she would mind picking me up in the morning. That "would not be a problem," so we set it up. I sat on my bed thinking this over. My Mom was addicted to alcohol and had stashed bottles all over the house. I should probably hide the hard liquor that I had. I recognized that I drank more than I should, but I never had any urge to try drugs or anything else like Jeff had. I got up and quietly hid the few bottles that I had before he woke up. I was sitting at my drafting table and asking myself what I should do when I heard him moving around in the kitchen. It was 5 o'clock in the afternoon. He had poured himself the last of the cold coffee and was trying to figure out the microwave. I showed him which buttons to push.

"How are you doing?"

He ran his fingers through his hair.

"I guess I crashed. I'm still kind of drowsy."

It was too soon to try to have a conversation about what I thought were his problems, so I let it pass. I made salads and cooked some spaghetti for dinner. (I had fixed the lid on the pan.) I pulled out a bottle of wine that I had left in the cabinet. Some wine would not be the same as hard liquor. We drank a few glasses together and ate dinner slowly. We just chatted about whatever came to mind. I told him about the disastrous night when I tried to cook spaghetti in my other apartment. He told me about what his friends had ended up doing in Salem after I left, and I told him a bit about my relationship with Melissa. Before we knew it, the time was 10 o'clock. It had been a good evening. I turned in, and he sat down in front of the TV again. He was not awake when I left in the morning, so I left the car keys on the table and a note with my office number.

The rest of the week went well. He was trying hard to find a place that would hire him, and there was always a new batch of brochures and papers on the table when I came home in the evening. He seemed to be getting along fine. He had filled out applications at a lot of places and was waiting to hear back.

171

Jeff was excited when I got in on Friday. One company had called him back and wanted him to start work on their shipping line – tomorrow! Jeff explained that it would be hard work because he had to tape up all the boxes that came down on a conveyer belt from about a dozen packers, then stick pre-printed labels on them, and finally stack each box for either UPS or FedEx to pick up. The pay was two bucks over minimum wage, which he didn't expect, so he was thrilled. The only bad note was that the hours would be 2 to 10 p.m. That would cut into his party time, but it would be OK for a while. The warehouse was about five miles away, so he would still need the car.

"Good news. Congratulations!"

Jeff was pleased with himself. I asked him if he had run into any problems during his interviews.

"I got some crap from one manager who wouldn't hire me because of my discharge. That was all."

"You might get more of that when you try to move up, but it shouldn't concern you now. Damn, let's go out and celebrate!"

We went to the same tavern that I had taken him to the week before. We ordered a large pizza and a pitcher of beer. He drank one glass quickly and then slowed down for the rest of the evening. He was proud of himself, and I was truly happy for him.

Jeff stuck with the job and didn't express any discontent about it. Working on the shipping line kept him jumping. I stocked the refrigerator with beer, so he could have a few after work because he always had to unwind. The only times I saw him were at night. I needed to get my car back, but I could deal with that so long as he was doing well.

One night, after a month or so, Jeff didn't come home as usual. I waited up, however he didn't appear or call. I didn't see or hear from him for three days. Humph! I was concerned, but figured that if anything bad had happened, I would hear about it or he would let me know. And if he was having a good time, I did not want to stick my nose in his fun. He came home on the third night just brimming with news. Yes, he had been staying with a gal he had met at a nearby bar. Shelley was her name. Even though she was older, she had a great body and treated him well. She had a townhouse a few miles away and wanted him to move in with her. When his paycheck came next week, he would have enough money to buy some clunker – or maybe a motorcycle – whatever he could find.

All this was good news – no, great news! In addition, I could get my car, the loft, and yes, my life back. He packed up his things, threw them in the Mustang, and that was the last I saw of him for a while. He called at the office at the end of the week and told me the Mustang was parked in front of the loft. He had bought a motorcycle.

"It's nothing special and is pretty beat up, but the motor runs good. All I need is transportation, so it will be fine for now."

"Sounds great, Jeff. Good job! You have a phone number where I can reach you?"

He gave me Shelley's number.

"I want you to meet her, Dad. She's really sweet."

"I'm looking forward to it, Jeff. Drop by anytime."

"You bet! Seeya'."

Jeff disappeared for more than a month, but I was resolved not to check on him. It was his life, and I did not want to interfere. I was sure that he would call if he was having problems. Melissa wanted to meet him, so one day after work we went over to the warehouse. The receptionist said he was in the middle of a shipment, but we could go in for just a few minutes. There he was, practically buried in boxes, and working fast to keep up. We watched for a minute until he saw us.

"Hi, Jeff. Melissa here would like to meet you."

He glanced up and did a quick double-take.

"Wow! Nice to meet you!"

Melissa smiled and went up to him. The boxes kept rolling down the line, and he had to keep up.

"Your dad tells me you like the work."

"Yeah."

Without looking up, he shook a packing label at her.

"This is important work. Like this box is going to Singapore. Where the hell is that? Could be next door for all I know. Not everybody gets to ship to Singapore."

Melissa and I raised an eyebrow at each other.

"Well, we don't want to interrupt. Give me a call sometime."

"Great to meet you, Melissa. Seeya', Dad."

Melissa gave me an incredulous look.

"Important work?!"

I shook my head sadly.

"Yeah, there has to be a fried wire in there somewhere."

Jeff and Shelley dropped by on Thanksgiving morning to say hi. To my surprise, Shelley was indeed a very attractive lady. She was trim, fit, and a good 15 years older than Jeff. She was more the age to go out with me. Shelley was robbing the cradle, but that was Jeff's business. He seemed genuinely happy, and that was enough for me. She had brought me a plate of homemade cookies. I could only say, "Thanks!" and give her an appreciative smile. They had ridden over on the bike and parked it in front of the depot. We all went downstairs to look it over.

Jeff was indeed proud of the bike, even though it was nothing fancy and would be awfully cold this winter. I remarked that the back tire was almost bald.

"Yeah. I hope to get that replaced next month, but it's going to cost almost as much as I paid for the bike."

A thought hit me.

"Geez, Jeff. Don't take your motorcycle out when you're drinking. It's too damn dangerous – that bike can kill you!"

•

Control is a wishful fantasy.

•

"Don't worry, Dad. If it happens, it happens. It really doesn't matter. Seeya'."

I watched them climb onboard the motorcycle and ride off with a wave and a "Happy Thanksgiving!"

The rest of the year went without too many distractions. Melissa and I traveled together a few times, which was always good fun. The New York office needed me to submit plans to handle a significant increase in workload when the base closure program made it through Washington. How many new personnel would I need? What would the training requirements be? How much increased funding would be necessary? Etc. I buried myself in my work, continued to paint, and managed to keep my life under control.

Snag

175

Dark Days And Holidays

THE DAYS PASSED BY until the Christmas holidays came around. I was becoming increasingly bothered by my relationship with Melissa. The more attached I became, the more I was hurt by her relationship with John – and whoever else she was taking to bed. She had accepted a few photography assignments, but refused to discuss them with me. I couldn't help my continued attraction to her although our relationship was wearing me down. Melissa had told me many times how much she loved me, and I believed she was sincere. I certainly loved her. However, her love for me changed nothing about her relationships with anyone else. On the one hand, I didn't want our affair to end. On the other, however, I could not find a way to separate my affections for her from just having a damn good time. Well – if Melissa played by her own rules – so could I.

That decision lifted more pressure from my shoulders than I could have imagined. I had managed to tolerate her behavior without ever accepting it. I still had more than enough tensions to manage without Melissa to worry about.

My crew decorated the office with a frosty-blue, artificial Christmas tree, a few strings of blinking lights, and some tinsel. We had a small party before everybody took off for their vacations. I brought the fixings for a punch, and the others brought food. This was before the Government prohibited alcohol at office parties. The food was good, and the punch was making us merry. Each of us had drawn the name of a person to give an anonymous joke present to. We placed the presents under the tree for the others to find and open. I received a Groucho Marx pair of eyeglasses with a mustache and nose that I proudly wore during the rest of the afternoon. Glen got a dancing monkey on a stick with a rubber band – a perfect present for him. Helen received a mug with "Back Off!!!" on it, and Carolyn got a desk pad of Garfield cartoons.

Then Melissa opened her present – a pack of 12 pink, plastic elephants that were supposed to be frozen and put in drinks as ice cubes. Melissa gagged and went off on a rant about how she absolutely, positively hated elephant ice cubes! Someone had slipped one on her chair when she sat down at another party. It had burst and gave her a wet, cold butt, and ruined a good dress. Anyway, she had absolutely nothing good to say about them – not a "f--king thing!" She tossed them in a waste basket and had another glass of punch.

The presents got us all in the Christmas spirit. We ate the rest of the goodies, and the discussion turned to how we would run the Corps of Engineers.

Glen could always be counted on to suggest something that would make his life easier.

"We should replace our crummy K-cars with Cadillacs."

Helen smirked and looked at Glen.

"Private offices for everyone!"

Of course, Melissa wanted to spend more time working out.

"I need a home gym in my private office."

Carolyn was getting tired of pushing paperwork.

"I'll supervise our new secretarial pool."

I was going to say something about writing our own regulations, but couldn't let a good opportunity pass unspoken.

"No, Carolyn. That'll be my job!"

The suggestions received hearty laughs and applause. On those cheerful notes, everybody was off for the holidays. After Melissa left, I retrieved the precious bag of elephants out of the waste basket and put them in my coat pocket. They might come in useful later.

It was still a few days before Christmas. Melissa had invited me to go to an afternoon family gathering. John would be there too. I had not planned to go, but this event gave me the perfect opportunity to carry out my plan for her Christmas present. I went looking very Christmassy in a bright green tie and flashy red Santa Claus hat. After a couple of stiff rum-nogs, I made the excuse that I had to leave to get to another party. Melissa never bothered to lock up her cottage and that became my destination.

I got to her place with no problem, except that by then the drinks were giving me a powerful buzz. I went in, took the little elephants out of the bag, and hid each of them in places that would be very difficult to find – until

177

Melissa managed to bump into them. I hid one in the pocket of her bathrobe. Another slipped into her pillow case. Another wouldn't be found until she flipped her mattress. Yet another got into the toe of one of her spiked heels. Another found its way into her panties in her dresser. One even buried itself in her sugar bowl. And so on. I became more and more excited as I found perfect homes for all the others. I finished up, stealthily stumbled back to my car, and successfully made my getaway.

All was well – until I was driving out of Melissa's cozy, little New England village. I was rolling along, still dressed in my Santa Claus hat and green tie, singing Christmas carols at the top of my lungs, when – damn! A cop roared up behind me with his lights blinking and siren screaming.

I pulled over on the shoulder. He walked up to my window with cautious steps, as if he was stalking Public Enemy Number One. He was an over-the-hill town policeman with silver hair, a bulbous nose, and a fleshy face with a complexion like a russet potato. His wide belt and heavy brass buckle held back a beer-belly paunch that was struggling to be free. At his age, catching out-of-towners speeding through his little town was the same as retiring with pay.

"You know you were going 47 in my 30 mile per hour zone back there?"

"No, Sir. I totally missed that. I'm very sorry."

He gave me a nasty smirk.

"Who the hell do you think you are? Santa Claus?"

I had totally forgotten about my Santa hat. I was sweating from racing around Melissa's cottage, and my face must have been red as a Christmas light. I'm sure I looked as if my festivities were still in progress.

"No, Sir!"

I shook my head and the fuzzy bobble at the end of my hat flipped back and forth, and the cop was trying hard not to smile.

"OK. Get your registration and insurance and step out of the car."

I found the paperwork in the dash and climbed out as steadily as I could.

"Now, hand it over with your license."

I handed over the registration and dug in my back pocket for my wallet. When I pulled it out, a plastic bag fell to the ground. Damn – it was the bag that I had carried the elephants in! The cop reacted and reached for his pistol. If he hadn't had the strap snapped on his holster, he probably would have drawn on me.

"That bag better not have drugs in it, Mister!"

I raised my hands shakily.

"No, Sir!"

I shook my head again, but this time I caught the tassel first.

He squared his stance around, deliberately unsnapped the strap, and kept his hand on the pistol grip. His slate gray eyes kept staring straight at me.

"Bend down slowly, Mister – very slowly. Pick up that bag and hand it over."

I crouched down, picked it up, and gave it to him. He held it by a corner like it was a piece of evidence and looked it over. He brought it up to his nose and sniffed it.

"So, what the hell is this bag for?"

I took a deep breath.

"Sir, that bag – in that bag were 12 pink, plastic elephants that I just took over to a friend."

The officer tilted his chin up and looked over his nose at me.

"You shitting me? You expect me to believe that?"

"No Sir. Um – No. I mean yes, Sir! They were ice cubes. It's going to be a surprise – a joke. That's the truth."

He looked at me scornfully. The Santa Claus hat was very hot now, and I was dripping with sweat, but I did not dare try to take the thing off.

"A damn surprise! I can smell booze on your breath from here. How much have you had to drink?"

"Just a couple."

The jig was up.

"You live where, Mister?"

"Littleton, Sir, about 15 miles up the road."

He stared at me for a moment.

"Then I suggest you get in your sleigh, Santa, and drive the fuck home to your North Pole – very, very carefully! Your story is so damn dumb, I know you didn't make it up. If it wasn't Christmas, I'd arrest your ass anyway. Just don't let me catch you speeding through here again with that stupid hat on!"

"No – yes, Sir. Thank you, Sir!"

I didn't stick around to give him time to change his mind. When I glanced in my rear view mirror, he was sniffing inside the bag again just to make sure.

The next day, I was sitting at my drafting table around noon. I heard the loud thumping of boots climbing the stairs to my loft. The door swung open and banged against the wall. I looked up just in time to see a flying herd of pink, plastic elephants about to hit me in the face. Melissa dragged me away from my drawing pad and pummeled me with a barrage of slaps to my face and hits to my shoulders and chest. I had to put my arms up to block her blows. She became even more furious – swinging away, cussing me, the elephants, and the horse's ass I rode in on. I finally had to get her in a bear hug to save myself.

I tried to play stupid and asked innocently what the matter was? She just started laughing and cussing me out again at the same time.

"Goddamn bastard!"

I tightened my hug.

"How about a drink, Dear?"

"Damn right! You – you –! I could only find nine of the damn things. Where the hell are the other three?"

I shook my head and gave her a shrug.

"Gosh, I have no idea. I was plastered at the time."

Then I told her my saga of being stopped on the way home. She looked at me strangely and burst out laughing again.

"Goddamn well serves you right! The cop's name is Morris. If you had been any real trouble, he would have run and hid in the woods."

I mixed a drink and handed it to her.

"Want to go to bed? It's Christmas, after all."

"What the hell do you think I came over here for?"

Despite that bright moment, I had come to dread the holidays since my divorce. Every year, I missed the good times with Marge and the kids at Christmas. She always made sure the decorations were put up and everything was cheerful. We didn't hold back on the presents, and it was a happy time for us all.

My thoughts always turned to that lonely Christmas on Yankee Station off the coast of North Vietnam. My mind dredged up and recycled the most prominent memories – and images of the war – and my accident. I could never get away from them, even in the best of times. I kept wondering what my life would have been like if I hadn't had the accident? What if I hadn't had to live through all that fear and pain? Would I have stayed in the Navy? Hell, I was 42 years old and could be retired by now!

That evening, loneliness and depression swept over me. I tried calling Mom, but she didn't pick up the phone. She was probably too inebriated to answer it. I didn't want to unload my troubles on my brothers or my sister. They had no idea how bad my problems had become. Melissa had only known the positive side of me, and I worked to keep it that way. There was nobody I could talk to. Mom probably had the right idea. I passed the night away drinking until nothing mattered and collapsed in bed to sleep it off.

Of course, the hangover made everything much worse in the morning. I heated a stale cup of coffee in the microwave and sat at the kitchen table trying to think of happy things, but everything came with problems. I was happy with my job, but almost all the money I earned was committed before I could enjoy any of it. I had the relationship with Melissa, but I would self-destruct if I let it continue. I was glad Jeff was here and doing well. However, I was deeply concerned that drugs had impaired his ability to function. I could not see him building a gratifying life for himself. Shelley and Jeff had invited me over for a gathering of friends and relatives on Christmas day, but I declined. I made some poor excuse, although the truth was that I was uncomfortable at any function where I didn't know most of the people. I would always be trying to explain myself and I probably would not relate to any of the others, anyway. If I went, I would make myself invisible and observe everything without really participating in the party.

Yes, my conduct was antisocial and irrational. As before, however, I did not identify my awkward behavior with any specific problem – like PTSD.

I had to make some corrections in my life, so where could I start? My problem with Melissa could be easily solved if I found another girl friend. That was the obvious place to start. It was time. I made a deliberate decision to read the local papers for stuff like singles listings and events. I thought of joining a running group or a hiking club, but outdoor activities would have to wait until spring. I made a mental note to check bulletin boards at art stores for notices of local painting groups. I needed to become involved in activities outside of the office and my narrow circle of friends.

Further, I asked myself two questions that I had frequently asked myself in the past.

"If I could do anything I wanted, what would it be?" and "If I could be anyone else in the world, who would I want to be?"

Those questions had led to real estate after I got out of the Navy and to the period after my divorce when I decided not to do anything significant at all. They had also prompted me to check out the art school when I was desperately trying to deal with my outrageous boss at GSA. I rejected my dream of running away – of just escaping and building a new identity on some tropical paradise. Truthfully, I found it difficult to resist that fantasy. I did not have the courage, however, to make it happen. At the moment, the only alternative that I found attractive was becoming an artist – that's what I truly wanted to be. But that was still impractical and simply impossible.

The next day was Christmas Eve. Matt called late that evening, and we wished each other a Merry Christmas. He asked about Jeff, so I filled him in with what I knew and gave him Shelley's phone number. Matt and Jeff had always been close growing up. For better or for worse, Jeff had been Matt's role model.

"Don't worry Matt, Jeff always finds some way to land on his feet and take care of himself. By the way, I hope you got the check I sent you?"

I had sent him $50.

"Sure did, Dad. Thanks a lot!"

"I wish it could be more. So, how's everything going with you? Any girlfriends out there?"

"Nope, sorry Dad. I'm just trying to keep up in school. This is my junior year, you know. I can't wait for it to be over! Otherwise, everything's going OK."

"Well, keep plugging, Son. It may seem boring now, but this will be awfully important later on. Anyway, thanks for calling and have a Merry Christmas."

"You too, Dad."

Other than a few cheerful calls from my brothers later that day, Christmas passed unnoticed. But the holidays weren't over. December 30th was Marge's and my anniversary. Then, I had to contend with New Year's Eve and also my birthday on January 2nd. I always had difficulties with anniversaries. They reminded me that I had accomplished nothing in my life that I had set out to do – nothing that I thought was significant, anyway. I was painting a lot, but as soon as I stopped for the day, each of those annual milestones would bring back their own package of sad, lonely, or disturbing memories. I became morbidly depressed. I mostly stayed indoors, painted, read books, napped, and watched TV. Over and over, my mind mulled all the "could haves," "would haves," "what ifs," and lost opportunities of the past.

Did PTSD play a role here? I still had not heard the term. However, I believe now that it left me emotionally defenseless and allowed the memories and issues to be amplified to extreme and dangerous levels.

I caught a display ad in our town weekly newspaper about a singles "party" at the ballroom of a classy hotel on New Year's Eve. There would be a DJ, a buffet, and a pay-bar. The specified ages were from 21 to 45 years old. Hell, I was only 42, so that worked. I got dressed and bundled up. It was a cold, icy night outside. I disregarded my anxieties of placing myself in a room full of total strangers and headed out to celebrate.

I arrived, paid my money, and went inside. The "music" was loud, and dancers were jumping up and down like they were a flock of exotic cranes acting out their mating rituals. I looked around and soon realized that I was probably the oldest guy there. Oh well, the safest thing would be to go get a drink. That helped calm my nerves that were in danger of being shattered by the noise. I checked out the buffet, which amounted to a few platters of left-over cheese and vegetable sticks. The hot wings and meatballs were, of course, already eaten. All that were left were heating pans full of greasy sauce, used toothpicks, and chewed chicken bones. I leaned against the partition and scanned through the crowd to see if there was possibly some lady who might interest me. I came up cold.

OK, there wasn't any point holding up the wall. I finished my drink and turned to walk out the door. A gal who had been standing there caught me before I got away.

"Excuse me – do you have the time?"

I was about to glance at my wrist when I noticed that she was wearing a rather large watch herself. I looked up and started laughing. She rolled her eyes and starting laughing with me.

She was a few inches taller than I was and a good deal heavier. But she was younger and had long, auburn hair falling around a good looking face with a warm, frank smile. She was dressed like a '60s flower child – decorated with a floor-length, flower-print skirt, a purple velvet vest over a red silk blouse, a knit scarf, and a pair of red and black cowboy boots. She looked very much like a colorful gypsy in thrift store hand-me-downs. Oh well – I couldn't think of anything better to do. I looked at my watch.

"OK. The time is time to get the hell out of here."

"Can I come?"

I took her by the arm, we grabbed our coats, and out we went.

"Where are we going?"

I thought for a moment.

"I need to get out of my place for a while. How about yours?"

She was agreeable to just about everything.

"All I've got is a jug of cheap wine."

"Good enough in a pinch. I'll follow you. OK?"

She tilted her head and looked at me slyly.

"Hmm, I don't think I've ever taken a guy home without first knowing his name."

"Buck. What's yours?"

"Rogers. Follow me."

Her real name was Andrea. She lived in a subdivision house in a mill town about 20 miles away. We went indoors and shooed the cats off the deep, cushiony sofa. I sat down, and my lap was immediately chosen by one of them for a bed. I don't know why cats have always liked me. Maybe I smell like catnip – or maybe kitty litter. Andrea handed me a glass of wine and gave me a soft kiss on my cheek for starters.

She told me that she worked in an office processing medical claims. I told her I worked for the Army Corps of Engineers, and she burst out laughing. Her passion in life was to bring peace and love to the world. She couldn't imagine herself going out with someone "in the freaking Army." I had to spend some time explaining my job, but eventually she caught on. I told her I was an artist at heart and not a soldier. She fancied herself to be a poet, so I asked her to read some of her poems while we got into the wine. She handed me a drawing pad, so I could sketch her portrait while she entertained me.

Between her poetry, my sketches, and the cheap wine, it was turning into a mellow evening. As she read to me, I thought to myself that I could do that, even though I had never tried to write poetry in my life. Whoever else Andrea turned out to be, she was my first inspiration to write poetry, short stories, or anything creative.

We were in bed before the New Year's Ball dropped in Times Square. I was clearly not a match for her size, but I tried valiantly to keep my flag flying. I was a bull rider who deserved a blue ribbon for exploding out of the chute and staying on past the eight-second buzzer. I was battered and bruised and felt grateful that I had survived 12 rounds in the ring with the female, heavy-weight equivalent of Joe Louis. The Times Square crowd was cheering wildly on TV at the exact moment we collapsed in a tangled mass on the bed.

Andrea's robust snoring shook the lamps, rattled the pictures on her walls, and soon woke me up – really. I snuck into the living room, closed the bedroom door, and slept on the couch with the cats. Early in the morning, I made some coffee, and wrote my first attempt at poetry:

•

FOR ANDREA

I cast off my anchor long ago
And searched the wide world to and fro
Across the seas to distant shore –
To find a broad who doesn't snore!

•

She came wandering out after a while in her slippers and bathrobe.

"I smell coffee! Where's the coffee?"

I smiled and pointed to the kitchen. I wrote my phone number and the poem on one of the sketches I had drawn and left it upside down on a side table.

We sat for a while and talked about how wonderful our night had been. She went back in the kitchen and made a large breakfast with her special home fried potatoes with peppers and onions. She subscribed to the forgotten theory that the best way to a man's heart is through his belly. It soon began to snow outside, so I gathered my coat and asked her to write down her phone number. I told her I had left mine on the table and departed after a crushing bear hug and an affectionate kiss. I gave her a pat on her ample breast and walked carefully down the snowy steps to my car.

Yes, the evening had been fun. I smiled all the way home to my loft. There were three inches of snow on the ground when I arrived, and I didn't have long to anticipate Andrea's response to my note. My phone was ringing as I unlocked my door.

"Goddammit!"

She was just starting to wind herself up.

"Goddammit!"

Then she started to laugh.

"Goddammit, Blake! You worthless …!"

Then I started laughing, and we both couldn't stop. Finally, she sniffled and had to catch her breath.

"Give me a call some goddamn time, you son-of-a-bitch bastard!"

She hung up, and I sat down to watch the Rose Bowl Parade on TV. The sun was shining in Pasadena. The sky was clear, palm trees were swaying in the breeze, and the crowd wore sunglasses and short-sleeve shirts. It was an impossible contrast to the gloomy, frigid, snowy day outside my window. Marge, the kids, and I had once gone to see a Rose Parade. Instantly, my thoughts left Andrea and went to Marge in those happier times. I became despondent again and had to turn off the TV. I was very tired and lay down on my bed to take a nap. I felt like I was riding on a roller coaster of emotions. I would be high one moment when I was painting, or when I was thinking about Melissa, or now Andrea, but my mind would always wander back to past mistakes and memories. Automatically, it seemed, my mood came crashing down and was crushed in the vice of depression.

Cat Window

I did not learn until 25 years later that Bipolar Disorder – or dramatic mood swings – develops in people with PTSD as much as 40 percent of the time! In any event, New Year's couldn't pass soon enough.

•

If it's sunny on TV, it should be sunny everywhere.

•

Poetry And Destiny

1986 STARTED MUCH LIKE 1985 ENDED. The job was hectic with all the work that had to be done to make up for time lost over the holidays. We barely had a moment to catch our breaths between assignments – more accurately, we were each juggling over 20 cases that all had to be kept moving toward completion at the same time. When one action was completed, two more would seem to take its place. In addition to my own assignments, I had to supervise and review everybody's work. If I had to travel, it was rarely for more than three days at a time. Any longer than that, and I would come back to a desk over-loaded with more problems than I had left behind. Melissa and I were still able to schedule a few days together occasionally, which made all the work less of a chore.

Andrea and I continued to spend time together on weekends. I found myself writing more poetry. It was a great way to spend time in the evenings when I was tired of painting. My poems were becoming longer – like my 26 page epic "How the World I Saved." The first few stanzas went like this:

•

HOW THE WORLD I SAVED

It started as an accident really
The time the World I saved
The strange events that follow tell
How the path to peace I paved.
No one in their wildest dreams
Could make the absurd prediction

That I saved Mankind from certain death
Using its own feline addiction.

Every nation has a Cat, you know
To serve its Head of State
Every dictator, president
Whatever potentate.
I was the dedicated White House Cat
I through the halls would run

Midnight black and a proud alley Cat
And my name was Washington …

•

Later in the saga, I wrote this section thinking of Melissa. DaDa is the female
Kremlin Cat:

•

… DaDa was in Georgetown
At the PussyCat Salon
She threw out the old, indulged herself
And slipped high-fashion on.

Her hair is spiked French vanilla blonde
Tattoos and studs in each pierced ear
Hip boots match her ruby eyes
And her pink leotard so sheer.
She wears a chain-link garter belt
And jewels from all her friends

She holds a spangled riding whip
Her whiskers have day-glow ends.

Her tail is colored rainbow
Her nails are lavender
We surely will dream sweet dreams tonight
With visions of her curves slender.
The crowd in awe makes a path for her
As the Capitol steps they climb

And each deliberate front paw move
Sways her hips in rhythm time! …

•

I did not totally ignore Andrea, however and wrote this especially for her:

•

PASSIONS

Swallows tossing swift moon shadows
Still breezes stir the air

> Passions swell within her breasts –
>
> If only I was there!

•

My early attempts at poetry were more like storytelling with verses that rhymed relentlessly. The best result, however, was that I developed a sense of rhythm that later made it into my other writings. Humor also played a big role in my style. I came to believe that poems need a good punch line, just like a good joke. I did not turn to more thoughtful, introspective writing for several years.

1986 started on an even keel, except that the IRS launched a new campaign against me. I had been dutifully making payments as specified in our agreement, but someone had apparently not gotten the word. I had actually got the balance that I owed down below $10,000 from its high of $18,000. If I had the money, I would have been glad to pay off what I owed just to get them off my back. Collection letters kept arriving that threatened to attach everything I owned, including the seat of my pants. I called the IRS many times and tried to explain what was going on. Every time, the person I talked to would say, "Oh, no. That's not right. I'll take care of it." But after each call, another demand letter would appear a few days later.

I became so paranoid that I fully expected an IRS truck to back up to my door at any moment. I had visions of them pirating away my important files and records, all my art work that had become part of my soul, my furniture, and my clothes – down to my socks and underwear. Andrea had a basement at her place, which became the emergency repository of my most important treasures and a couple of get-away suitcases – packed ready to go. I was becoming more and more anxious. I made up my mind that if the IRS came, I would cash my last paycheck and disappear. How difficult could it be? So what if I ended up wandering the streets and highways with pennies in my pocket? I would sure be teaching the IRS a lesson – damn right!

Andrea found this all very amusing, but I was an emotional disaster. I would go over to her place for some company to calm me down and cheer me up. She was sympathetic because she was working through her own set of problems with the Government. One of the IRS agents who I had talked with was finally successful, however, in turning off the collection letters. I received a written apology, which helped return my life to normal. My cherished cache found its way back to the loft, and I was able to go outside without constantly looking behind me to see if the Feds were sneaking up to haul me away.

One wintery Saturday morning, Melissa came over unannounced. I offered her a drink, but she uncharacteristically shook her head and declined.

"I want to talk with you, Roger."

"Sure, what's on your mind?"

All sorts of scenarios ran through my thoughts. Was she quitting her job? She had been treated for an ulcer recently, so was she sick? Was she dumping me – or hopefully ditching John? She had given no indication of any of that. I was totally in the dark.

Melissa sat on a chair and looked down thoughtfully. Finally, she sighed and looked up with a half-smile.

"I want to get married. Will you marry me?"

I burst out laughing.

"You – you want to get married? No way!"

"Seriously, Roger. Will you marry me?"

I looked at her. She was completely sincere. She cocked her head to one side, lifted an eyebrow, and waited for an answer.

"What brought this on? Are you breaking up with John?"

"No, I just feel like I'm missing something in life – like I'm not a whole person. All I need to know is if you will marry me?"

I stood up and paced around for a few moments. Then I sat down, took her hands in mine, and looked her in the eyes.

"Melissa, I would marry you in a damn heartbeat, but I have to know if you would still be seeing other guys?"

She didn't hesitate with her response.

"Oh yes. Nothing would change. I just want to get married – it's between you and John."

Wow! I wanted nothing more than to marry her, but the whole idea seemed crazy.

"I don't see what you see in John. How can you even think of marrying that guy?"

"Oh, he's so sweet and understanding. He never objects to anything I do. We're great together."

I realized that what she said was true – as she viewed the world anyway. Melissa would keep sleeping with other men, regardless of how I felt and as much as I didn't like it. It had been that way since I met her, and she would always be the same. I sat and tried to contemplate this for a moment. I had to make up my mind.

"Melissa – my dearest Melissa – I love you and want to marry you so badly, but I just can't. Every time you go off with someone else, you break my poor little heart. I'm sorry, but no. I hope you understand."

She thought for a moment.

"OK, Roger. That's what I thought."

"You're really going to marry John?"

"We'll see. I wanted to ask you first."

With that, she got up and left. I sat down and shook my head. I didn't try to fight the tears that fell down my cheeks. I knew I would never meet another woman as outrageously captivating as Melissa. But I also knew that she would drive me insane. Nevertheless, I felt that I had passed up a grand opportunity and was left again with an empty, lonely heart.

I worried that my decision might change her behavior and performance at work. When Monday came around, however, she gave no indication that anything had changed because it hadn't for her. I didn't ask her how things had ended up with John, and she didn't offer to tell me. She worked as hard as ever, we got together once in a while, and our relationship continued as though nothing had happened.

One evening, out of the blue, Jeff came over.

"Just wanted to check up on you, Dad."

"I'm doing fine, thanks. And how's everything with you?"

"Pretty good. I'm getting real tired of my job, but I've met a developer who's building some homes near Shelley's. He wants to hire me this spring to do some framing as soon as the weather warms up. That will get me outdoors, and I'll be earning much more money. I'll like that a lot."

"Sounds good, Son. And how's everything between you and Shelley?"

"Great, Dad. I really love her. I know she's older, but it doesn't matter. She's hotter than hell!"

"'Hotter than hell' is a very good thing."

"Melissa still treating you right, Dad?"

"Oh yes, just fine."

Jeff looked down. There was something bothering him, but he was having difficulty getting it out.

"Um – I'm having a problem I want to talk with you about."

I was pleased that our earlier conversation had sunk in.

"Sure, Jeff. Tell me – what's on your mind."

"Well, Dad, lately I've been going into bars and having a few drinks. Then when I'm talking with some guy, we might disagree on something, and I'll get pissed off. I get so angry, all I want to do is start a fight and knock his fucking head off. I never used to be like that. I actually got thrown out of a place last night and was told never to come back. Something's wrong with me, but I don't know what it is."

"Do you think it might have something to do with the Marines, Jeff? Maybe something in their training that makes you want to be violent? I know you were angry at them when you left."

"Maybe, Dad, but I'm not even thinking about the Marines when I do this. Something wells up inside me, and I want to fight anyone I can get my hands on."

I was perplexed. I couldn't remember any time that I had felt that way. There was nothing in my experience that I could relate to his problem. But I had seen Jeff out-of-control angry when he was doing drugs.

193

"Are you into any drugs, Jeff? You know there were times when you flipped out in Oregon."

"No, Dad. None of that. Shelley has got me straightened out."

"Wow! I'm really glad to hear it, Son. Hmm – how much have you been drinking?"

"Two, maybe three – four at the most."

"Just beer or hard liquor?"

"I've graduated to the hard stuff, Dad. You know – bourbon and gingers, vodka tonics, rum and cokes."

"You're still underage. Where the hell are you getting served booze?"

"There are plenty of places. The bartenders don't care – they only want the money."

I shook my head and frowned.

"That's got to be it, Son. You can't drink hard liquor the same as beer. Then you add the sugar from the mixers and, jeez! Your body is obviously not able to handle it. You're probably also drinking too fast and getting swacked. That alcohol and sugar combination can hit you like a brick."

Jeff thought for a moment and then nodded in agreement.

"You might be right."

"Look, son, I'm not being critical or trying to give you a lecture. God knows I drink my share of booze. But I pace myself. Hard liquor is for sipping. You can't guzzle it down or it's going to land you in a world of trouble."

"Good advice, Dad. I'll watch it. Thanks."

"I hope this helps, Jeff. Just be careful – and gosh! I know I've said this before, but whatever you do stay off that motorcycle when you're drinking!"

"OK Dad. Thanks again. Seeya'."

I went downstairs and watched as he drove away with a wave. I was glad he had come to me for advice, but more worried now than ever that he might ignore the warnings and do something stupid.

May came around, and I got an invitation in the mail. Damn if it wasn't to Melissa's and John's wedding! That conversation had long passed and been forgotten. I asked Melissa into my office the next day. She looked absolutely fresh and delicious as always.

"You're going to do it, aren't you?"

She was positively bubbling.

"Yup, sure am. I hope you'll come – at least to the reception."

"I'll have to think about it. You know John's not my favorite person. I'm sure he feels the same way about me."

"Well, just do it for me then. This is important, and I'll miss you if you don't show."

I could only shake my head.

"OK. I'll try, but it's going to be awkward. Can't I just give you a dumb gift and a kiss to send you on your way?"

Melissa smiled sweetly.

"You can, Roger, but I'd really like it if you came."

I frowned and waved her back to work.

The more I thought about it, the more depressed I became. I should have ignored my problems with her other guys and accepted her proposal. So what if I would be miserable some of the time? I was already miserable. I would be married to Melissa, and the times we were together would more than compensate for the times she was out playing around. But no. That wasn't true. I had made the right decision, even though it was damn sad. She was like a brilliant diamond with a serious flaw. Whenever I tried to admire its beauty, all I would see was the imperfection. In any event, their wedding day finally came, and I decided to show up briefly at the reception.

The grass was lush and green, the flowers were blooming, and it was a beautiful, warm afternoon. The reception was held in the large garden of her

195

family home. Melissa was radiant and looked spectacular in her grandmother's wedding gown. I stuck around for a few drinks, but felt very much like the odd man out. I gave her a kiss and a fond "good luck." I had made my appearance and left quietly.

That evening, I was moping around, not doing much of anything. The time was probably around eight o'clock. Melissa came clumping up the stairs – I could recognize those clumps anywhere. She swung the door open and marched in angrily. I was dumbfounded.

"My gosh! What's the matter?"

"Goddamn John. He passed out! It's my damn wedding night, and I'm going to get screwed by someone. That someone is going to be you, so let's go to bed!"

I smirked and had to laugh.

"Serves you goddamn right! But OK. Let's do it."

It was an amazing night. Melissa held nothing back, and I savored every bit of every moment. We finished with a drink, sat naked in bed, and reminisced about our more special and brazen moments together. We had known each other for less than a year and had packed in an awful lot in that very short time. I loved her more that evening than at any time since we had met.

The lazy summer days were passing by without any notable event. Jeff was a framer now and very proud of himself. Life was good. He and Shelley were doing fine, and the extra money he was earning helped out tremendously with their finances.

Jeff came over with Shelley to celebrate his 21st birthday at the end of July. I had called Matt and told him about the party and what time to call. I had also called Shelley and asked what Jeff would like for his birthday. She told me he wanted a leather tool belt and some framing tools for his job. Good suggestion, so I had gone down to the local hardware store and bought everything they suggested – leather tool belt, framer's square, tape measure, and scribe – all professional quality. In addition, I slipped $121 in an envelope and put it in the package with the belt.

Shelley brought a cake, and it was party time. We popped a few beers, toasted his 21st and gave each other warm hugs. He opened his presents and was genuinely pleased. The tools bolstered his confidence and made him even more proud of himself. Now he could become a skilled framer. Matt called, and they had a cheerful brotherly conversation. Jeff was a man now with the whole world opening up for him. His happiness was amply evident in every move he made.

I got to know Shelley a bit. She was born nearby, had lived here all her life, and had lots of family in the area. The farthest Shelley had been from home was the New Hampshire coast, only a few hours away, so she wanted to travel with Jeff to the West Coast sometime. She was pleasant and worked as a receptionist in a local investment office. I could see why Jeff enjoyed being with her. It was getting dark outside when she and Jeff hopped on the bike. He was wearing his new belt with all the tools securely in place. They rode off with a "Seeya', Dad," and a couple of big smiles.

"Seeya', Son. Congratulations again. Take care guys."

It was Saturday night, eight days after Jeff's 21st birthday. I was in bed sleeping soundly. I heard the telephone ring in some distant world, but didn't want to answer it. The phone kept ringing. I finally sat on the edge of the bed and picked it up.

"Hello?"

I was none too pleased. I glanced at the clock. It was just past midnight.

"Is this Mr. Roger Blake?"

I was still trying to rub the sleep out of my eyes.

"Yes."

"Sir, are you by any chance a relative of Jeffrey Blake? We found your name and phone number in his wallet."

"Yes, I'm Jeff's father. What's going on?"

I didn't like the direction that this conversation was going.

"Sir. This is Sergeant Johnson with the Groton police department."

Oh Lord, I thought. What the hell has Jeff done now? I had visions of him getting into a fight and tearing up some bar.

The officer sighed.

"Jeff has had an accident, Sir."

"How bad is it, Officer?"

"I'm very sorry to have to tell you, Mr. Blake, but your son is dead."

I suppose everybody dreads such a call in the middle of the night – or anytime for that matter. I can only say that it is just as bad – or worse – than can possibly be imagined. I gulped for air. He was doing so great! My God! I had just hugged him the other day.

"I'm – I'm – trying to think clearly, Sergeant. What happened?"

"He was driving his motorcycle on River Road about three miles out of Pepperell and tried to get around a car on a curve. The driver of the other vehicle said that he lost control, went off on the shoulder, and hit a tree."

"Oh damn!"

So many thoughts were racing through my head that I had to take some time to collect myself.

"Where is the body? Can I see him?"

"Yes Sir. He was taken to the Worchester Hospital. I see that your phone number is in Littleton. Do you want me to pick you up?"

"No – no thanks. I'll be OK."

"Are you sure? I would be glad to drive you over."

"I appreciate it, but I can manage."

"Just go in the emergency entrance then. Should I tell them you're coming?"

"Please. I should be there in less than an hour. Thank you, Sergeant. Thank you for tracking me down and calling."

"You're welcome, Mr. Blake."

He paused for a moment.

"Please take your time, Sir – there's, uhm, no point in hurrying."

He hung up and left me holding the disconnected phone and staring at the floor. Finally, the buzzer went off, and I hung up the receiver. I thought of calling Marge, but decided that I better see the body first. I would also call Shelley later.

I sat for a moment and tried to gather my thoughts. I had to dress and get going. I shook my head. Damn! It had to be the bike, the bars, and the goddamn booze. I became very angry with myself for not preventing the accident somehow, but could only wring my hands knowing that it was too late. What more could I have done? I had warned him. Maybe I could have been more forceful. No. If I had, he would have rejected me. Youth believes in its own invincibility.

I have to get dressed and go see him. I need to hug him one more time and say goodbye. Keep moving, Blake. You have to do this.

I arrived at the hospital and identified myself as the father of Jeffrey Blake. A nurse came forward and asked me to follow her. We entered an examining room, and there on the table was his body covered with a sheet.

"We need a positive identification of the body – if you don't mind, Sir?"

"Of course."

She pulled the sheet back. Yes, it was Jeff. There were some cuts on his face and an indentation which must have been a crushed cheek bone. The nurse started to cover him up again. I put my hand up.

"No, please. Can you leave me alone with him for a few minutes?"

"Certainly, Sir. I'll be outside when you're finished."

She closed the door softly behind her. I put my hand over his cheek. His body was already cool.

"I'm sorry, Jeff. I'm so very sorry."

I stared around at the ceiling half expecting to see his ghost up there looking down at me. I wanted to see his smile and carefree wave. I wanted to hear him say, "Seeya', Dad" one more time. But none of that happened. I sighed and patted his head. I bent down and gave him a long hug. Finally, I kissed him lightly on his forehead.

"Seeya', Son."

I slowly slipped the cover back over his face and went back outside. The nurse suggested that I have his body taken to a funeral parlor nearby.

"I'll be pleased to take care of it for you, Sir."

"I appreciate your generosity. Thank you."

I turned and slowly walked out the door. Outside, I felt the delightfully fresh night air. I was aware of everything around me. I needed to remember this experience – to emblazon every detail in my mind.

It was time to get home and make the phone calls. On the way, however, I wanted to find the crash site. I drove slowly through the night mists until I saw the single skid mark in my headlights. I stepped out of the car, took out a flashlight, and followed his track onto the gravel shoulder. Gravel and motorcycles are a deadly mix. It was easy to see where Jeff had struggled to wrestle the bike back onto the pavement before he hit the trunk of a small tree. The bark had been scarred by the impact of the motorcycle, and there were a few bits of broken glass and a gasoline stain on the ground to identify the point of his death. I knelt shakily at the base of the tree and tears started to flow. My memory was flooded by all the problems and good times that we had known. The happy image of him on his 21st birthday stuck in my mind and wouldn't disappear. What a waste – what a goddamn, terrible waste!

I got home and reluctantly dialed Marge's number. This would be the most difficult call I had ever made. Matt picked up the phone.

"Hi, Matt. This is Dad. Is Mom there?"

"No. She's out somewhere. What's going on?"

"Did she leave a number or anything? I need to talk with her."

"No, she didn't. Can I take a message or something?"

I didn't want to tell Matt first – especially if he was alone. There was no telling what he might do.

"If there's a problem, Dad, please tell me."

I took a deep breath. It wasn't fair not to tell him now that I had inferred that there was, in fact, something wrong.

"This is terrible news, Matt. I wish someone was there with you."

"I'll be OK, Dad."

I told him everything as gently as possible.

"I'm so sorry, Matt. I know how close you were – how much you loved your brother."

Matt was silent when I had finished. I waited for a few moments, but he didn't say a thing.

"Are you all right?"

"Yeah, Dad. I've – I've got to hang up. I'll talk with you later."

I was left with a bad feeling in my gut. I called some old friends in Salem who were also very close to Marge, Jeff, and Matt. I explained the situation and asked if they would please drive over to Marge's house right away and stay with Matt. I frankly did not trust what he might do. If they could track down Marge, that would be good too.

"Absolutely, Roger."

Then it was time to call Shelley. She was devastated and burst into convulsive sobs. She had known he had gone off to his favorite bar for a couple of beers. At about 11:30, she became concerned and called to check up on him. His voice was slurred, and she was having trouble understanding him.

"You don't sound real good, Jeff. Let me come down and pick you up. I'll drive you home."

The tavern was only six miles away. He responded in his macho way.

"Oh, no. I'm OK. I'll leave in a little while. Seeya'."

Those were the last few words that she had with him. About half an hour later she heard sirens of police cars and an ambulance as they sped by. The thought crossed her mind that Jeff may have had an accident, but she had no way of knowing. I gave her my sympathies and told her that I would call when I had more information.

Then Marge called. She was almost mute and was obviously suffering from shock. Our friends were still with Matt when she got home. He was OK, but had retreated within his private thoughts and wasn't talking with anybody.

201

After running through the details of the accident, Marge and I agreed to have the body cremated, and I would go back to Oregon for a memorial service. After that, I wanted to fly above Mt. Bachelor – Jeff's favorite ski mountain – and scatter his ashes over the rugged ridges and peaks of the ski bowl. I wished I could be there to console her, but that was not going to happen.

Finally, at about 4 a.m. I poured myself a drink and sipped it while I waited for the sunrise. The first rays of sunlight were filtered by a hazy layer of humidity. I imagined that it was rising somberly over the trees and hills – a sad gesture to one of its own. It was a new day, but the light would take a long time to chase away the dark shadows from the night before.

I waited until a decent hour and called Melissa. She came racing over and stayed with me for much of the day. We went over to the police department to get the accident report. They estimated Jeff was doing 56 miles an hour when he skidded off the pavement and much less when he hit the tree. He had left only 20 feet of skid marks on the road and another 70 feet in the gravel. They determined that he had simply failed to react quickly enough to make the curve.

Then we went over to the hospital. Blood tests revealed that Jeff's blood/alcohol level was 20.6 percent – more than twice the legal limit. The medical examiner reported that his neck was broken, skull fractured, and spine shattered – not to mention major lacerations, and massive internal injuries. The hospital listed the cause of death as, "Impact with a tree." Melissa and I looked at each other. We both knew that the real reason was alcohol.

Our last piece of business was to visit the shop where the motorcycle had been towed. The tow truck operator on duty let us into the compound. The bike had some obvious damage, but the guy said it could be repaired. I told him if he wanted the bike, he could have it in exchange for the towing bill. That was fine with him. We were about to leave when I glanced at the rear wheel. It had the same bald tire that was on it when I first saw the bike. I could not dismiss the thought that if Jeff had changed the tire – or if I had replaced it for him – maybe he could have gotten out of his skid and walked away. Damn!

Melissa and I went back to my apartment. I told her I was taking a few weeks off, and that she would be Acting Chief during my absence. I would call the New York office in the morning and tell them what was happening. She mixed me a drink, but I took a few sips and poured it down the sink. It was the first time that I could remember that booze did not taste good.

A few days later, I flew to Oregon and met with Marge and Matt at their house before Jeff's memorial service. Her parents were there, along with her boyfriend, Jerry. Her cousins had also come and even her brother, Terry, who I had known in pre-flight training. My brother, Brian, joined me from the East Coast.

I was not looking for a warm reception and did not get one. The mood was strained – to say the least. They had decided, years ago, that our failed marriage was my fault. Now, I felt that they had no problem blaming me for not looking after Jeff more closely. Other than Matt and my brother, they were all on Marge's side of the family, so what could I expect. I was able to take Matt aside, and I tried to assure him that I would be there if he ever needed me. "Please call me any time, Matt." We hugged and I turned my attention to the rest of the room. I made the rounds, shook hands sadly with everybody, and left.

I was expected to speak at the service – it was only me and the minister. The large church was full of the relatives and many mutual friends who Marge and I had known before our divorce. All of Jeff's friends had come, and many others who I did not know. I had written a three page, small type, single-spaced eulogy. It was long, but I believed that the tragedy of Jeff's death could serve as a lesson for everybody there – especially Jeff's friends.

I started shakily, then took a deep breath and didn't mince any words. I spoke about Jeff's 21st birthday. I went through the dreadful details of the accident and the police reports. I read from the medical examiner's report. I told the gathering about Jeff's excessive drinking and his new-found taste for hard liquor. I relayed how his girlfriend had tried to persuade him to let her pick him up and how absolutely devastated she had been when I had told her the news. I recounted how she had heard the sirens on their way to the accident scene.

I talked about Jeff's lack of regard for his life. How he had said, "Dad, if it happens, it happens. It really doesn't matter."

"Well, life really does matter, Jeff. Your life mattered to everybody in this hall!"

I paused and looked over the gathering, which was silent except for some quiet crying here and there. I finally read further from my prepared remarks.

203

•

"... What kind of person was Jeff? What traits did he have that made him vulnerable to the accident? Jeff's priorities were very simple:

- A cold beer in the fridge.
- A fast set of skis, hot wax, and deep powder.
- A new fishing reel.
- Good friends.
- Good times, and
- The freedom to live life his own way.

He worked hard and played hard. Life was a game – a game to be embraced. If there was a party, Jeff wanted to be there. He was generous, good natured, and kind. But he was also rowdy in the name of excitement and fun. He lived life to the hilt and frequently stepped over the line between taking considered risks and being reckless. The difference is that being reckless leaves no margin for error."

And I finished with:

"... Let us remember Jeff's fine qualities as a human being. There's not one of us here that can say that in Jeff's terms, his life was not fulfilled. He lived his shortened life his way, but I'm sorry – life damn well does matter! I pray that none of you here have to learn that lesson the way Jeff did.

"So, while it hardly seems enough, all that is left to say is, 'We love you, Jeff. Seeya' later, Son – later.'"

•

Matt and I climbed into a light, single-engine aircraft at the small airport in Sunriver, Oregon. I had explained to the pilot the purpose of our flight. The plane rattled and shook as we rolled down the runway. I had tried to dismiss my anxieties and fears that I would not be able to manage flying in what I perceived as an under-powered, accident-about-to-happen with wings. My preparations didn't work.

I was instantly fearful that the engine would quit, or that we did not have enough power to fly at this high altitude, or that wind gusts on top of the mountain would drive us onto the barren rocks below the rim. Horrific images of my accident in the Navy raged through my mind. I held on tight to the canister between my legs and closed my eyes.

"Do this for Jeff. This plane had flown many times up there without an accident. Be calm – this will all be over soon."

I took a deep breath and opened my eyes. Outside the ground was dropping away beneath us. The flight smoothed out, and we were on our way.

"OK. I'm doing fine. I can get through this."

The plane took a long time to climb above Mt. Bachelor. We finally swung around the volcanic crater that formed the ski bowl. Matt and I pointed out to each other many of the peaks and crags that we had climbed together. On our second pass, I slid back the window and poured some of Jeff's ashes into the clear mountain skies. I handed the canister to Matt, and he did the same.

"Here you are, Jeff – back again on your favorite mountain. Remember us down here and protect us with your love. You will remain forever in our minds and hearts. Farewell."

I left Salem early the next day and flew back to Massachusetts. I buried myself in my work and only went out for important business trips. My mind had built a defensive shield around itself. I remained quiet and moody. I'm sure I presented myself as a morose and lost individual. Depression would come over me when I wasn't occupied, or as soon as I entered my loft for the evening. Melissa, Andrea, and occasional contacts with my family were my personal safety net. Time eventually worked its magic to enable the acute hurt of Jeff's memory to drift from the present into my dimmer recollections of the past.

I don't recall any major events that happened during the remainder of 1986. That's a very good thing.

•

Pushing the boundaries of life is a quick way to lose it.

•

Chapter *26*

1987 – Age 44

Nothing Matters 'Till It Hurts

IF SOLDIERS MUST SURVIVE the fog of war, I would describe my state as enduring the fog of life – or struggling through the murky haze of events as they swirled around me.

I spent most of my time at work because it was the one thing that took my mind off of Jeff. I was only half-heartedly going through the motions, however, and did not care what happened at the office one way or the other. My friends were supportive and did their best to cheer me up, but they were tiptoeing on egg shells around me. The last thing I wanted was sympathy. I couldn't even get excited about painting or writing. I tried to take up jogging again, but found that my back couldn't take it. My mind was drowning in a numb morass of hurt and guilt. I withdrew from social contact as much as possible.

After months of gloomy isolation, Melissa took charge and dragged me up to her grandparent's farm in Maine for a long weekend. The trip was the first outing I had taken since I lost Jeff. We had a relaxing time picnicking, canoeing, eating lobster and clams, and visiting places that she remembered from her youth. I had forgotten how good it was to be with her.

Coming home in her mini-van, we were driving on the freeway, surrounded by weekender traffic heading south from Maine and northern New Hampshire. I asked Melissa to get some water from the back. I thought she could just reach over the seat and grab it, but the cooler was in the rear by the door. Melissa had on a skin-tight T-shirt and her skimpy cut-off shorts. Nothing else. Oh yes – she was wearing pink panties this time.

She scrambled over all the luggage, equipment, food, and freezer bags. People driving next to us were watching her every move. She got to the back and lifted up two water bottles triumphantly. Drivers started beeping their horns and giving her enthusiastic thumbs up. Then she turned around to climb over everything again to get to the front. Her butt was sticking up in the air, and the car behind us started honking, blinking its lights, and swerving in its lane while Melissa wiggled her rear-end back at them.

Drivers who could see what was going on were going crazy as she made her way to the front. We were both laughing and waving back. Her finale was

206

diving over the front seat and slipping under the dash with her legs kicking in the air. Have I mentioned how really great her legs were? Her cheering spectators were hysterical. After a good deal of exaggerated squirming and kicking, she finally made it upright again. We toasted each car beside us and the one in the back. I'm sure her audience would have paid admission to see a repeat performance.

Life was never dull when we were together. Later that summer, we were coming back from a meeting in Stamford, Connecticut. I was driving a government station wagon, and we were both dressed in proper business suits. Traffic came to a stop-and-go standstill through New Haven. The guy in the car next to Melissa's side looked over and rolled down his window. He started bouncing up and down in his seat, wagging his tongue, and panting at her. She just rolled her eyes and ignored him. Traffic in our lane started to move so I sped up as well. The other guy accelerated to stay next to us, but he drove smack into a large speedboat on a trailer that was still stopped in front of him. Melissa gave him a dainty wave as we left him with his grill planted in the boat's engine compartment and his radiator spewing steam. I wondered how that guy would explain his claim to the insurance company.

Andrea and I had drifted apart and had a final falling out. Our evenings of reading our writings to each other had become competitive, and Andrea claimed that I did not like her poetry – or thought that mine was better. She was right, but I had tried hard not to show it. I said that her writings were just different, and I liked them fine. She was offended, however, and I could not turn her feelings around. Our times together had been good fun, but had dragged to an end.

One evening in November, I got a call from Matt. I had heard that he had dropped out of high school and planned to enroll at Chemeketa Community College to get his GED.

"Hi, Matt. So how's Chemeketa?"

"Not good, Dad. I'm having a really rough time."

"Gosh, Matt. I'm sorry to hear that. Is there anything you want to tell me about?"

"It just seems I don't remember a lot of things I ought to know. Other students are breezing right through this stuff, but I'm lost. I can't seem to catch up."

"I'm really concerned, Matt."

Until the last few years, Matt had been a bright student and earned good grades in everything.

"Have you tried counseling, or maybe a tutor?"

"I have a counselor. She says I should take my senior year over. I don't want to do that, Dad. Those kids would be much younger than me – I would feel like an old man sitting in their class. Frankly, I'll probably drop out and pick up my GED later. I'm really burned out on school anyway."

"What does Mom say, Matt?"

"Well – she's always on my case about something. If it's not school, it's about my friends, or going out to look for a job. She's probably right about the job, though. I'm thinking that will be the right thing to do."

Matt was clearly struggling and I felt totally inadequate. I wished I was there to give him some support, but that was not possible. His learning problems had to be caused by drugs. He couldn't remember things he ought to know because his mind had never been "present" to learn them in the first place.

"None of this is good news, Matt. But there's not much point of staying in school if you can't understand what you're trying to study. You've got to do something, however. You can't get a good job if you don't have a diploma or a GED. Is there any way I can help?"

"Well – frankly, Dad. I'm wondering if I could move back East and live with you for a while."

"Gosh, Matt – have you talked with Mom about this?"

"Yeah. She thinks the move would be good. Actually, I think she wants to get me out of the house and away from my friends."

"Well – sure. Please realize though, that my place is pretty basic. I can support you while you find work, but you'll have to get a job to help out with expenses."

"I understand all that, Dad."

I was apprehensive. Jeff's death was still weighing heavily on my mind. My life was relatively calm and manageable at this moment, and I didn't need to take on any problems that could change that. I had been thinking recently of my father. He led a reclusive and lonely existence, but functioned better without family interference. I was feeling the same need for seclusion. It was the lonely part of seclusion, however, that kept me from cutting everybody off. I still needed the friendship and companionship of close friends and family. What mattered right now, however, was that I needed to support Matt. I resolved that I would manage whatever adjustments were necessary to help him get started.

"OK, Matt. Let's work something out."

Matt moved in a few weeks later. It was a pleasure getting to know him again. For all his problems, he was still a warm and considerate fellow to have around. It had been three years since we had spent any time together. He was 19 now – too old to be a teenager, but not quite old enough to be a man. I drove him around the area and showed him where Jeff had worked. We stopped in at my office, and I introduced him to everybody. He was a big hit, especially with Melissa who demanded to know how such an ugly father could possibly have such an attractive son.

Then Matt asked to see the spot where Jeff had been killed.

"There's not much to see. Are you sure you want to go there?"

"Yes, Dad. I really would."

It wasn't hard to find. The skid mark was still there – a dark line pointing to the tree that ended his life. I parked on the shoulder, and we got out to take a look.

"You can see here where he left the pavement. That scrape in the bark is where his motorcycle hit and probably flipped him into the trunk. He was going too fast to have much of a chance once he hit the gravel."

Matt studied the scene for a moment and wiped some tears from his eyes.

"He should have dumped the bike. He would have gotten busted up, but might have survived."

We stood there silently for a few minutes. Matt was wrestling with his memories and deep sense of loss. He finally kicked the gravel and turned to get back in the car.

"OK. I'm done. Let's get out of here."

The first interview Matt had was with a canning company down the street from the loft. They needed a laborer on the shipping dock and hired him immediately. The job really got him motivated. His goal was to earn enough to buy a clunker, so he could get around without having to borrow my car. It wasn't long before he bought a beat up excuse for an old Datsun sedan. Then he began to come home late at night, and I saw less and less of him on weekends. He always came back cheerful though and acted like nothing unusual was going on. He said he was only "... going around with a couple of new friends." I felt he was too old and mature for me to lay down rules and curfews, so I let him do what he pleased. I tried not to be suspicious, but I took his late nights out as a warning sign that needed to be watched.

The holidays came and went. This year was no different from the rest – all I wanted to do was get them behind me. But having Matt around made it easier, and I tried hard to put on a good show for his benefit. At times, however, he slipped into an even deeper depression, and I couldn't reach him at all. Jeff's death was still a burden for Matt – just as it was for me. When I asked him if there was anything he wanted to talk about, he would shrug his shoulders and shake his head without saying a word. I bought a small tree – for the first time since my divorce – and we had a fun evening decorating it. We went out for a good dinner on Christmas Eve and exchanged a few presents on Christmas morning. All that was superficial, however. It did nothing to help Matt's mood after the holidays were over.

"I wish I could turn back the clock, Dad – on so many things."

I wasn't much help because I had the same feelings of regret. And I could only guess what the "many things" were that he referred to.

•

Regrets are negative reminders
that we should have done something positive.

•

Red Flags And Rocky Roads

BUSINESS TOOK ME OFF ON A TRIP for a few days in the middle of January. I did not anticipate the disaster that awaited me when I got home. Broken glass lay scattered on the floor. Dirty dishes, pots, and pans were piled in the sink. Paints and brushes were missing from my studio. The place was rank from smoke and spilled alcohol. There were plates with ashes and mashed out stubs of pot. The few bottles of liquor that I had kept in a cabinet were emptied. It looked like a team of acrobats had slept in my bed. It must have been one helluva party!

I was still livid when Matt came in from work that night. He apologized again and again. He hadn't expected me home until the following night and intended to have the place cleaned up by then.

"What about the broken stuff? Art supplies are missing. The booze is gone. What the hell is going on here?"

"I'm sorry, Dad. I'll replace what's broken and the other things. I don't know anything about the stolen stuff."

"Who did you have over, Matt? Dammit, I live here too – there are lots of people I don't want coming in here!"

Matt looked at me hopelessly.

"Just some friends from work, Dad. I didn't expect it to get out of hand. I'm sorry!"

"Some friends! It looks like a bunch of whacked out druggies had a convention here, for chrissake!"

"They were just friends, Dad."

Matt was getting testy, and my rant was not being helpful. I sighed in resignation and looked him straight in the eye.

"This went too far, Matt. We can't live together if I have to worry about what you're going to do whenever I go away. No more drugs. No more Goddamn parties. If this is what you want to do, you'll have to move out tomorrow. Understand?"

He nodded and went to the sink. He stood there with his arms spread on the counter while he looked the mess over. Then he shook his head, rolled up his sleeves, and started to wash things up. I gathered a garbage bag of trash and lugged it outside to the dumpster. My final indignity was having to change the sheets on my bed. We didn't say a word to each other for the rest of the evening. I slammed my door and went to bed.

Life soon returned to something approaching normal. Matt, however, was more reserved than before. He would not talk about his job, his friends, or what he was doing out so late at night. I did not know whether he was uncomfortable because of my harsh words, or embarrassed because of the party, or if he felt I was restricting his lifestyle, or if perhaps he had something bothering him that he wouldn't talk about. It was likely a combination of all those things. I tried several times, but simply could not penetrate his shell.

A few weeks later, I had to go down to New York District for a meeting. I called that evening to check up on him. He answered the phone, and I knew he was in a very dark mood as soon as we said hello.

"What's the matter, Matt? What's going on?"

He paused for a moment before he replied.

"I got fired from work, Dad."

"Why? What happened?"

"Someone was taking tools from the warehouse, and they blamed me."

"What proof did they have, Matt? They can't just fire you for something you didn't do."

"The shift supervisor claimed it was me. He's lying and probably stole the crap himself."

I honestly did not know what to think, but I had to support my son.

"It's not as bad as all that, Matt. Listen, I'll be home in a couple of days, and we'll decide where to go from here. Are you going to be all right?"

"Oh, yeah, I'll get over it. But it won't be that easy to find another job. The next business will want to know what I've been doing for the last few months, and I can't use this company as a reference. This really sucks, Dad."

"Look, Matt – we'll get through this. Here's a couple of numbers for me ... I'll be back soon, but call me if you need to talk. OK?"

"Thanks Dad. See you when you get back."

Our conversation left me very concerned. After Matt had arrived, he had told me how depressed he was about Jeff when I had called and told him what happened. He said he "didn't know what he would have done" if our friends hadn't come over until Marge showed up. Tonight, there was the same hopeless tone of despair in his voice. I decided that I needed to find him some help. The logical person for me to ask was Melissa, so I gave her a call.

"Hi Roger. What's up?"

I told her about my conversation with Matt, and asked if she would go over and make sure he was OK.

"Just do what you can to cheer him up, please."

"I'll go over right now."

"Thanks a lot."

I breathed a bit easier and passed the rest of the evening in front of the TV. I phoned Melissa at work the next morning.

"So, how was Matt? Everything OK?"

She giggled.

"Sure, he was great."

I had to think about that for a moment. She sure didn't act like there was a problem.

"Matt wasn't depressed? He was OK?"

"Oh yes. He was very depressed when I got there. But he's OK now."

She chuckled again. She was being coy – like she was playing with me.

"Melissa, goddamn it! Don't tell me ..."

"Sure, Roger. You asked me to cheer him up, and that's what I did!"

It took me a few moments to catch my breath.

"Goddamn, Melissa! You know that's not what I meant! How in the hell could you screw my own freakin' son?"

To her, it was the most natural thing in the world.

"Oh, he was really lonely and needed a boost. You know, he's one of the sweetest and most tender lovers I've ever had. He was great!"

"Shut the fuck up!"

I slammed the phone down. My heart was pounding so hard it could have blown apart. I could not believe this had happened! I felt betrayed by the two people that meant the most to me in the world. Melissa had crossed the line. Nothing would ever be the same again between us. I was emotionally torn to shreds. Nobody would ever get this goddamn close to me again!

Melissa was the one who seduced Matt. He should not be held responsible for what she had initiated. It was impossible, however, to live with the thought that this would happen again as soon as my back was turned. How could my trust ever be repaired? How could Matt and I ever stay together after this? It wasn't possible. I didn't want to kick him out, but I felt like that was the only option. Worry gripped me when I returned home to confront him in person.

It was a bitterly cold night, and the packed snow crunched under my feet as I walked up to my apartment door. I expected to have to wait up late to talk with Matt, but his car was parked in front of the loft. I noticed a hole in his driver side door when I walked by. It had definitely not been there when I left. My careful inspection revealed that it could only have been made by a good-sized bullet. Matt's bags were packed in the car. What the hell was going on here?

I came up the stairs and dumped my luggage on the floor.

"Hello Matt. I want to hear about that bullet hole in your car, but first we have to talk about Melissa."

Melissa had apparently already told Matt about our conversation. He sat down and shook his head dejectedly.

"I'm really sorry, Dad. We had a couple of drinks and – it just happened."

"Melissa's responsible. I guess I should have known better when I asked her to come over. Shit – I hope she cheered you up anyway!"

Matt smiled.

"Oh yeah."

I frowned and looked away. I was the only one who thought this was a problem.

"Well, I'm still having trouble with that, but we'll have to come back to it later. Now, what's with the bullet hole and your bags in the car?"

"Dad, can we have a drink? We're both going to need it – I damn sure will!"

I hated conversations like this. I mixed a couple of whiskeys and sat down across from him.

"OK, shoot – sorry, no pun intended."

Matt gave me a smirk. He took a swig of his drink and looked at me with a resigned expression written on his face.

"OK. You know I've been staying out late."

I took a drink, nodded, and waited for him to continue.

"Dad, I got involved with a gang. I've been dealing drugs."

He downed his drink and went over to the counter to mix a second one. I finished mine and let Matt pour me another as well. How in the hell could I respond to that? Hysterics were not going to do either of us any good. Matt was opening up and obviously telling me the truth. This was dangerous ground, but I had to listen and hear the rest of what he had to say. I had no idea where this was going.

"How long has this been going on?"

"Since before Christmas."

"OK – and the bullet hole?"

"I've been selling in a territory claimed by another gang – the Puerto Ricans. They control most of Boston and will force anyone out who tries to come in. They're ruthless – murder doesn't mean a damn thing to them. At first they didn't know who was selling in their area, but they've obviously figured it out. That shot is the only warning I'm going to get."

"For chrissake, Matt. You are going to get yourself killed! This may sound pretty crude, but I don't want another dead son on my hands. I don't think I could cope with it. What are you going to do?"

"I can protect myself."

He pulled a shiny, semi-automatic pistol out of a handbag sitting on the floor.

"Goddamn, Matt. That won't do you any good if a gang comes after you. Put that thing away!"

He put the pistol back in the bag, but did not zip it up. He looked at me seriously and sighed.

"I have to leave town."

"Just like that?"

"You were right, Dad. This shit will get me killed."

"Where will you go? How are you going to survive?"

I could not believe this was happening.

"I've got money – from the deals I've made. I'll probably head back to Oregon eventually."

I slumped forward in my chair and rubbed my forehead. I was too damn angry to cry. It was clearly too dangerous for Matt to stay. The only option was to accept his decision and let him go. Maybe someday he would grow out of all this and get a better start.

"Please don't deal in drugs anymore, Son. You have choices – there are so many options you haven't tried."

"I have tried other things, Dad. Nothing seems to work."

"Come on, Matt. You can rebuild your life. It will take work, but you can do so much better."

"I'm sorry, Dad. Drugs are the only thing I know how to do."

I couldn't think of a thing to say. Matt broke my heart, leaving without some other course to pursue. I could only look at him apprehensively and wonder what his future would bring. He checked his watch.

"I need to get away from here tonight, Dad. I've got to leave."

I nodded, stood up, and walked him down to his car. We gave each other a warm hug.

"Take care of yourself for God's sake. I love you, Son."

"Love you too, Dad. Be seeing you."

Matt climbed into his Datsun and drove away into the frigid night. I stood there and wondered if we would ever get together again. Given the path Matt had chosen, I half expected not to.

There was still Melissa to deal with. I went to work early the next morning to speak with her before anybody else came in. I gave her a dirty look, hung up my coat, and waved her into my office. We sat in my guest chairs and stared at each other for a moment.

"What you did is inexcusable. It's – it's fucking outrageous! Do you even have a clue how much you hurt me?"

"Come on, Roger. It's nothing. You should be proud of your son. He was wonderful! I think it's cool that father and son both screwed the same woman."

I was floored. Melissa just kept brushing the problem off. I was being hit by a barrage of negative emotions. Mainly, however, I was just sad.

"Well, Melissa, you've wrecked our relationship. I hope your fun was worth it."

She leaned closer and studied me for a moment before she replied.

"Get over it, Roger. This should pull us together, not push us apart. I certainly don't feel that way."

"Regardless, it damn sure isn't going to happen again. Matt left last night."

It was Melissa's turn to be shocked.

"What happened? Not over this for Pete's sake!"

I described everything that Matt had been going through.

"My God! I can't believe it. Do you think he'll be all right?"

"I hope so. He should be into Pennsylvania by now. I don't even want to guess what will happen later."

Melissa looked at me in disbelief.

"Are you all right? This comes at such a bad time – can I do anything to help?"

"I'll manage – you've done quite enough. Right now, I've got work to do."

I got up and walked around the desk. I opened the nearest file, sat down, and flipped through the pages.

"Shit!"

She pushed her chair back, wheeled around, and left the room.

Matt's departure left me wondering how my boys' lives could have gone so wrong! Was it me, or my absence from the scene after the divorce, or something I didn't provide while they were growing up? The bottom line was that their lives should have turned out much differently. So why was all this happening?

My difficulties with Jeff had started at an early age. He rebelled against everything I stood for, even my attempts to be a better father. I had hoped that my work ethic would set a good example. I had joined him in outdoor activities that we both enjoyed. But my efforts had never been enough for Jeff. He couldn't grow up soon enough. He always demanded more – and right now was already too late. Doing drugs and alcohol was just another way he had found to assert his independence.

Matt and Jeff had always been close. The two of them together served as a stronger counterbalance to my authority. But I felt a closer affinity to Matt. His disposition had always been easier to get along with. Matt had started his downhill slide after Jeff introduced him to drugs and his grades got worse as his addictions took their hold. He was no longer interested in physical activities – even though football might have turned his life around. And now he was dealing in drugs with the belief that it was his only option.

Things might have been different if I had been more successful in some of my real estate enterprises. Maybe Marge and I would still be together. Maybe I could have provided them with a better lifestyle. Maybe I could have taken them out of the drug culture that permeated their schools. Maybe – maybe – maybe. But I had not been able to make "maybe" happen.

I had done my best, so why beat myself up over all this mess? Their lives were their own, and they had made their own choices. It was not all my fault, but a deep sense of failure and abject regret settled over me. Any sense of achievement, gratification, or pleasure from my life was obscured by a dense cloud of these personal disappointments. I felt like a damn punching bag. All I did was try hard to do the right thing, get knocked down, and have to struggle back up to repeat the pattern again.

Melissa was still a friend, but no longer a companion. When I got home after work, I just sat and stared vacantly at whatever was around me. Art and writing weren't happening. Work meant nothing, but was the only thing that got me out of bed in the morning. Along with depression came a feeling of remorse and hopelessness. I felt that I had no control over forces stacking up against me. There was no use trying to find a way out. My best efforts would never be enough and were doomed from the start.

This was the same despondency that I had dealt with many times since the Navy. My thoughts would drift frequently to the accident, but I still did not connect my despair directly to any of its lingering traumas. I recognized my depression when it was tightening its grip on me and managed it as best I could through work. Whenever I became frustrated or overwhelmed at the office, however, I was reminded of my helplessness while struggling in the back of that cockpit. Work reminded me of the accident, and the accident reminded me of work. The way to defeat the cycle was to achieve positive successes at the office, but they were, for the most part, minor compared to the problems that kept dragging me down.

One day in late September, however, a call came through from New York District. The Chief of Real Estate had retired early because of health problems. The Assistant Chief was being promoted to his position, and they asked if I would be willing to come back down to New York and be the Assistant Chief? I thought about it for a couple of days. This would be a promotion and put me in line for the Chief's position. The job would come with a heavier workload and more responsibility, but I was ready for a new situation – so why not? I accepted the offer and started to get organized for the move.

I asked Melissa to come into my office and told her what was going on. I was recommending her for my position and thought she would do very well. She thought for a moment and shook her head.

"I don't have a good feeling about this, Roger."

"Why not?"

"We have it pretty good here. The pressure in New York is unbelievable – nobody deserves that kind of stress."

"I could use a change, Melissa. The District will snap me out of my funk, and the City is an exciting place. I think it's just what I need."

"OK, but I wish you wouldn't go."

Of course, one of my main reasons for going to New York was to get away from Melissa, so I dismissed her concerns.

A few weeks later, we were all gathered to say goodbye and good luck to each other. It had been a good run from a business point of view. The field office was functioning smoothly, and I had no problem leaving it in Melissa's hands. It was time to move on. I had found another loft space on the second floor of a commercial building in Hoboken, and my things were being picked up the next day. New York was anxious for me to start as soon as possible. I had the feeling of turning a page on a lot of memories as I walked out of the building. Hopefully, the disappointments would stay behind and positive opportunities would open up for the future.

I had just begun to unpack boxes in my new apartment when the phone rang. I picked up the call and to my surprise, it was Matt. I hadn't heard from him since he driven away that night in Massachusetts.

"Hiya' Dad! How's it going?"

"Great, Matt. Really good to hear from you. I've just arrived here in New Jersey. How the hell are you?"

"I'm doing pretty good Dad, thanks. Mom told me about your move. Don't laugh, but I'm wondering if I could come back there again and try to get a fresh start?"

"Fill me in, Matt. What's happening back there?"

"More of the same at home, and there's no real job market back here. New York would have a lot more opportunities for me to check out."

"Matt, I haven't even unpacked my suitcase. I've got to get settled in my job and have a little breathing space here."

"I know, Dad. I'm sorry, but I'm getting a little desperate. You're the only one I can turn to."

"You know there are going to be rules. I'll kick your ass out at the first sign you're not living up to them. You'll be on your own."

"I understand, Dad. No parties and no drugs."

I sighed. Everybody deserves a second chance.

"OK, Matt. Give me two weeks and then you can come."

"Thanks, Dad. You have no idea how much I appreciate this."

We signed off. I was grateful that he was OK, but it was going to be hard to have Matt in my life right now. I would have my hands full just with the office. Oh well, nothing's easy. Just take it one step at a time. Hogwash! I always had to have things put away neatly in their tidy little boxes. I didn't like surprises. I wanted my life to be calm and predictable. It was important, however, that I do everything I could for Matt. Maybe something good would come of it this time.

Matt arrived just after my two weeks breathing period was up. He said his trip back to Oregon had gone without a hitch, but he hadn't been able to find any work. The constant pressure to find a job and live on his own had become too difficult for him. His attitude, however, seemed more realistic and responsible this time around. We were both optimistic that somewhere in the big worlds of New York City and Hoboken he could find a positive opportunity.

That evening, Matt casually mentioned that Marge and Jerry had been living together for several months. I could hardly stand it. Here I was, still struggling to pay alimony while she was being supported by another guy. True, our divorce agreement stated that I would pay money until she remarried, but this was a new twist. I could only think that she was not getting married because she was receiving alimony from me. I called some acquaintances in Oregon and lined myself up with an attorney who told me that we could probably do something about it. This live-in situation amounted to an "unanticipated change in circumstances." There was no mention of a live-in situation in our divorce agreement. The attorney offered no guarantees, but he agreed to handle the case – for a $1000 retainer, of course.

•

Abusing a person's good nature should be a criminal offense.

•

Self-Portrait – 1988

There Is No Greater Fool Than One Who Believes His Own Lies

I FELT THE PRESSURES of my new position from the moment I walked into the office. I was no longer one of the beleaguered specialists just trying to survive without being drowned by the constant flood of cases and actions. My boss, the Chief of Real Estate, was already past the age when he should have retired. The position had made him tense and nervously hyper. He was required to spend much of his time in meetings where management decisions were made, but no real work was ever done. Most of the nitty-gritty details and decisions ended up on my desk.

I now carried the title of Assistant Chief, Real Estate Division, New York District. It was my responsibility to effectively control all the elements that kept the cases flowing. I also had to provide answers and guidance on how all real estate matters were to be conducted. I set higher standards than the office was used to and received a good deal of push-back and animosity in return. Everybody soon learned, however, that it was easier to do good work than to try to buck me. Most of the workers in the office were motivated individuals working hard to do a first-rate job. There were a few deadbeats, however, with whom I constantly battled. Any attempt on my part to be conciliatory was viewed as weakness to be taken advantage of. They persistently tried to find ways to make my life difficult, and I responded with letters of reprimand and threats of dismissal. I never was successful getting any of them fired, but I made their lives just as miserable as they made mine. Otherwise, I was very pleased and proud of the rest of the hard-working employees in the office.

My time at the Ft. Devens Field Office had given me only a glimpse of what was to come in my new position. I had supervised four employees at Ft. Devens. Now I had over 60. The thousands of properties that we managed, together with hundreds of new actions, threatened to overwhelm our existing planning systems – which were merely tickler files and manually developed monthly reports. Piled on top of the active cases were conferences, legal issues, planning, and project reports. But we could hardly create reports without data. Staying ahead of the ever-changing stream of information was a major effort all by itself.

Computers were just being introduced into the Corps of Engineers – almost 10 years after they had initially hit the market. Training courses were scheduled for everybody in the District. I did not know the slightest thing about them, other than they were to be used to generate documents. Our Realty Specialists – who had relied on our secretarial pool to get documents typed – would now have to do their own typing. I sat through the training course and became interested in the data management capabilities of this new resource. A few of our accounting staff had already become programmers, so I gave them the assignment of designing spreadsheets that would – for the first time – be able to present an accurate analysis of our workload, individual productivity, and budget requirements. It was an enlightening revelation. We knew definitively how resources were being spent and where adjustments needed to be made.

The Real Estate Division finally had an accurate model of what was happening. New York District had a reputation, throughout the Corps of Engineers, as being a money pit where workers sat on their hands all day and programs went to die. We could now document, however, that we had a higher work load and completion rate per Realty Specialist than several other Districts in the Corps. This information was not well-received by some people in Washington, who were responsible for distributing program resources. They were used to allocating generous funding and personnel allotments to their preferred Districts, and NY District was not on their favorites list.

Our conclusions were initially dismissed as summaries based on gerrymandered data. Central Office in Washington designed its own spreadsheet requirements. When we adapted our data to the new spreadsheets, our documentation proved correct. I should have learned a lesson from this, however – that it does no good to be right if you annoy your bosses in the process. But I was a slow learner and started to develop a reputation as a maverick – someone who had to be dealt with rather than worked with. I became fiercely protective of the Real Estate Division staff and proudly carried the District's banner to Washington whenever I had the chance. I just presented my facts. If diplomacy meant that I would have to kiss everybody's butt, I wasn't interested. I wasn't one of those federal employees whose main goal was to make sure I had a job to come back to in the morning. If the truth hurt – too bad.

Matt had found work with a company that did theatrical lighting for conventions and trade shows. The work was intermittent, but Matt made good money when he was on a job. Being a tall, strong, young man he was able to handle the scaffolding and heavy lights without a problem. He liked the job a lot – especially the fashion shows when he got to meet some of the models.

"I've had sex with some of the most extraordinary women in the world, Dad!"

"Well, in that case, Matt, we share the same taste in women."

Matt's company became involved in laser light shows, which were the new fad. He got to travel to places as far away as the Mid-West and Florida to put on events. He seemed to be well on his way to success, so we decided to move into a better apartment. The one I found would cost almost twice as much money, but we could afford it with Matt contributing about a quarter of the expense. It was in a new high-rise in Jersey City, was convenient with a ferry stop and a subway station a few blocks away, and had a grand view of lower Manhattan across the Hudson River.

One evening I got a phone call from John, one of my older brothers. He had a junker sitting in his garage that he would be happy to get rid of. The engine was smoking badly, and it was little better than a rusty bucket with wheels, but would we want it? Sure. Matt could use it to get around, so why not give it a try. We picked it up and drove to Hoboken without a problem – except that about every 30 miles we had to dump in a quart of oil.

All was well until we drove it to the local supermarket. Matt got in on the passenger side, and I sat down on the driver's seat. I was reaching for the ignition switch when – WHUMP!!! The rusted floor gave way under me, and I landed on the asphalt still sitting in my seat. I was left holding the steering wheel at eye level and laughing so hard that I couldn't possibly get up. Matt had to come around and pull me out. So, what to do? We were able to lift the seat up and slip a couple of 2x4s under it. But I felt that this was just the beginning of the car's problems.

"I think we better get rid of this thing before it kills us."

Matt agreed so we took it to the nearest junk yard. They wanted to charge us $50 as an environmental waste disposal fee. That was the law, but it was not going to happen. As we were driving out, we passed three, rough looking men walking up the road. I rolled down my window and waved them over.

"Hey guys – want to buy a car?"

There was some scratching of heads and skeptical looks.

"How much?"

"One hundred dollars."

I told them about the seat and the bad engine.

"Ah – too much, Sir. We don't have that kind of money."

"OK. How much have you got?"

They dug in their pockets and put it all together.

"We have $43."

"Sold!"

Matt and I jumped out. He took off the license plate while I took their money and signed off on the title. I let them keep the $3.

They piled in and waved out the window as they drove away – belching thick clouds of black smoke. I gave the money to Matt.

"Here you go, Son. Spend it on one of your girlfriends!"

When Matt wasn't working on the weekend, we would generally go into Manhattan for a couple of drinks and a good dinner. We enjoyed wandering around Greenwich Village and watching all the counter-cultural weirdness pass by. I would tell him about the nonsense in my office, and he would entertain me with stories of the intimate successes in his life. Our favorite watering hole was a micro-brewery just north of Canal Street that had the best beef ribs on the planet. One night, we got on the subject of Jeff. I told Matt how much I missed him, and what a shame it was that he died just after he had gotten his life together.

"Yeah, Dad. I really miss him too. Sometimes I feel like he's still with me up there – watching and telling me what to do."

"Wow! That's a really neat thing to say. Have you always felt that way – since his death, I mean?"

"Absolutely. You know how upset I was when you called and told me about the accident?"

"I remember. I was scared you might do something."

Matt paused and took a long swig of beer. He looked down at his glass, then tilted his head back, and finished it off.

227

"Yeah, Dad. I was seriously thinking of suicide. I probably would have done it except that the folks arrived."

This was the first time Matt had stated it directly. I shouldn't have been so shocked, but he had just driven the fact home.

"For chrissake, Matt! You're the only one I have left of the family. I don't have Marge. I don't have Jeff. You are it!"

"It's OK, Dad. Thanks. I got over it."

"OK, but suicide is too damn permanent. Don't even think about it!"

I studied Matt for a moment. He was off somewhere in his own distant world.

"OK, Son. Let's have a toast to Jeff. Here's to you, Jeff. We love you, man."

We emptied our glasses and ordered another round.

Back at the office, just as I felt that matters were somewhat under control, my boss had a stroke. The poor man had not been able to handle the intense pressures that had been thrust upon him. He never made it back to work and resigned. Our District Commander called me into his office and appointed me Acting Chief while they went through the normal hiring process. I had hardly learned my own job. No one else was qualified, however. They did not want to appoint an Acting Assistant because I might have to slip back into that position. I was wearing both hats now. Truthfully, I did not feel ready for the promotion. I said I would do my best, however, and hopefully I could hold all the loose ends together. That was about all I was able to do.

My immediate supervisor was a Lieutenant Colonel, with whom I soon developed a fine rapport as my counselor, advisor, and sounding board. I could always discuss my many business problems with him. My biggest issue was lack of time, which neither of us could do anything about. As Assistant Chief, I had been able to put some thought into each case that came across my desk for review. That was simply not possible now. I had to suffer through the same interminable meetings as my predecessor, many of which had nothing to do with real estate. I typically spent nine or ten hours in the office each day and had to take work home at night and on weekends.

Another significant complaint of mine was how the Legal Division and Real Estate had to interact. Many of our cases had to be reviewed for "legal sufficiency" before I could sign off on them. Several attorneys were assigned to review real estate cases, but I had no control over which case was assigned to which attorney, or the quality of his work. I could not critique their performances or write their evaluations at the end of the year. Their arrogant argument was that nobody in Real Estate had the knowledge and expertise to review an attorney's performance.

I discussed these issues in depth with my supervisor, but I could not convince upper level management that the organization needed to be changed. These problems might appear to be trivial, but they actually caused significant harm and delays to Real Estate's ability to perform.

For the next year and a half, I stumbled through treacherous mine fields of frustrations, disappointments, and intermittent triumphs. At the professional level, I was successful. On a personal level, I was deeply dissatisfied and depressed. This was not a life I wanted to live. The pressures were no longer a challenge – they were insurmountable barriers to gaining fulfillment and gratification. I stayed in the job because there were positions at higher levels that were much more manageable. All I had to do was hang on until someone up the chain left and gave me a chance to move higher. I was also earning good money, and I still needed the income to pay off Marge and the goddamn IRS. After that, I could see myself making a change to something that was more in line with my temperament. My creative fantasies became more urgent as pressures escalated at the office. I dreamt of hiking mountain trails, or of sitting out in a field with my easel, or drifting through life with my writing pads and pencil. A few weeks' vacation a year was nowhere near sufficient time to escape the insane environment of the job.

One weekend, I made time to go to the country to see Mom. She had written this note to the family a year earlier, to celebrate Christmas 1988 when she was 76 years old – (the grammar and punctuation are her own.)

•

> "Hurray for the age of the computer & space travel! When I was 8 years old, in Andover, Me. we had no phone, no radio, no TV or VCR, no electricity, no refrigerator, 1 bathroom for 10 people! We depended on our Model T Ford for transportation. On our farm we had one barn for 4 horses, 2 cows, & 2 pigs. In another barn there was a pony-cart, 2 buggies (one with a roof & another without) & 2 big sleighs for our jingle-bell winter parties.

> "I remember one summer morning, after breakfast, my father announced that a <u>real</u> wall telephone was about to be

229

installed, in a few minutes! Then a bell clanged merrily (we thought it could be heard a mile away.) We children gathered around on tiptoe & listened breathlessly to my mother's indignant words: "Yes Mrs. Marsden (she was the post-mistress) this <u>is</u> the Poor House. (i.e. Poor was Mom's family name.) BUT Mrs Marsden – which switch is the right switch for Ipswitch? – it's the Ipswitch switch that I desire. You've switched me to Norwich, <u>not</u> Ipswitch, you've switched my switch to the wrong wire! And so, to avoid further hitch, please tell me which switch is Ipswitch & which switch is Norwich, THEN, I'll know which switch is which! SILENCE. ...

"Happy New Year, from MAW"

•

I arrived early Saturday morning and stayed with her all day to make sure she didn't get into the booze. I promised that we could have wine with dinner if she would stay sober until then. I wanted to ask her about her early years and her life with Forrester which she had never discussed with me. We got dressed up and went to a popular restaurant not far from our house. The place was packed, and the tables were placed very close to each other. We ordered our meals and sipped wine while we waited.

"So Mom, what was it like growing up in such a grand lifestyle?"

She seemed to almost physically leave the present and look wistfully into her distant past.

"It was like living in a fantasy, but those times were gone. They were never coming back."

I sensed that that subject was out-of-bounds.

"So, what about Forrester? What attracted you to him?"

I noticed that a fellow sitting at the next table had picked up on our conversation and was leaning closer to hear what this elegant, soft-spoken lady had to say.

"Oh, I thought he was a wonderful writer, and that we would have many adventures together. He was always exploring places to find material for his books."

"So, you got married and followed him wherever he went."

"We stayed in New Mexico for a while, then went to Oklahoma, and finally to the Northwest. Forrester soon left me, however, for months at a time, and I had to support myself. He always said that he had to be alone."

She finished off her glass of wine, so I ordered another. Mom was taking her time and reflecting deeply on each memory.

"But you stuck with him. When did he start giving you trouble?"

"Oh, it didn't take long. Right off the bat he made it clear that I was in the way and slowing him down. He was always complaining that he couldn't do things because I was along. And then he blamed me when his new books didn't sell."

"Interesting. But you had the twins, and then he went off to war."

"That's right. Our marriage was not working, so it was good for all of us that he went away."

"And I came along. I guess he came home for some R&R because that was still during the war. From what little I remember, it was almost impossible to deal with him after the war. If things were so bad, why did you continue to have babies?"

"I thought it would keep the family together – but things did not work out that way."

"What was Forrester like as a person? Do you think the problems were related to his creativity?"

I had always felt that I had inherited my own creative urges from my father.

Mom paused for a moment to take another swallow of her wine.

"He viewed himself as essentially a writer, and was certainly disappointed that his books weren't more successful. But he was very disturbed after the War – way beyond having creative frustrations. He was – uhm – much, much worse than before he went."

The man next to us was still listening attentively to our conversation. He had shifted his chair even closer and glanced over now and then to look at Mom.

231

"Were you able to talk with him about the war?"

"No, he wouldn't discuss it. We hardly talked at all."

I had expected these types of answers. Most of this I had already heard or deduced, but I still wanted to know more about what Mom had been thinking.

"But my sister arrived. You were still having sex with the man. What was Dad like in bed?"

Mom sat up, stiffened her back, and took another drink. She raised her voice and spoke firmly and loudly.

"He was a sexual deviant!"

The guy next to us choked and sprayed a mouthful of wine across his table. The rest of the room couldn't escape hearing and looked over in amusement to see what was going on. I was delighted. It was an incredibly rare moment that Mom ever expressed such intense emotion. She just sat there – ramrod straight and exceedingly proud of herself. She had, at that one moment, gotten even for all the years of neglect and abuse that my father had heaped on her. I could not stop laughing and had to work to catch my breath.

"Bravo, Mom! Well – you brought the house to its feet with that one!"

I didn't dare ask what was behind her declaration. Our dinner orders came, and the rest of our meal was delightfully pleasant. The rest of her secrets remained buried in the past.

My court date in Oregon arrived later in the spring. I took leave and flew out for the event. We all assembled in the courtroom. Marge did not once look at me or acknowledge in any way that I was there. The atmosphere was anxious and tense. The judge looked over the documents and announced that he was acquainted with Marge's boyfriend, Jerry. He did not know him well, but the two of them had played golf together a few times at the country club. He did not know Marge. He offered to recuse himself, but said that he thought he could make a fair decision in this matter. After a brief consultation, my attorney and I agreed to go ahead. I couldn't afford to fly back and forth to Oregon, and it would be four to six months before we could get another court date.

Both attorneys made their arguments, and the judge went to his chambers for a few minutes to consider the case. After about as much time as was necessary for him to take a leak, he came back with his judgment.

"Although the defendant is living with someone now, she may move out tomorrow. Therefore, no change in alimony is allowed. Case dismissed!"

My attorney was dumbstruck. I was furious. Marge and her attorney escaped the courtroom without saying another word. I could not let this stand. It just wasn't fair! I caught up with Marge on the court house steps.

"Marge, you may have won the legal battle, but this is immoral as hell! I'll make this offer. I'll pay you one-half of what you have been getting and that's it. If you don't agree, I'll never pay you another goddamn cent. I'll disappear where nobody will ever find me. Believe me, I really don't care. That's your choice!"

Marge looked at me with contempt.

"OK."

She turned and walked away. It was like I had been talking to a stranger. That was not the victory I had expected, but at least I didn't leave empty handed. It was a long flight home, and I had plenty of time to think about what I had said. It had been a spur-of-the-moment statement, but I meant every word of it. If Marge hadn't agreed, I would have checked out and left town with what I could carry on my back. I would have most certainly been happier than I was at the Corps of Engineers.

I went back to the interminable meetings and crushing workload, but all I could think of was how wonderful it would be to escape to anywhere. My work at the Corps seemed petty and pointless. What would I gain by staying – other than more frustration and aggravation? The answer was nothing – just more of the same damn thing. Some sense of obligation kept me there, however. I picked up where I left off and settled into work again. Truthfully, however, I begrudged every minute I stayed at that office.

Matt came to me one evening and said that the laser-light show fad was dying. He was not bringing in as much income and had to move back in with his friends at the lighting company, which cost him almost nothing. That meant that I would also have to move out of the comfortable apartment. Oh well. It had been too good to last. After a bit of looking, I was able to find another small unit in Hoboken. Not fancy – but it was OK. It even had a small yard with tall weeds to hack away at when I got really frustrated – which was most of the time.

One element of my life that had been sorely missing was female companionship. I was wavering in my sworn promise not to become involved again. I still found a trim figure in a pretty skirt appealing and longed to come home to a soft touch and tender kiss. The problem was finding a gal who was compatible with me. I went through a couple of false starts, which were sad failures.

One warm evening in the summer of 1990, I found myself sitting next to a good looking lady on the upper deck of the ferry from the Financial Plaza on lower Manhattan to Hoboken. I glanced over and no, she wasn't wearing a wedding ring. By the end of the trip, we knew all about each other's jobs and relevant personal history. Her name was Janine. She had never married, was not attached, had a master's degree in fine arts, and worked for the State of New York screening veterans for benefits programs. She also owned a townhouse in Hoboken, and – sure – she would like to get together some time.

Janine, however, had a network of devoted friends who advised her every move. To get close to her, I had to first be vetted by one of them named Janet, who lived in Cambridge and was a psychologist. She had a heavy East European accent that I could not narrow down further. I found myself in Janet's apartment one afternoon, while Janine made some excuse to go out shopping.

Janet and I were making small talk when she suddenly hit me with one of her Psych 101 textbook questions.

"Janine tells me that you were in Vietnam, Roger. Did you kill anybody?"

I looked at her for a moment in disbelief.

"You can forget the psychological bullshit, Janet. The personal stuff is between me and Janine."

She was clearly disappointed.

"You won't talk about it?"

"No, Janet. Let's talk about you. I judge from your accent that you're not from the States."

She was deflated and distressed. It turned out that she was from Poland. When Janine got back, Janet was asking me why she hadn't been able to find a good man.

"What do you think is wrong with me?"

"I suspect that you try to psychoanalyze every guy you meet. Nobody is going to put up with that."

"Is it really that obvious?"

"Yes, Janet, it really is."

Janine had another friend who she was very close to. She would say, "Baumgart said to do this, or Baumgart said I shouldn't do that." I suspected that he did not approve of another guy interfering on his turf with Janine. Sometimes, when she was trying to make some decision, I could see that she was conflicted and clearly trying to reconcile information that I was giving her with advice she was getting from her friends. She seemed to not trust herself to make personal judgments about relationships.

Speaking of trust, Janine told me months later that she had pulled my military records off her computer at work. She had access to all veterans' files though her job. When I expressed amazement that she would even consider checking my private records, she laughed it off and said that everything I told her was true, so there wasn't a problem. She regarded it as nothing I should be concerned about. I, however, filed it away as a possible future problem.

After a few dinners and excursions, Janine and I got down to the serious business of love making. She was nervous at first. That was until I had to look for a flashlight and opened the drawer in her nightstand. She dove over the bed to stop me, but out popped a sundry collection of sex toys. It turned out that Janine wasn't nervous about making love – she merely had some decidedly kinky preferences and was worried about how I would react. Never let it be said that I wasn't willing to try something new.

One night we were going at it with particular abandon. As we were reaching our moment of inspired ecstasy, I gave one grand final thrust and – WHAM!!! I smashed the top of my head into the crossbar of the brass headboard. I collapsed in a heap of intense pleasure and horrendous pain. My skull felt like I had been hit by a jackhammer, but the rest of me felt like I had been reborn. I knew my pain was serious, however, because my vision was still spinning several minutes later. I couldn't see straight or balance well enough to walk. But I was also not able to stay awake, so I took two aspirin and slept it off 'til morning.

I woke up with the same problems in the morning and had an unbearable headache. My head had hit that brass rod so hard that I thought I might very well have done some serious damage. Janine bundled me up and drove me to the emergency room of the local hospital. The young admissions clerk started asking me questions.

"What is the problem, Sir?"

"I hit my head last night. I'm dizzy, my vision is blurred, and I have a wicked-bad headache."

"How did you hit your head, Sir?"

"I banged it on our bedstead. It's – um – brass."

She glanced up and thought for a moment.

"We really need to know exactly what happened, Mr. Blake."

I shrugged. She needs to know, so I'll have to tell her. Janine was eagerly nodding her confirmation the whole time.

"Oh – I see."

The clerk had sparks dancing in her eyes. She gave us a delightful smirk and asked us to please take a seat. She got on the phone, and we could hear someone laugh from one of the examining rooms down the hall. After several minutes, a nurse pushing a gurney came over and smugly asked me to lie down.

"Please be careful now. We don't want to hurt anything."

She fussed over me with a sly smile. I climbed on the cart and the nurse made an exaggerated show of tucking a blanket around me and fluffing up a pillow to gently support my head.

"You're a celebrity now, Mr. Blake. Be prepared to get a lot of attention."

Janine was left waiting in the reception area. The nurse wheeled me into the on-call doctor's office who, to my relief, was a guy. I explained the whole event to him and had to listen as he too burst into laughter.

"I'm sorry, Sir. Not many funny things happen around here. I know you're hurting, and we'll take an MRI to see what's going on. But I suppose if you're going to have an emergency, this would be the best kind to have!"

More goddamn chuckles. Har – har. I was not amused. They placed me in the hall exposed to whoever walked by. Every few minutes a new nurse would look me over and ask if I needed anything. One patted me on my leg and said, "Good show!" Another asked, "Is it really true?" The best comment, however, came from a well-built gal several years older than me who leaned over close to my ear and whispered, "I wish I had a man like you!"

This must be how legends are born. I would be having a lot of fun if I wasn't feeling so awful. In any event, the MRI revealed that everything was still intact, and that I would probably survive.

"Just a bad concussion, Mr. Blake. Stay off your feet for a few days. Here's a prescription for the pain. And by all means – um – be more careful next time!"

I don't know about being "more careful," but I did recover. Janine and I went to Broadway plays, gallery openings, and antique shows. One of her passions was skiing. She generously bought me a pair of skis, and we were on the slopes in Vermont on the first day of the season. Our friendship grew rapidly over the next few months. One night in early December, we were sitting around in my small apartment. Janine was nervously picking at the fabric arm of my sofa.

"Where do you think our relationship should go from here, Roger?"

I was very fond of her, but hadn't thought much about it.

"Maybe we should live together for a while and see what happens."

She became even more agitated and threads from the sofa were floating down through the air.

"I don't want to just live together. I've done that too many times!"

"Oh, so what do you want to do?"

"I want to get married, damn it!"

I was floored, but couldn't see anything wrong with it. I needed some excitement in my life, so why not? She was generous, a good cook, and a great lover. Hell, we had been going together seriously for three whole months now.

"OK. Let's work it out."

Well – here I go again, I thought. This is going to be interesting. I moved in with Janine, and we proceeded to make plans. Janine wanted to get married right away, so we decided to have two weddings. First, we would secretly get married in Nevada for ourselves, and we would have a second ceremony later for her family who lived in Florida. It was a bizarre arrangement, but that was what Janine wanted, so it was fine with me. I was along for the ride.

One incident occurred during the holidays, however, that gave me reason to pause and reconsider. It was not a deal breaker, but it turned out to be an unfortunate omen of problems to come. Janine was a successful investor in real estate, and very conservative with a dollar. I was neither. I had explained my financial situation to her, and that I was managing my bills, but I couldn't handle luxury expenses such as dinners out, shows, or anything unnecessary and expensive. Janine obtained some credit cards in both our names so that I could charge things when I needed to – so long as I paid them off, of course.

Just before Christmas, I hit a sale at a museum store in Manhattan. I was looking for a present for Janine and found a wonderful pair of hand-stitched, needle-point, Christmas stockings. They were large, colorful, and beautifully crafted – the best I had ever seen. The price for the pair was like $120. I didn't have the money in my pocket, so I charged them without a second thought. I snuck them home proudly and squirreled them away until Christmas. Unfortunately, the bill came before Christmas. Janine opened it and looked at the charge closely.

"What's this? I didn't know about this!"

"You didn't have too. It's a Christmas present, so don't ask. Give me the bill, and I'll pay it."

"The museum store – they're outrageously expensive! Take it back and get a refund."

I was trying very hard to keep my cool.

"It was half-off, and I'm not taking it back. It's a present, so just drop it."

I could not figure out what her problem was, but she didn't miss a beat.

"What is it? How could you spend so much money?"

It was time to end this conversation. She had already blown whatever happiness either one of us might get from them. It didn't matter what the hell the present was.

"They're a pair of really beautiful Christmas stockings, but I'll find someone else who will appreciate them!"

I went upstairs and left her stewing in her bills. What I was just beginning to see was her need to have control over money and everything else in her life – including me. Unfortunately, I came with a warning label – "Attempt Control at Your Own Risk!" But I dismissed the episode as just the pressure of the holidays and our upcoming secret wedding.

Oh yes – I gave Janine a scarf for Christmas.

Frost

Too Quick – Too Soon – Too Bad

EVERYTHING WAS SET for our trip. Through a travel brochure, I had found the "Oldest Wedding Chapel in Nevada" in the foothills west of Carson City. We packed our bags and waited for the holidays to end.

Our wedding reservations were for the morning after we arrived in Reno. The first thing that went wrong was that the airlines lost one of Janine's bags, and it did not arrive in time for the wedding. She had bought a classic western gown for the ceremony, but it was circling around on a luggage carousel in Mexico City. She threw on a denim skirt, a silk blouse, a pair of cowboy boots, and off we went.

The chapel was a one room, wood-frame structure with charming Victorian trim. The bell in the steeple was missing, but that didn't matter. The peeling paint and missing pieces of siding just added to its quaint appeal. After all, it was the "oldest," or more likely was built just to look old. Granite boulders framed a wonderful view of the plains dropping away toward the east. Massive ponderosa pines filled the air with the intoxicating fragrance of the High Sierras.

The minister was half an hour late. He was a tall, wasted man with deep, craggy features. He was also unshaven, unwashed, and almost unable to stand on his feet. He wore rumpled jeans, cowboy boots, a black jacket which was threadbare and covered with dandruff, and a black shirt with its collar askew. His breath could have curled the slats off the dingy, chapel walls. We had also hired a photographer who arrived in even worse shape than the rent-a-preacher.

We all gathered in front of the pulpit, the photographer snapped off a few pictures, and the minister started to read the text of the ceremony. He soon got lost, however. All he could do was slur over a few passages from memory.

"Do you – ah – Janine – shuspect this man?"

"Accept, dammit. Yes, I do! Now get on with this."

"And dooz you, Roger –"

"I dooz. Let's take a few more pictures and get out of here."

"I now postect shoose man and schwife."

I particularly wanted a picture of Janine in her boots. The photographer took a few more shots. He then took the film out of the camera, put it in its plastic case, and handed it to me.

"But ..."

"Good luck."

"Wait a minute!"

"No prints – just negatives. It's in the contract."

The guy swayed his way to his car, jumped in, and drove off before we could complain any further. Janine was furious. The minister was already sneaking around the back.

"We paid goddamn good money – for that?"

I was keeping my head down. I thought the whole scene had been hilarious.

The rest of our vacation was a lot of fun. Janine was a better skier than me, so most of my time was spent trying to catch up. The snow levels were down that year, but the scenery was grand, and the weather was ideal. Our vacation was as delightful a change from the office as I could imagine. I went home and back to the job with a great deal of regret.

I walked into work and was hit by mounting pressures and tensions caused by a new influx of "critical" assignments. Base closure legislation had passed through Congress, which meant that we had about 800 housing units that had to be sold. Some of those were in New Jersey, but the majority was in the territory covered by the Ft. Devens Field Office. We got an additional allotment of only one Realty Specialist and one Appraiser to do all the field work. All the support, accounting, and legal work, however, would have to be done by existing personnel at the New York office. I was steaming mad and claimed time and time again that we desperately needed additional resources. Nobody was listening, however. My boss finally told me that I better shut up because I had received all the allotments I was going to get. My complaining was just making everybody angry. OK. I could take a hint, but the facts did not change, and our workload remained unmanageable.

I made a last ditch appeal to the District Commander to have two attorneys assigned directly under my supervision for the duration of the base closure program. My valid argument was that there were too many details that would be lost by having two levels of management in the disposal process. We would effectively be doing the same job twice and delaying sales. My request was denied, but the Commander resolved the issue by making matters worse. Because a large percentage of the work had to be done by the Legal Division, after Real Estate completed the field work and found a buyer, Legal was given the authority to close the finished deals. The change meant that they could do whatever they damn well pleased, and that I was left with the ultimate responsibility for the program, but no control over how it was handled after it left my office. I was twice as upset and continued to object, but was told firmly to give my problems a rest.

On the home front, however, things were going reasonably well. Incidentally, the photographs of our wedding came back, and they were either out of focus, blurred, or missed the subject entirely. Neither of us was surprised. Anyway, Janine and I were making plans to do a lot of antiquing that summer, and even start some kind of an antique business on the side. Her only vehicle, however, was a Honda Accord, which wouldn't hold much. So, she bought a Ford Astro Van for hauling around furniture and other purchases.

I got a call from Matt one evening. He said he was in St. Louis with some guys for a lighting job, and he had been rolled by a couple of thugs down by the waterfront. All of his money had been stolen.

"Can you help me out, Dad? I need about $200 for bus fare and meals until I get home."

"Bus fare? Weren't you riding in a company van or something? How did you get there?"

"Yeah Dad, I was, but I guess they left when I didn't show up."

I sighed. His story was suspicious, but I thought I should give him the benefit of the doubt and let it go.

"OK Matt. I'll send you $200 by Western Union. Get the info and let me know."

Besides the pressures of the office and my growing worries about Matt, life with Janine was a lot of fun. After we got the van, she asked what I thought of having a second home that we could escape to on weekends and vacations. Great idea. How about Maine? That was a wonderful region for antiquing. I had always fantasized having a small getaway place for some peace and quiet.

I made a few excursions on the weekends and found a lovely, small house on Chebeague Island off the coast near Portland. It was only ten years old, secluded, and solidly built for all-season living. The drawbacks were that it was not on the shoreline and did not have a view, but that was why it was relatively inexpensive. Chebeague was a charming New England fishing community. Other than retirees and summer people, most of the islanders were lobstermen and their families. The house also came with a beat-up "island truck" and a 14 foot open skiff with an outboard motor – which by itself made the house worth buying in my opinion. Janine and I flew up the next weekend to look it over. She approved, and we made an offer on the place.

But this is where our marriage started to unravel. I believe you always learn most about someone when they are reacting to some kind of pressure. Committing herself to that kind of expense made Janine very anxious. We discussed and evaluated the whole idea many times. I became so concerned that I thought we should back off from the purchase. I could live without the place if it meant subjecting our relationship to too much stress. We discussed my concerns – but no – Janine decided to go ahead with it. When it came time for signing the purchase agreement, I was looking it over and found some error in the language.

"You really shouldn't sign it until that provision is corrected."

"You don't tell me what to sign. I'll sign whatever I damn well want to!"

She announced this in front of the realtor and her assistant. Her comment hit me out of the blue. I looked at her sideways and didn't say another word until we got into the car.

"Janine, do not ever talk down at me like that again – particularly not in front of others. That's not acceptable."

"I'll talk down at you whenever I please."

I had no idea what was causing this scornful outburst. She shut down any attempt to talk the problem out. I was furious and really wanted to back out of the property.

"OK, I don't want the place. Cancel the deal."

She didn't say another word, and neither did I. When it came time for closing and writing the down-payment check, I again objected, and said that I didn't want to go ahead with it. Janine bought the property anyway. She later told me that she thought it would make me happy. Actually, I loved the place, but our relationship never recovered from the way she had humiliated me.

Matt called again. This time he was in Naples, Florida.

"What are you doing down there, Matt?"

"A guy from the shop and I came down to try to get jobs, but I'm broke and not going to make it."

"Can't you even get some kind of a fast food job or something?"

"I probably could if I had transportation, but without that and a place to stay, I don't have a chance. And I – um – can't stay here. I'm sorry, Dad, but can you send bus fare again?"

"Hold on a minute, Matt."

Janine and I were flying down to Gainesville that weekend to finalize wedding plans with her family. I asked her if she wanted to drive down to Naples with me to pick up Matt and fly him back with us. Sure, that will be fine.

"Matt, we can pick you up there on Sunday. Are you going to be OK until then?"

"That would be great, Dad. Thanks a lot!"

I got his address and hung up. By the time we caught up with him, it was clear that he had been having a rough time. The first thing we did was buy him two double-cheeseburgers and a large milkshake.

"So, what happened, Matt? You don't look well at all.

"Things just went bad, Dad."

"Things?"

He looked at me hopelessly.

"Yeah – things – Dad. I really don't want to talk about it."

Florida Woods

"OK, then – things."

I left it there. I was sure he was dealing drugs again, but didn't want to press him in front of Janine. We made it home, and Matt disappeared to the lighting company again.

Summer came around, and Janine and I were officially declared husband and wife by a competent minister. It was a small wedding, but a pleasant one in Gainesville. Matt was my best man and my brother, John, represented the rest of my family. Matt looked dashing in a blue blazer, slacks, penny loafers, and a necktie – which I had the pleasure of tying for him. I was actually shocked to see how good he looked, and I think he was too. Our honeymoon amounted to a few unexciting days on the beach at St. Petersburg because Janine said that we had spent too much money on our Nevada wedding.

Back to the office. If things were frantic before, now they were frenetic. We had new critical superfund sites, flood control, and beach erosion projects that all required land acquisitions before any work could be done. Everything else was on top of that, including our massive obligation to sell all the excess military housing. Then I found out that some of my projects in New Jersey had been transferred to the Philadelphia District in my absence. I made it clear that I believed the New York District was being punished because the Central Office hadn't provided the resources for us to do the job. I took the transfers personally – as just one more insult I was expected to swallow.

About a month and a half later, I got a call from a friend at the Division level.

"Um – Roger, this is a heads up. Apparently, Legal closed on too many properties, and we have an anti-deficiency judgment coming down."

I had never heard that term before.

"What the hell is an 'anti-deficiency judgment'?"

"It's where you spend more money than has been allocated to you. There's a law that prevents any government agency from spending more than they have on hand."

"OK. You guys control the money and are sitting on plenty of funds to cover us. Why can't you just send some of that over to the District, and we'll go on like this never happened?"

"Believe me, I'd like to. We would be all right if the properties hadn't already closed, but a deficiency has occurred. It looks, Roger, like you will be holding the bag."

"Me? So, how's this going to happen?"

"I'm hearing that the Commander is writing you a Letter of Reprimand."

"This is so much bullshit! I'm given the responsibility for the program, but not given any authority over the people who are doing the work. Then they spend more money than they're allowed, and I'm the fuckin' one to catch the blame. This really is a bunch of crap!"

"I agree, Roger. As I said, this is a heads-up. I hope it doesn't come down like this."

I hung up and had to stand away from my desk. I walked around my office in frustration. I could not take it anymore. This was a disgrace – way beyond unreasonable! It was also an insult to my professional management. I would not allow a Letter of Reprimand to stain my record. Period!

The Commander's secretary soon called and wanted me upstairs immediately. I took a couple of deep breaths and headed for the executive offices. The Deputy Commander stopped me before I went in and tried to calm me down.

"Think about what you're doing, Roger. Don't do anything you will regret!"

"I'm the only one who is thinking straight around here! If a reprimand comes down, I'm gone."

I was fuming. I went in and stood in front of the Commander's desk.

"Yes Sir?"

The Colonel looked up and offered me a seat. We went through the details of the problem and his decision to give me the Reprimand.

"You're just looking for a scapegoat to blame this on, Colonel, but the blame should be placed on the Legal Division."

"It's not as bad as it could be, Mr. Blake. I added a provision that the letter would be removed from your file at the end of one year. No one would ever know it happened."

I would know, however, and was disgusted. I very calmly went over my case again. I might as well have been talking to the wind.

"Well, I'm sorry, but that is my decision."

"Well then, Sir, you can roll your fucking letter into a tight little ball and toss it out the window. I'm not going to stick around to see it!"

With that I stomped out of the Commander's Office and went down to Personnel. The comments on this Resignation Statement read:

•

"July 19, 1991 –

Unable to effectively meet the responsibilities of my position because of unrealistic and uninformed demands of higher level management and inadequate financial, legal, and manpower resources for Real Estate Division programs. Inaccurate perceptions regarding the quality and volume of work produced have resulted in redistribution of programs to other districts despite the excellent work product of my office. The above factors have become intolerable and forced my resignation."

•

I had not made that decision as casually as it may appear. A long time had been spent to reach this boiling point. All I had needed was a push, and I was out the door. I knew what I was throwing away – a secure $60,000 a year salary with good benefits for starters. What I was gaining was much more important – some peace of mind and a new life, whatever that would bring. It was a bittersweet moment that I fully embraced.

I expected Janine to be distressed when I told her, but that didn't happen. She just wanted to know what my plans were. I told her I had cashed in my 401K and that the check would come in three or four months. It would be a sizeable sum of money. I would pay off the IRS and Marge, and work on finding something else to do. I would also be running short on funds before the money arrived, so would she please allow some bills to go on our credit cards? I would pay off the charges out of the 401K money. She was agreeable, and the issue got dropped.

I became Janine's go-to handyman for maintaining some housing units that she owned in Hoboken. I painted vacant apartments, made minor plumbing and electrical repairs, and helped whenever I could. Once, she took a call from a tenant that told us that her ceiling was leaking badly due to Hurricane Bob that was passing over the area. I bought two gallons of tar and climbed three stories up to the top of the building on a shaky, metal ladder. It was attached by a few corroded screws that were set in old, crumbling bricks.

I fought to stay on my feet in the gusts of wind and heavy sheets of rain. The roof was in such bad shape that it could have been leaking anywhere. I filled up holes and cracks around an old chimney and spread what was left of the tar around as best I could. After managing to make it down, I went to report to Janine. She was sitting at her desk shuffling bills when I came back in – dripping wet and covered with tar. She glanced up and looked me over.

"How's the roof?"

"You need a new roof, and that ladder is about to fall off. I wouldn't send anyone else up there until it is replaced."

Happy Face for Sale

Janine just grunted and went back to her papers. I didn't mind helping out, but I did expect some gratitude for my efforts – like a thank you. But she didn't say thanks, or ask if I was all right, or say sorry that I had to spend my day spreading tar in a hurricane. There were other times when I did work on her rentals and got the same non-appreciative treatment. I've said before that if there's one thing I hate – it's being taken for granted. This was not going to stand, but I took our marriage commitment seriously, and it was too early to think of bailing out. Maybe Janine would become more reasonable when things calmed down – I hoped.

I needed to get away and went up to Maine for a weekend. I gathered up my mother and took her along, although she was getting very frail. She was now 77 years old and needed assistance to move around. Nevertheless, I wanted to take her for an excursion, which I hoped she would be able to enjoy. With some neighborly help, I got her on and off the ferry to the Island. Mom was game for anything – she just needed assistance doing it.

The next morning, we climbed into our dilapidated truck and drove down to the dock where my skiff was anchored off shore. I rowed out to get it, started the motor, and brought it to the dock. Mom got on her hands and knees and backed herself aboard. She looked tiny in the heavy, wool sweater and rain gear I had found for her at the house. I put her up in the bow where she could get the full sense of being out on the open ocean.

Our destination was Eagle Island, a state park that was once the home of the renowned Admiral Robert Peary. The historic site was left as it was in 1920 when Admiral Peary died. Mom was eight years old then, and she no doubt grew up with the exciting news that this adventurer had discovered the North Pole. He and other explorers were national heroes.

It was about a two mile run to the island across some open ocean, and we ran into some heavy swells. I slowed down, but spray kept coming over the gunnels and washing over Mom. I had to yell over the roar of the motor and the splashing waves.

"Are you doing OK up there?"

She was gripping the gunnels so hard her knuckles were turning white. She turned around to reply, but didn't have to say a word. Her expression of sheer delight spoke for her excitement and joy! Everything the world needed to know about Mom was written on that beaming smile. All of her reserved reticence was gone. It was like she was born to be out on the open seas – living the adventures that only the natural elements could provide. Her face was wet from the spray, but I have never seen her so radiant and energized. Her grin spread from ear-to-ear as she gave me a quick glance and a nod and turned forward to catch the next large wave.

Mom climbed out with the assistance of the dock manager and was hopping around with excitement. She grabbed my arm when I got next to her after tying up the boat.

"Let's go – I want to see everything!"

The Peary house was built like the bridge of a ship and captured magnificent views of the ocean in three directions. Mom went around staring out the windows, looking at old photographs, and running her hands over the time-worn furniture. We then walked down to the rocky shore and watched for a long time as seabirds swooped and dived into the waves. Surf crashed and foamed on the rocks. Mom was totally lost in the experience.

Our ride home was tamer because we were running with the swells. I went slowly, however, because I had seen what this moment meant to Mom – what it meant to us both actually. She would lean forward with each wave as it lifted the bow and rolled under the boat. She would then shift back as the boat rode down into the trough and thrust its bow into the next one. In her mind, she was probably on some tall ship exploring uncharted seas and distant shores.

I have many memories of Mom in her middle years, and from some photos taken in her youth, but the boat ride was the moment that I will cherish most. I'm sure that is also how she would like to be remembered. It was a glorious weekend. All things have to come to an end, however. I had to bring Mom home and get back to my life in Hoboken.

We hadn't heard from Matt for a while, so we invited him over for dinner one evening. He liked Janine, and she enjoyed having him around. She now had a step-son and figured that she had a stake in him.

"So, how's the lighting company, Matt?"

"Oh, it's going OK, Janine. Well, honestly – it's not going anywhere at all."

Janine and I both looked at him with concern. Matt seemed reluctant to be talking about his problems while Janine was present, but she pushed the issue.

"That bad? What's the matter, Matt?"

"Yeah, that bad. The company's not getting many new jobs. I don't know what's going on, but I'm not making enough money to be able to stick with it."

"Have you looked around? There's got to be other jobs out there."

"I've been looking, but everybody wants at least a GED. It looks like I'll be washing dishes for the rest of my life."

I asked him my favorite question.

"OK Matt, if there is one thing you'd want to do, what would it be?"

"Make a ton of money."

Janine shook her head and asked without hesitation.

"How are you going to do that without an education?"

"Hmm – I guess I'd have to start with a GED."

Janine leaned back and studied Matt seriously.

"So you agree that you need a GED, Matt. What would you need to do to get one?"

I hadn't seen this coming. Matt thought about it and replied quietly.

"I guess I'd have to go back to a community college. But I don't want to do it in Salem."

I could understand why he didn't want to be in Salem with his old friends and all their problems.

"How about the one in Bend, Matt? You love that area."

"Sure, Dad. That would be good."

Janine stepped back in and firmly made the decision for all of us.

"OK, we'll pay for your books, tuition, and set you up. All you have to do is study hard. How does that sound?"

I watched approvingly. Her generosity was a major factor that kept us together.

He was totally surprised.

"Wow! I'd love that. Thanks!"

Matt stayed with us the night before he left. He seemed excited about the new opportunity and the move back to Oregon. At the end of the evening, I took him aside as he was getting ready for bed.

"Don't blow this one, Matt!"

He looked at me seriously and put his arm around my shoulder.

"You too, Dad."

He nodded in Janine's direction.

"Don't blow this one!"

Marge met him in Portland and helped set him up in Bend. She also had him meet with a local psychiatrist, which we agreed was a good idea. Matt found a group of students who were sharing a house and moved in with them.

Everything appeared to be going well. Then Matt called one evening right after the semester started. Janine and I were reading in the living room.

"Hi Dad. I just called to chat."

He sounded distant – like he was trying to think of what to say.

"Sure, Matt. Tell me – how are things going?"

"Well, Dad, honestly not so hot. I don't see how I'm going to do this."

"You're registered – right?"

"Oh yeah. That's no problem."

"And you've got your books – right?"

"Yeah, Dad. I've got my books. But I've been looking through them, and I don't remember any of this crap. It's just like before. I'm lost!"

"That's OK, Matt. They will start you where you left off. Don't worry about it."

Matt was quiet for a moment.

"I guess I'm just depressed, Dad. I don't think I'm cut out for this."

"You can call Mom, Matt, if you need anything."

"Nah, Dad. I crunched her car fender right after I got back. I can't talk with her now."

"Ouch! That's really too bad. It sounds like you want to tell me something, Son. Do you need some money? Is that it?"

"No Dad. I'm OK. I'll need to get a car, but I'm planning to get some job after school to earn money for that."

"Mom said you got together with a psychiatrist. How did that go?"

"OK, I guess. She gave me a list of questions to answer for the next session."

"When is that, Son?"

"I'm supposed to see her in – let's see – three days."

253

All this time, Matt's voice seemed unnaturally subdued and reserved – like his mind was drifting.

"Well, don't miss that meeting, Matt. She could be really helpful."

"OK. Well – like I said – I just called to chat."

"Anytime, Matt. Take care now."

"Sure. Thanks – goodbye, Dad."

He hung up the phone. I sat back and looked at Janine.

"Something's wrong. I should go out there and see him."

But I shook the feeling off and put my faith in the psychiatrist. It was early in the morning three days later. I answered a call from Oregon, and this time it was Jerry.

"What's up, Jerry?"

"I've got sad news, Roger – There's no easy way to say this. Matt committed suicide last night. He shot himself. I'm terribly sorry."

"Ah – crap! Give me a minute, Jerry. I can't think – is Marge OK?"

"She's taking it hard. She couldn't talk with you right now."

"Do you know what happened?"

"I talked with the guys he was staying with. They said they were partying and didn't realize what Matt was doing. He had been drinking a lot and went outside. There was a rifle by the door, and he must have taken it with him. Apparently, he just laid down in a hammock and shot himself."

"I'm sorry – I'm having trouble with this, Jerry – I've got to call you later."

I felt dizzy and totally lost. I had no idea what to do first. I needed to talk with Janine, but she was at work. I didn't want to tell her over the phone. I had to get out of the house. I had to gather my wits about me. I had to do something!

I went outside and walked down to the ferry landing. Why was everybody so happy? I was detached from each of them, from the crowds, and even from myself. I saw myself walking down the sidewalk acting normally, but feeling unbelievable sorrow. The world was oblivious to my pain. How could life go on around me like nothing had happened?

The ferry arrived, and I climbed the ladder to the upper deck. I stood by the rail and watched the ships churning their way up and down the Hudson. The air felt invigorating, but all energy had been bled out of me. I sat down and stared blankly at the seagulls flying effortlessly around the ship. I could only think of Matt and the knowledge that another sad journey had begun. I got to Janine's building and gave her a call.

"Something terrible has happened. I'm in the lobby – can you come down?"

She walked off the elevator a few minutes later. I was leaning against the marble wall, unaware of the crowds that were moving around me. I looked at her sorrowfully and shook my head.

"It's Matt. He's committed suicide."

"Dear God!"

We hugged each other tightly. I was wracked by sorrow and couldn't let her go. My emotions took a long time to subside enough to allow me to step back.

"I'll go upstairs and tell them I'm taking the day off. Will you be all right for a few minutes?"

"I'm OK."

She returned, and we walked back silently to the ferry. We took our seats, and I sat there wringing my hands.

"He was supposed to see the psychiatrist today. I knew something was wrong when he called. I should have gone to see him. What a damn fool I've been!"

I went on and on like this. Janine kept trying to comfort me, but I could not release my guilt. We got home and went to bed. I needed desperately to hold her – as if she was the last thread that my life depended on. I could have stayed in that dimly lit bedroom for the rest of my life and did not care if I ever saw another sunrise again.

But rise it did. We made plans for my second memorial service in Oregon. Janine insisted on coming. There was a quiet family gathering before the ceremony. I was able to introduce Marge to Janine, but I don't recall having much conversation with Marge after that. My brother, Brian, flew out to be with me. I was introduced to one of Matt's friends, who had come over from Bend. He was a clean cut, regular kid, who had been close to Matt. I thanked him for coming and offered to take him up in the plane the next day while I released Matt's ashes over Mt. Bachelor, where Jeff's were also scattered. Marge had said she didn't want to come. He said he would like to do that.

Jerry gave me a copy of the death certificate. It stated the cause of death as "Self-inflicted gunshot wound to the head." Once again, however, I knew that drugs and alcohol were the real cause.

He also handed me Matt's wallet and a crumpled note.

"They found it on a table by the hammock."

I checked the wallet and it was empty – no money, driver's license – nothing. How very strange, I thought. I didn't have the heart, however, to investigate the matter. Nothing I learned would bring Matt back. I unfolded the paper carefully. There were some badly scribbled words on it that were mostly illegible. There was only one phrase that made sense.

"Sorry Dad ..."

There wasn't much Janine and I could do except acknowledge everybody's grief, have a few brief chats with others, and leave. I found this eulogy harder to write than Jeff's – probably because suicides are harder to talk about than accidents. I will simply quote from what I read:

•

> "There are no simple solutions in life, but honest communication is a long step in the right direction. One parent just told me that he knows '... 90 percent of the time, he is being told only what his children think he wants to hear. They're very good at it.'

> "If I can offer a bit of advice to the young people here today – don't be afraid to express yourselves. Make your parents listen. Don't bury your turmoil and frustrations deep inside.

"To the parents – listen. Be sensitive and alert. Don't be judgmental. Your children's problems are very real to them, even if you don't agree or understand them. Don't settle for appearances. Find out what is really going on. Get help if you need it.

"Matt was not only my son, but a frequent companion and friend. We shared our secrets and experiences in ways that few fathers have the honor and joy of doing. And when I needed support – which was frequently – he was always ready with whatever he could provide – whether labor, love, understanding, or a good natured smile.

"Matt gave life and purpose to some difficult years that I went through. I will be forever grateful for the time we shared together and will miss him with all my soul. I only wish he had been able to share his problems with others to the same extent that he was able to listen to me.

"I really do not want to close this brief message, but I must. Farewell, Matt. Thank you for our times together. May your new life be happier than your last. You will always be in my thoughts and heart.

"We love you, Matt. Goodbye and seeya' later, Son – seeya'."

•

Janine and my brother had to return back East. I drove out to Bend to make my final goodbye to Matt and picked up his friend for the flight. It was a crisp autumn day. The only problem I had was with the pilot. I had to explain several times what was happening, but he couldn't figure out why we were doing this. He just kept asking questions that I had already answered. I finally got angry and laid into the guy.

"It's a goddamn funeral. I'll tell you where to go. Now – shut up and fly!"

The sun was low as we flew over the rim of Mt. Bachelor, and the final rays were lighting up the rocks with an orange glow. We circled the bowl and slowly dispersed the ashes. Sadness gripped me. My two boys had ended up here. Their lives, which had once been so full of promise, lay wasted on the rocks and steep slopes of the mountain. Matt's friend tossed out some ashes and began to cry. I consoled him as best I could and then finished the rest of our task. All that could be said had been said. All that could be done had been done. Matt's journey was over – as was Jeff's before him. The sun that had shone brightly on the rocks began to dim. It was time again to put the pain of recent events behind me and return to the problems of the present.

My time back in Hoboken was spent trying to develop a plan for the future. I knew a couple of things. First – I wanted to work only for myself – under my own name. Second – I wanted to be an artist. No – I wanted to be a great artist. I had no interest in anything less than that. There was no other choice. I was basically beginning from scratch, so the only thing that mattered was that I got started.

I looked around Hoboken to see what studio space was available. I found a couple of buildings that catered to the artist community. The quality of the art didn't come close to New York's, but the creative energy was there. If I could get a start, maybe other things would happen. I just needed to wait until my funds arrived. Until then, I was treading water.

The weeks passed, and I rolled along thinking everything was going well. It was late November, and the time for my 401K money to arrive was a few weeks away. I was excited about being able to set my new life in motion. Then without warning, I got hit by a surprise, and the bottom fell out of my plans. I tried to charge something insignificant on a credit card, and it wasn't accepted. I tried another card and got the same result. I called both companies and was told that the accounts had been closed. I confronted Janine, but all she did was shrug.

"So, you cancelled them and didn't bother to tell me?"

"That's right – this morning."

"Why? For chrissake? I'll be able to pay these off next month. That was our agreement. Please reinstate them, Janine. This is stupid!"

She shook her head without looking at me.

"No. I'm not going to do that."

I thought for a minute and tried hard to control myself.

"Janine, I know why this is happening. One of your friends is advising you to do this. Who in the hell is it?"

She stiffened in her chair, but said nothing – which I took as admitting that it was a fact. It had to be the truth.

"OK. You knew I was relying on the credit cards for the next few months, but you didn't even discuss what you were going to do. You could have at least talked with me about this if you had a problem. You've just killed whatever trust we had together and ruined our marriage. I hope your friend's happy. I hope you're happy!"

She just sat there with an expression of stoic resolve. I'm sure she expected me to accept it and go off in a huff.

"Janine, I'm moving out tomorrow. I'm packing up all my stuff in the van and going up to Maine until my payment comes. Add up what I owe you, and I'll write you a check when I get back."

There were no hysterics, no attempts to change my mind, no expression of regret, nothing – just a blank face. I kept expecting more, but she never offered an explanation.

"OK. That's it then."

I went upstairs and started to pull out boxes for tomorrow. The next morning, I took my paintings off the walls and packed up my files, documents, art materials, and baggage. It wasn't too difficult and everything I owned was stowed easily into the van. It wasn't until I was ready to go that Janine came close to me.

"I wish you wouldn't leave, Roger."

I looked at her and couldn't believe what she had said, and that she had taken so long to say it.

"Janine – for chrissake. I say again – you blew our trust. Trust is everything in a relationship. It's not just about the credit cards, but I'll ignore the whole thing if you change your mind. Maybe we could patch things up. I think you acted on bad advice. Whoever gave it to you was terribly, terribly wrong. What are you going to do?"

"No, I can't do that."

"Bullshit!"

That was the last straw. I had given her every chance to change her mind. I shook my head and went out the door in disgust.

Winter had arrived on the coast of Maine. Ice covered the trees, rocks, and fallen leaves with a brilliant layer of flashing crystal. The weather was too frigid to take long walks along the shore, so I mostly stayed inside by the fire and spent many hours thinking about the last year. My breakup with Janine was no surprise. I had ignored too many incidents, warning signs, and stressful tensions.

I began to connect my anger and willingness to leave the Corps of Engineers and these events with Janine. Why was I unable to deal with the situation at the Corps in a more reasonable manner? Why was I unable to relax and just let the crisis roll over me? Why was I so willing to ditch everything and walk out on a good job that could only have gotten better? Should I have tried harder to stay with Janine? Why was I so incapable of restraining my anger? Despite these frank questions, I could not come up with any answers other than my actions simply reflected who I was. No, I was right to cut my losses and leave.

My time sitting in Maine soon came to an end. My money was deposited, and I wanted to get out of town. The settlement was substantial, even after the early withdrawal penalties. Marge finally got her money and so did my persistent friend – the IRS. Janine would have to wait until we got together.

Unfortunately, a Nor'easter was blowing down the coast, and the ferry to the mainland wasn't running because of ice flows in the channel. The only option was to hire a lobsterman to take me ashore. I found one who was willing, but the tide would only be right at 4 a.m. the next morning. If I didn't get off the island now, it could be a while because most of the lobster boats were being taken out of the water for the winter. The island taxi delivered me and my boxes to the pier. Winds gusting to 50 miles per hour drove freezing spray horizontally into my face. One frantically swinging light illuminated the dock and the small boat as they pitched and rolled in the blackness and angry seas.

The lobsterman cupped his hands and yelled into the howling gale:

"Toss me the boxes!"

I heaved one to him over the water, and then all the others followed. I had dressed warmly, but was still turning blue from the cold. He was a small man with a bushy, ice-encrusted beard, and was jumping around like a grasshopper. I clambered aboard, and we set off into the storm. My cartons were stacked on the stern and getting soaked with spray. I was shivering in the small cockpit, even though I was almost hugging the exhaust stack. If we had been caught by the full force of a wave, all my belongings would have washed overboard to sink into the foaming white caps. At that point, however, I was so frozen that I didn't care. I had no idea how the lobsterman kept from freezing.

"H-h-h-h-how can you work in such dreadful conditions?"

"This ain't so bad – gets a lot colder than this! Ah jus' keep movin'!"

I could barely hear his gleeful yells over the frigid gusts, crashing waves, and throbbing engine.

The dock where we had to unload was catching the full force of the gale. I gave myself a Hail-Mary pass, jumped onto the platform, skidded on the slick deck, and almost slid over the other side. The skipper motored the boat up as close as possible to the pier and rapid-fire pitched the boxes to me. He had to make a couple of runs at the dock, but nothing was lost. I could hardly move and have never been so frozen in my entire life. The lobsterman gave me a jolly wave and off he went to haul in his pots.

I arrived at Janine's the next day. I had stopped off at a Goodwill Store and left off trash bags full of all of my business clothes that I wouldn't need anymore. Janine was keeping the van, and I was taking the Honda. She and I settled our accounts, and I wrote a check for what I owed her. I offered to take over the contracts on the van and even the Maine house.

"No. I can't trust you to make the payments."

Floating with the Stars

This was just after I paid her over $5000. I don't have any proof, but, again, I'm sure she said that on the advice of her "friends."

Then she repeated herself as if nothing had happened:

"I wish you wouldn't go, Roger."

I shook my head in disbelief. Nevertheless, I gave her a goodbye hug.

"Thanks for the good times,"

I meant it, but walked out the door anyway.

My getaway destination was – as before – Taos, New Mexico. It was midnight on Christmas Eve as I crossed the Texas/New Mexico state line west of Amarillo. The clear night was filled with countless stars, and nobody but me was on the freeway. I turned on the radio and started to listen to Christmas music when two shooting stars flashed through the sky ahead of me. Emotions flooded over me, and I had to pull over. I sat alone on the side of the highway under the infinite sky and cried.

Rio Grande Gorge - Near Taos, New Mexico

•

Take two Taos three times a day for depression and pain.

•

Perception And Reality Are On Opposite Ends Of The Insight Scale

YOU MIGHT HAVE READ the previous chapters without having a thought about PTSD. Or you might be asking yourself – whatever happened to Blake's "Secret Life With PTSD?" Well, the symptoms of PTSD were at work here, and you have been reading about them.

My actions might have seemed normal, considering the pressures and dreadful circumstances. That would be a reasonable assumption if you did not know me. However, my short-fused temper and willingness to cast successes aside is not something the more sensible and rational me would have done.

If I thought my judgment was better, nobody could persuade me otherwise. When I was directed to do something that I disagreed with, I would argue and complain to the point of making myself ineffective. People who disagreed with me were adversaries. Any affront to my professionalism was unacceptable. I was always right. I needed to be in control of decisions, but found it unacceptable when restrictions were placed on me. If I had to jump off a bridge to prove my point, I was always ready to take the leap. Without PTSD, I believe I might have been more flexible and effective.

My nature had been easy-going and cooperative. Essentially, I consider myself to be reflective, introspective, and – very importantly – creative. I used to be able to address matters reasonably and make practical adjustments to get things done. The actions I have described are not indicative of who I know myself to be. They do represent, however, who I had become. Anger and intolerance affected every major decision I made. Despite the extreme pressures of some of my jobs, I should have been able to keep a lid on my emotions and act more calmly towards the challenges of my daily life.

I mentioned earlier that work reminded me of the accident and the accident reminded me of work. There were times when I reacted to business as though it was the same as the accident. I acted as though I was always facing a dire, do-or-die crisis. I gritted my teeth and grimly forged ahead through difficult situations. I trusted no one. My negative emotions were frequently reflected in my decisions and actions. I was still having occasional nightmares about the Navy and the accident. Those never went away. In addition, I was now having nightmares about the Corps of Engineers, my boys, and all the other frustrations I was experiencing.

Nevertheless, when I looked at myself and seriously tried to find reasons for everything that had happened – I felt I was simply not up to the task. I should have tried harder to be a better father. I couldn't handle stress. I wasn't cut out for the professional world. I still did not relate these problems to any past trauma. I thought I was merely going through life, reacting normally as each crisis overcame me.

PTSD was the determining factor during these latest defining events. It prevented me from becoming a success. It effectively drove me away from pursuing any kind of a professional career again. I was not able to handle my marriage. PTSD had woven its heavy net further into the fabric of my mind.

It was a new year, however, and it was up to me to patch the shredded remnants of my life back together – once again.

•

Depression is a disaster waiting to happen.

•

The Most Insurmountable Walls Are Built Within Our Minds

I HAD GRAND INTENTIONS of embarking on my career as an artist right away. Instead, I rented a one-room house outside Taos that had adequate living space, but no room for anything else. Everything I owned had arrived with me in the Honda and a small trailer. My ambitions and creative energies, however, had remained back East. I was gloomy and depressed and shut myself in for the winter. I did not go out except for trips to the grocery store. I briefly helped an old friend remodel her garage into a studio, but soon went back into seclusion. Nothing interested me. Nothing excited me. Nothing intruded in my life.

It wasn't until spring, when the snows released their grip on the high country, that I found myself wanting to circulate again. As before, it was art that drew me out of my restrictive shell and into the real world. I slowly started to go to galleries and museums. Motivation was still lacking, however, and I drifted for the next two years.

I worked as a night manager at a bed and breakfast in Santa Fe. I rented a small studio space and painted. I met a wonderful lady named Barbra at the B&B and went back to New Jersey to live with her. I took over her basement and continued to paint. She was generous and sweet, but I sorely missed the high mountains, magnificent skies, and more manageable lifestyle of the West. I soon said, "Thank you. I'm sorry but ..." and moved my well-traveled circus back to New Mexico.

Then Mom died. She had become increasingly frail after I left and had slipped into a non-responsive coma caused by dementia. She passed away comfortably and quietly.

An inheritance came to me, which amounted to approximately $100,000. I was determined to turn it into an income producing asset to last me for the rest of my life. I knew real estate and art, so why not open a gallery? I found an old house in the historic mining town of Madrid, some 25 miles south of Santa Fe. The village had a number of quaint shops and galleries, which appeared to be surviving well. The property came with a small cottage in the back that I could live in. The main building was a substantial Victorian structure, with high ceilings and plenty of wall area, which would make excellent gallery space with some work. I believed I could make a go of it. I wanted to offer quality, contemporary art – similar to what could be found in Santa Fe, but at a more reasonable price. I bought the building, spent too much money on renovations, and opened my doors.

I met a lady named Cia who became a wonderful companion and lover. She was also a terrific salesperson and an important asset while the gallery was getting started. The first time we went out, I took her to a wild game restaurant in Santa Fe. She then told me she was a vegetarian. I sure know how to endear myself to women!

Cia had high personal goals for herself, however, and was dedicated to her own path of growth and fulfillment. Gallery sales were much too mundane to hold her interest, and she eventually left to pursue greater things. We were both born dreamers and nothing was more important than achieving what we perceived was our purpose in life. Our divergent paths sadly pulled us apart.

I missed her, but the gallery remained exciting for me. I was painting and occasionally sold one of my own pieces. New artists were always coming by and offering to place their works on consignment. Sales were good. I expanded into Native American arts and offered pottery, fetishes, and fine turquoise jewelry. The gallery looked great. Most of my sales were to the tourist trade, but I was gaining repeat customers and a respected status in the local art scene. People from Santa Fe and Albuquerque came to see what I had to offer. Buyers frequently told me that the appearance of the space and the merchandise reflected a fine sense of design. The business lasted for almost two years.

New Mexico's vacation and tourist industry is a seasonal proposition. I was prepared for that. What I could not handle, however, was a bad snow season plus a prolonged downturn in the national economy. The few skiers and tourists that showed up were just looking. Dozens of galleries in Santa Fe were closing. I was losing too much money, so I either had to sell the business or take on a partner. I listed it for sale, but got no offers. Taking in a partner was not a mistake, but who I took in definitely was. She came on board, and I soon despised her as much as she scorned me. We ended up suing each other over control of the gallery and settled out of court after some very nasty negotiations. In the end, however, she got the business and liabilities, while I got out with enough money to pay my legal bill and last me for about a year. I would have lost everything if I had tried to keep the business going, so I suppose I came out ahead. At least my attorney was happy.

I decided that I wanted to try my hand at making contemporary jewelry. From my gallery experience, I had a good idea of what would sell and making it did not seem that complicated. I said to myself, "I can do that!" I read a few books on technique, set myself up with the equipment, and found a remote cabin with a studio in the mountains 70 miles northwest of Santa Fe. I spent months hammering out rings, necklaces, pendants, and bracelets set with semi-precious stones. I was able to get my work into a few galleries and sold them on a steady basis, but the return never came close to recovering the expense and time invested in each piece. It was time to think of doing other things.

One day the phone rang, and it was Melissa on the line! This was the first time we had talked since I had left the Corps of Engineers over two years ago.

"Hi Roger. What's up?"

She spoke as though we had never been apart. We had done business frequently after I had moved down to New York and had, for the most part, gotten beyond the problems we had together.

"Jeez, kid. I'm fine – and how in the hell are you? It's been forever."

Her voice had less than its usual mischievous enthusiasm.

"Practically forever. Listen – I was thinking of coming out to see you. I was wondering if next week would be OK."

"That would be great! I've got a friend coming up next weekend, but I have all week free. I'd love to see you."

"No, I'll want to have the weekend too."

"Melissa, this gal and I are lovers. I can't tell her not to come because I have an old girlfriend who will be visiting me."

"Well, I guess it isn't going to work then. If I come I want to have you entirely to myself."

"I'm sorry, Melissa. I would love to see you for a few days, but I'm not interested in another relationship with you."

There was a pause while she said to John, who had apparently been listening to her end of the conversation.

"Roger's not interested."

267

I was not quick enough to tell her that that was not what I meant.

"OK, Roger. I just thought I would give you a call. Goodbye."

She left me holding a dead phone and wondering what the call was all about. Part of me regretted that I did not give her the weekend too, but deep down I was still upset by what she had done with Matt. I let it go. I couldn't make everybody happy.

While I was pondering what to do next, my favorite question popped into my mind again as if it had been scheduled on my yearly calendar. "If I could do anything I wanted, what would it be?" Art was not possible at this time because the entire economy continued to be bad. Trying to get back in business was out of the question. I had talked with major galleries in Santa Fe to see if they might need someone with sales and management experience, but the answer was always no. Cia had left and gone to California for a teaching job. There was nothing to keep me in New Mexico.

One glance at the classifieds in the paper made it clear that by far the highest number of want ads were for over-the-road truck drivers. "30 cents a mile to start." "Best equipment and benefits." "Coast-to-coast runs." Etc. I would have to go to a driving school to learn how to operate an 18-wheeler, but a job was guaranteed after completing the training. The romantic notion of cruising around the country at someone else's expense had always been appealing. What really felt right was the isolation of being in a truck. The fewer contacts I had to make with the outside world, the better. My only responsibilities would be to get where I was supposed to be at a scheduled time and not crash into anything along the way. I should be able to handle that. What could be better? Nobody else was hiring – so why not?

I sold all my jewelry equipment, benches, furniture, everything else I had accumulated from my gallery – even my car. My files, artwork, and a few items I hadn't sold went into a storage locker. I got on a bus to San Diego and signed up with a truck driving school.

Driving an 18-wheeler seemed unexpectedly like flying an aircraft. Getting in the cab of a big truck felt the same as sitting in an enclosed cockpit. They both smell of hydraulic fluid. The constant noise and vibration of the engine reminded me of being strapped into an F4. I became very anxious and had nightmares of crashing and burning, just like what I went through in the Navy, even though I was the driver this time. One dream that kept repeating itself was that I was sleeping in the back of the cab, when my air-brakes would slowly fail. The truck would start rolling backwards down a hill, but I was powerless to get up to stop it. It backed itself around corners and sped up as we came closer and closer to a cliff. I woke up as I fell over the precipice or was about to crash in a flaming explosion on the rocks below.

I would be left anxious, sweating, and wondering why in the hell this was happening. Why was I pursuing this career? By now, however, I had spent too much money on the school to back out. Dammit – I could get through this. Two months later, I had my Commercial Driver's License (CDL) and was in Tulsa, Oklahoma, going through orientation with my first trucking company. It took about a year before being behind the wheel of a big-rig became second nature.

I drove over-the-road for the next seven years and crossed the country so many times that I lost count. I knew every pothole and crack in the freeways between Los Angeles and New York City. I delivered mail on overnight runs between Norfolk and Knoxville. I worked for companies that had thousands of trucks and some with only a few. True to form, I went through 12 different companies – if you count one company twice – with all kinds of equipment and loads.

Dispatchers tend to treat drivers like property. I was an asset to be exploited and squeezed for every damn cent the company could make off me. I have never been able to tolerate such treatment. One company hired me and put me in a brand new truck. I then sat for two days, despite my frequent calls and reminders that I did not have a load. They were costing me money that I could not afford. On the morning of the third day – with still no load in sight – I quit.

If I complained about getting too many local runs that took a tremendous amount of time and energy, but paid next to nothing, the dispatcher would shuffle me to the bottom of the list and make me sit. Some companies would think nothing of giving me runs that were legally impossible to make given the Federal DOT hours-of-operation regulations. I would have to find a way to fudge my logbook to make it happen. I was in trouble if I got an unreasonable dispatcher who would rather get angry than consider my problems. I wouldn't keep my mouth shut when I was assigned a bad deal, and that would make them less sympathetic the next time. My short-fused temper became worse than it had ever been. The times I quit companies were usually because my dispatcher and I had reached a heated impasse.

I could write a book about all the near mishaps and many issues I had while in the trucking business. I've had to unload trailer loads of tires and appliances. I had two accidents where cars hit me. I was coming down an icy mountain highway one night, when my trailer jack-knifed sideways and almost pulled me off a cliff. A car once ran over a freeway center divider, hit the berm on the shoulder, and sailed airborne a few yards in front of my cab.

269

Forget all the romance of being an over-the-road trucker – it's a damn hard life and a hairy business.

After I unloaded a trailer in Virginia one time, my back was hurting so badly that I took a few days off and went to the VA hospital in Hampton Roads to have it checked out. They X-rayed it, but – as when I got out of the Navy – nothing structural was discovered. The doctor gave me some muscle relaxers and said he hoped that they would help. The fellow at the front desk who was checking me out asked if I had one of their new computerized identification cards. I hadn't heard of them, so I asked what I had to do to get one. He stood me up before the camera, took my picture, and a few minutes later the clerk handed me the card.

"New equipment. It's digital. You can use this ID at any VA facility in the country. All your records will be instantly accessible by computer."

"Great idea!"

I checked out my photo and tucked it into my wallet.

Back pain was a problem that I wrestled with during my entire trucking career. Besides unloading trailers, sitting for hours at a time became painful. When my back was hurting, it was difficult just to climb into and out of the cab. I dealt with it by taking generous amounts of over-the-counter pain killers.

Trucking was intense, stressful, boring, and exhausting. I drove an average of 3000 to 3400 miles a week. Less than that was not enough to justify spending my time on the road. If I got to 4000 miles – that was great. 4800 miles was fantastic economically, but would leave me a blithering wreck. And yet I still had to function safely regardless of how I felt. After vacations and down time, I would usually accumulate around 120,000 miles per year, which would relate to around $50,000 in earnings.

From my first day in the business, people would look at me and wonder why I was doing it. Even the fellow who signed me up at the driving school asked, "Are you sure you want to do this?" Other truckers would say, "You don't look cut out for this," or "you don't look like a truck driver," or "you should be doing something better than this." It was more than keeping showered and shaved, or wearing a clean T-shirt. They were telling me that I was different than them – that my culture was different from theirs. My education and business experience showed, and that made many truckers uncomfortable. I never considered myself an intellectual or academic and never acted like one, but that's how I appeared to them. Other truckers would frequently call me "Doctor" or "Professor." I would just shrug those comments aside, get back in the cab, and head on down the road.

One of the best things about being an over-the-road driver was getting out of the truck for a while. It was like stepping into a different world. I had chosen a solitary life, but longed for companionship. I would occasionally be able to take time off and visit my three brothers and their families on the East Coast. Intelligent conversations, home-cooked meals, and a few moments of peace were elements that were rare in my life. Brian and Gretchen would place me in front of magnificent roasts and bottles of good wine as we passed delightful evenings. John, Terry and I usually caught up with each other at local restaurants and taverns. Tony and Judy – who is also an artist – took time to show me the galleries and the university museum in Charlottesville, Virginia. I also made a point of taking in art shows and exhibitions wherever I had the opportunity.

Albuquerque was frequently on my route as I crossed the country between Southern California and the East Coast. My much-removed cousin Connie had lived there most of her life. She had a colorful background as a racing jockey, before women were accepted in that profession, and was now a western artist and craft person. She was a tough, spunky woman in the mold of a true ranch lady, and I enjoyed her company immensely. We got to know each other when I had taken some time off from the Corps of Engineers to visit my old haunts in New Mexico and she had been very supportive while I tried to make a success of the gallery in Madrid. I would give Connie fair warning a day or so before I was passing through on I-40, and as I approached Albuquerque I would give her a call.

"Hi, Cuz'. I'm coming down the hill. Got a bed tonight?"

"Come on by – the gate's open."

Sometimes, I could take a couple of days off, but more frequently I was only able to spend the night. Stopping at Connie's was special because I could sit on her patio, watch the hummingbirds buzz around the trumpet vines, and smell the flowers and fresh mown grass. Her doggies always excitedly jumped all over me when I parked my rig in front of her house and walked down the driveway. Connie would sometimes prepare a feast of home-cooked food, or we would go out for dinner and a few excellent margaritas at our favorite Mexican restaurant. One Christmas, I was treated to an outrageous display of lights that would have put Rockefeller Center to shame.

"Just keepin' the lights on for ya'."

To my entire family – many thanks for treating me so well!

Each time I dropped in on them, I felt like a sailor returning after years of being at sea, or a soldier coming home from war. Back on the road, my thoughts were always about how I could somehow bring this to an end and do something – anything – of significance. Driving the endless highways had become a mindless addiction, and my life was wasting away with each mile I left behind.

During my third year of trucking, I was driving through Massachusetts not far from where Melissa lived. I decided to pull into a rest area and give her a call. Maybe we would be able to get together for a few minutes.

"Hello?"

It was John who answered the phone.

"Hi John. This is Roger. Is Melissa there?"

There was a pause on the other end of the line.

"You haven't heard, have you?"

"Heard what, John? Is there a problem?"

"Yeah – uhm – Melissa died almost two years ago, Roger. I tried to let you know, but the phone numbers she had for you were disconnected."

"For chrissake, John. What happened?"

I could not believe this.

"She had pancreatic cancer and went into a coma. I had to have her unplugged after a week or so."

"Jesus, John. I can't believe it. I don't know anything about pancreatic cancer, but wasn't there anything they could do?"

"Nothing. It's usually fatal. Hers was so advanced, it was too late to try chemo. And she kept drinking through the whole thing. I tried to get her to quit, but she wouldn't do it."

There was nothing I could say. All I wanted was to slam my phone on the dashboard.

"I'm speechless, John. Thanks – uhm – I've got to go."

I sat there in my truck as emotions and memories poured over me. I lowered my forehead on the steering wheel and shook. Melissa was one person who should have lived forever. Shock, anger, pain, and profound sadness gripped me. Only after getting out and pacing around the truck for about an hour, was I calm enough to get on the road again. The realization hit me that this was why she wanted to see me a few years ago. Melissa knew she was dying and wanted to say goodbye. True, she had disappointed me, but there would always only be one Melissa in my life. She was a star that burned too bright – an angel who flew much too low and fast!

For some time, I had grown tired of just sitting all day and driving. I couldn't figure out a way to paint even small watercolors in the truck. The light was bad, painting was too messy, there wasn't enough room, or after a long day on the road, I was too tired to feel creative. But photography had always interested me. From what I had read about digital photography, the quality had advanced beyond the fuzzy shots from the earlier cameras. I didn't know what a pixel was, but I bought a 5 mega-pixel camera. I couldn't do anything without a computer, so I bought a laptop as well – which I also didn't know anything about. To cap everything off, I needed a wireless card so I could send emails and get online from inside my truck – for what reason, I had no idea except that I had read that the internet was fun. The camera came with a basic photo editing program, and I was in heaven.

I started taking pictures at truck stops, loading docks, rest areas, or wherever I stopped. Occasionally, I saw a subject by the side of the highway, but missed it as I whipped past. I would drive to the next overpass – turn around – drive back to the last one – turn around again and stop on the shoulder where I had seen the shot. It cost time and fuel, but I didn't give a damn. I had my photo.

I sent a few photos to family and friends and always got good responses. The occasional photo escalated to a daily email with a caption sent to readers I gathered from around the country. I bought an advanced editing program, and my images became much better. With referrals, my list grew to over 150 addressees. The messages were sometimes clever, or humorous, or reflective, or expressive of my view of the world. Sometimes I would email poetry or even short stories. I would take my pictures during the day and dream up material for the next day while I was driving down the highway. When I stopped in the evening, I would work on the photo, add the caption, and put together an email that would go out in the morning. It was a perfect way to be creative and productive while I was on the road.

The following is my favorite of the hundreds of emails I sent out:

•

JERRY LEE AND CATHERINE

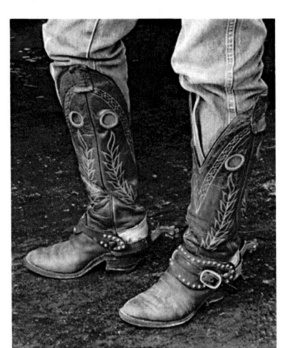

High-tops

A SPIFFY PICKUP and horse trailer pulls up while I am fueling at a truck stop outside San Antonio. This lanky fellow steps out – crisp as a new $100 bill and dressed like he's off the set of a John Wayne movie. What really gets my attention are his boots. You don't see classic, green high-tops very often.

"Nice boots! You're sure looking good today," I say, knowing at that moment there was no way I was going to let him leave without taking his picture.

"Not bad for an old guy, I guess," Jerry Lee responds with an easy smile.

I dive into my truck for my camera, get pictures of Jerry Lee and the boots, and a conversation develops about my photography, and the writings I send out with the pictures. We're into mutual experiences when Catherine comes around from the other side. She's decked out in her silver and turquoise, looking pretty as a centerfold model for Santa Fe Magazine. I take a photo of them together.

It turns out Jerry Lee Sewell is a veteran of the Korean and Vietnam Wars, speaks three Asian languages – including one I can't even pronounce – and a few others. He has also been a real estate broker/developer and lawyer. (You can tell because he's the one wearing the black hat.) But his business card now reads, "Clinician/Trainer – Schooling Horse and Rider." That's legalese for "let me introduce you to your horse," and you should whisper when you say it. But here's what you really should know.

In Vietnam, Jerry Lee had a 28 month Special Forces ("spook") tour followed by a 16 month go with the 1st Air Cavalry as a rifle company commander and later, battalion ops officer. He came home badly wounded and haunted by the war. Demons were stampeding through his head, and he responded by indulging in every self-destructive behavior he could imagine. Anything to dull the pain and escape his brutal memories. When he wasn't recovering from substance abuse, he was falling back into it. He would bury himself in his work, only to find the stress of dealing with clients and making deals as unbearable as his past. He was in and out of VA hospitals through the 70's, 80's, and 90's.

One day, about a year before I met Jerry Lee, Catherine Norman came into his life through an internet dating service. She is a retired ER and ICU nurse who finds dealing with horses fulfilling to her need to nurture. Jerry Lee also has a way with horses and loves working with them. They fell in love, but Catherine had dealt with enough human problems and didn't need another one.

She finally said to him – as only a good woman can – "Jerry Lee, I love you more than the sun and stars that shine. I love you so much I'm not going to stick around and watch you kill yourself. Either shape up or I'm leaving."

That got his attention.

Then his doctor told him, "Jerry Lee, you need to do something you enjoy. It's stress that's doing all this to you."

275

Now Jerry Lee knows that Catherine is the best thing to ride over his horizon in a long time. He also knows that his shrink gives good advice, and this was a great time for him to take it. So with the force of his will, the strength of his faith, and his love for Catherine, Jerry Lee pulled himself up by his green bootstraps and remade himself into the person I saw that day. Catherine and Jerry Lee are fully enjoying their late-life romance and life is as good as it's ever been for both of them. Romance is like a river running its natural course to the sea. And you can't rush a river – or Catherine.

I told Jerry Lee that I honestly didn't see how he held himself together through all those years.

"I believe God puts each of us on this earth to accomplish a purpose, and then calls us home. I hadn't accomplished mine yet, so he kept me alive through some pretty bad stuff."

Time and again I hear a similar message. An absolute faith and belief in a purpose greater than self enables someone to achieve a dream, meet an impossible challenge, or just survive.

Where there is faith – there is hope. Combine hope with motivation – it becomes a force.

•

It wasn't long before I became an expert at taking pictures while driving. Don't laugh – it was very simple. I would preset the camera at a medium zoom and put it on automatic. All I had to do was drive with my left hand, point the camera, and snap the picture with my right. If I saw something interesting coming up out the side window, I would roll it down, pick up the camera with my right hand, cradle it with my left elbow – which was fairly steady – and take the shot while always looking forward. I soon got the timing and angle of the camera mastered and rarely missed a shot. I never took my eyes off the road, and my photography never caused a safety problem. And I came up with some dramatic photos that otherwise would never have been taken.

I found that if my very first action in the morning was to review the photo and caption and send out the email, I would then be thinking creatively for the rest of the day. I was always looking for photos to shoot. Captions would compose and rearrange themselves in my mind. I was filled with creative spirit rather than destructive anger, depression, and sheer boredom.

For my first six and a half years of trucking I was able to avoid any serious accidents. I had banged up a couple of doors at loading docks, but that was it. One night, however, I had to exchange trailers on an unlit, dirt lot in an old industrial area of Philadelphia. The company I was driving for had what were called "drop-frame trailers," which can raise or lower their rear end to match the height of a loading dock. Rain had left the lot muddy and pitted with deep pot holes. The trailer I had to pick up had its rear wheels parked in water about eight inches deep. I climbed down from my cab and did my inspection with a flashlight. The floor appeared level with the ground, so I did not notice that the back had not been lowered. Huge mistake!

I hooked up and got on the road. I was ahead of schedule and feeling great. Philadelphia has some of the oldest freeways and lowest overpasses in the country. When I went under the first one – KAWHAM!!! I looked in my mirror and saw debris sliding down the highway. Before I could stop, I scraped the top of the trailer on a second overpass. I finally was able to pull over on the shoulder and climb out to see what had happened. Sure enough, the trailer was in its raised position. I had peeled back the rear frame and doors, which were now hanging off the end at a 45 degree angle.

I was walking back to my cab to call my company and 911 when I heard sirens screaming in my direction. A city police car came to a skidding stop next to me and a short, fireplug-sized cop jumped out. He charged around his car and started screaming at me with his hand on his pistol.

"Hold it right there, mister – don't move – let me see your hands!"

I did what I was told, but I couldn't figure out why I was getting this kind of treatment. Other police cars wheeled up and surrounded us. He was a captain, an older guy, and clearly in charge. He got very close and was almost spitting in my face.

"So you're the guy spreading all this shit on my freeway! – Did you do this on purpose, asshole? – Is this your first time driving a fucking truck? – What the holy hell do you think you're doing for chrissake?"

I was getting very tired of taking his crap, but he was the guy with the gun. I didn't say a word, just pointed to the rear of the trailer. The cop glanced over and was about to rip into me again when a state highway patrol officer pulled up. A young, tall, black officer got out and calmly walked over. He stepped between us, grabbed me firmly by the arm and guided me over to my cab.

"Get in. Don't say another word to this creep. This may be his city, but it's my

Oops – Damn

freeway. I've got jurisdiction. Stay in the truck and don't get out. Don't do anything he tells you. Understand?"

"Yes Sir. Whatever you say."

I was now thoroughly confused, but was happy to do as I was told.

He walked back to the city cop who was standing there fuming with his legs spread and hand still on his pistol grip, like he was ready to draw on me if I so much as blinked in his direction. They had a brief, heated conversation, and then the officer came back to me.

"Stay calm, Sir – you're doing fine. Now show me your license and registration and hand me your log book."

I had just updated it at my last stop, so I wasn't worried about any violations. I handed the paperwork over and he took a moment to flip through it, but it was all show for the other cop. There was no way he could have read any of it or checked the hours. He climbed up on the steps of the cab and handed it back to me.

"OK, Mr. Blake, here's what's happening. I've dealt with this old bastard before. What he's trying to do is get you pissed off so you'll do something stupid. One false move in his direction, and he'll arrest you for assault and impound the truck. Once he does that, it will take you months to get out of jail and cost your company thousands of dollars to buy the rig out of the impound lot. I suspect that the money finds its way into the police retirement fund. Don't say a word to him. Be cool and stay in your cab."

"Yes Sir. You've got a lot of nerve officer. I appreciate it!"

"I'm glad I got here in time. Now, explain to me what happened and how you are going to get this wreck out of here."

I told him about the trailer and explained that I needed to make a call to my company to find out what they wanted to do.

"Make the call. I'll hang out here until this gets resolved."

The company had a contract with an emergency salvage company that soon came and strapped up the trailer. The officer wrote me a ticket for driving with faulty equipment. He handed it over pretending to be stern and upset.

"Don't worry about this. It won't show up in anybody's computer. I'm sure you'll have enough problems to deal with without a ticket. Now, get the hell out of here, and let's not do this again."

I was amazed and thanked him as best I could. He gave me a nod as he got into his patrol car and drove away. I felt lucky to get out of there with my life.

He was right about having "enough problems to deal with." My company decided I was not a driver they wanted to keep around. They wouldn't fire me because I could then get unemployment or maybe cause some other problem for them. What they did do, however, was give me only short runs, and I had to sit for a day or more between load assignments. In other words, they made it uneconomical for me to stay with them – so I had to quit.

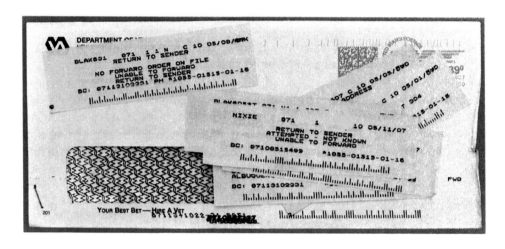

Return to Sender

Slipping, Sliding, Sinking Down A Slick And Ceaseless Slope

THERE IS A NATIONAL REPORTING AGENCY, which keeps track of every hiccup a truck driver makes. It reports on such things as late deliveries, employment experience, tickets, and especially accidents. Almost all national companies subscribe to this agency. After my last accident, I would never get a job with a major trucking company again.

What little cash I had was dwindling rapidly. I got behind on payments for my credit cards and pickup truck and was at the point of having to keep moving to avoid having it repossessed. I cleaned out my El Paso storage locker, which I had rented when I drove with the last company, and moved everything to a cheap motel with weekly rates in Amarillo. My clothes, some trucking equipment, a few boxes of files, some small paintings, my camera, and laptop were all stashed around my room. I had no income coming in and no prospects in sight. At the gnarly age of 62, one thing I could do was sign up for Social Security. At least it would be something to fall back on. With little cash, no earnings, and no job, however, I had to take whatever measures I could to stay afloat. My debts weren't great, but were too much when I had no income to pay them. I reluctantly walked into the federal courthouse and filed for bankruptcy. With that done, I kept looking for a job.

I talked with petroleum businesses, livestock haulers, and refrigerated cargo companies – anyone who hired drivers with CDLs. I even tried bus and tour outfits. No luck. Desperation was setting in. With each lead, I had to send in an application and employment history. Stacks of paperwork littered my small room. It all consumed time, energy, and money. How the hell did I ever sink this low?

Finally, I got a break. One of my email contacts – a retired couple – had a son-in-law in the trucking business in Canyon, Texas, about 20 miles south of Amarillo. He only ran two trucks, but one of his drivers had just quit. We had talked about a job with him before, but she now asked if I would I go down and talk with him.

Absolutely! We had a casual interview, and I met his family. They already knew about my emails, so that was not an issue. We talked at length about my accident, but got beyond that. Accidents happen. They had a run to

Los Angeles in a couple of days. Could I start then? Yes, indeed! I dropped what I didn't need on the road in a storage locker nearby.

Almost immediately after I climbed into the truck, it started to break down. A fuel injector went out in Los Angeles. The transmission needed to be adjusted. A shock absorber had a hole in it. The owner complained about me keeping the engine idling when I was sleeping, which is standard procedure in order to keep the air-conditioner running. Otherwise, the cab would heat up like an oven, and I would have been trying to sleep in over 100 degree heat. But that costs money, and the company had to be as tight as possible. I didn't fuel at the right truck stop, which could have saved them three cents a gallon. The son-in-law's wife screwed up and copied me on an email that she had sent to her husband. She said something like, "He isn't going to be around long." She apologized, but that did not negate the fact that she had said it.

The final blow was that the transmission started to slip and became progressively worse when I was pulling my first heavy load out of Los Angeles. I called the owner right away and told him the problem.

"Do you think you can make the delivery in Texas, Roger?"

"It's holding together, but I don't know how long it will stay that way."

"Why are so many things suddenly going wrong?"

He was obviously inferring that I was causing the problems.

"That driver before me had no experience and probably quit when he realized that he had burned up the truck."

 Whatever else he might have thought, I had been trucking for seven years and at least knew how to drive an automatic transmission. Obviously, he did not share my opinion. I was able to make the delivery and took the vehicle to a shop. I sat in a motel for three days while the transmission was rebuilt. When it was done, I got a call from the owner.

"Bring the rig back to the yard. You're fired!"

"Dammit, you can't blame me for problems that existed before I climbed in the truck! That's not my fault."

"You've bankrupted my company. I won't discuss it. Just bring the truck back and get out of here!"

I would have left the damn thing at the shop and let the owner deal with it, but abandoning a truck is not something anyone does in the business – even for the best of reasons. Anyway, my pickup was back at their yard, and I had to get it out of there. I drove the truck back and removed my gear. I tossed it in my pickup and left.

On my way to Amarillo, I dropped off my stuff in the storage locker in Canyon and stopped at Wal-Mart to get a few things to eat for the next couple of days. I had entered another world. People were bustling around, and the atmosphere was cheerful and friendly. I felt like I was walking around with a dark cloud hanging over me and had no business being there. I couldn't leave fast enough.

When something like this had happened to me in the past, I could usually develop some sort of a plan. This time, however, I came up empty. I still had a paycheck coming from my last few runs, and my first social security check was only a few weeks away. My problem was surviving till they came in. I had a little money in my pocket, but not much. I drove back to Amarillo and checked into the same motel I had stayed in before. I even got the same room in the back, so that my pickup would not be seen and repossessed. One fortunate thing about this mess was that I would be able to attend my bankruptcy hearing in two days. I had planned to withdraw my application after I got my last job, but now I really had no choice. It was late, so I had a granola bar and a soda for dinner and let my problems percolate overnight.

The new day was even grimmer than the night before. The dark cloud of depression that had hovered over me at Wal-Mart had followed me to my room. I checked my wallet and pockets and came up with $34 plus some change. I had run myself out of options. I would never tell my family what I was going through and ask for help, however. Hell, I couldn't even explain what had happened to myself. I had dug my own hole, and could not expect them, or anyone else, to pull me out. I would get what I deserved.

Why not go out by the side of the road with a cardboard sign saying, "Will work for ..." The motel was by the freeway, so I took a walk to see if I could find a good spot to hang my shingle. It did not take long, however, before the oppressive heat and traffic noise from the big trucks drove me back inside. Suicide crept into my mind as a final possibility. Death was becoming an attractive option compared to the mental anguish I was going through.

That afternoon, I picked up a discarded newspaper and took it back to my room. I checked the ads and saw that the company that I had the accident with was looking for drivers. I had nothing to lose and gave them a call. I explained the situation to the recruiter, and asked if they would take me back? He put me on hold while he checked with someone. When he came back on, he asked if I would be interested in a local driving job in Portland, Oregon?

"Yes, I've lived there before and would love that!"

"OK, Mr. Blake. You'll have to come down here and fill out an application. We'll take it from there."

"Are you sure – with the accident and everything?"

I was too excited to believe it.

"I checked with my boss, and he said OK."

Wow! Now all I had to do was get to their headquarters in El Paso which was about 440 miles from Amarillo. The rest would take care of itself after I got there. I did not have the money for gas, however. I tried Greyhound, but they wanted $75 for the ride. I decided to be at my bankruptcy hearing in the morning, drive back to my storage locker in Canyon, get what I would need in Portland, park the pickup somewhere, and hitchhike to El Paso. It wasn't the best plan, but I was determined to get there by any means possible.

The bankruptcy hearing was perfunctory. None of my creditors showed – not that any were expected. However, when I walked out of the court house I saw a tow truck backing up to my pickup. The bank had guessed that I would be at the hearing and would most likely have it with me. This couldn't happen. I had my essential clothes and living stuff in the back, and there was too much to carry. I had to drive to Canyon to drop this off and get my trucking gear out of the storage locker. I explained all this to the repro guy who was skeptical, but listened anyway. He was actually a pleasant man in his late 50s or early 60s – someone who would be a good neighbor or friend.

"I don't believe this! I've been doing this a long time, and you're the first person I've felt like cutting a break to. I may be stupid, but I can't dump your stuff out and leave you standing on the sidewalk."

After some discussion, he got into my pickup. We drove down to my storage locker, switched out my gear, and headed back to Amarillo. Along the way I told him about my prospect for the job and how I planned to get to El Paso. He looked at me skeptically.

"For God's sake, you'll die in this heat. The temperature is a good 104 degrees – a lot more on the highway."

"Only thing I can do."

Back in Amarillo, I drove my pickup behind his tow truck, handed him the keys, and was about to get out, but he put a hand up to stop me.

"Wait a minute. I need to call my wife."

He stepped out while he had his conversation. When he was done he motioned me out of the truck. I hopped out and lifted my two duffel bags onto the curb. They were heavy because I had my bedding, CB radio, and other trucking equipment in one bag; and my laptop, camera gear, and clothes in the other. I didn't want to be in Oregon without my camera and laptop. I was about to thank the man when he started to dig for his wallet.

"Look. We don't know you, but you're obviously going through a rough time. My wife and I would like to help you out."

He pulled out $75 and handed it to me.

"Here's enough for your bus fare."

"Thanks – thank you, Sir. I'll remember this for the rest of my life!"

I was damn near in tears.

"I really hope your job works out. Good luck."

He may be the only repro man in the country with a heart of gold. Many thanks again, and thanks also to your wife. Be well!

With that, I handed over the keys to my pickup and walked the short distance to the bus depot. I arrived in El Paso just before midnight. I asked the fellow at the ticket window if there was a cheap motel nearby, and he pointed me to a place with its lights on a few blocks away. The night manager asked $50 for a room. I told him I had $30. He held his hand out and took my money. I had bought a soda on the ride down and now had $3 to my name.

The next morning, I spent $1 on a candy bar and called the company. Sure, they would send a driver to pick me up. I arrived and sat down with the recruiter. Everything was OK.

"Just fill out the application since you've been away for more than 30 days."

I completed the paperwork and was asked to wait while he went to get it approved. Another individual finally brought the paper work back and took a seat across from me.

El Paso

"Mr. Blake, I'm the senior safety officer and have been reviewing your file. I'm sorry, but we can't take you back."

My life stood still while I fell into a state of absolute shock.

"But Sir. I was told it was OK. I spent all the money I had to get down here. I – I don't have anything else I can do. Isn't there some way we can resolve this? Someone I can talk to?"

"No, Mr. Blake. I'm the one who makes the decision. Your accident was just too expensive, and our insurance company won't cover you. I'm sorry."

Thoughts were racing through my mind. I wouldn't take another trucking job if it was offered to me. My other possessions were in Canyon, and I had to get there to drop off the belongings that were with me. I had no idea what I would do after that.

"I've got these two bags. Can you drive me somewhere? I need to hitchhike back to Amarillo."

He looked at me disdainfully, as though I had now become a pest.

"We can do that. Wait here. It will be a few minutes."

•

Great expectations lead to major complications.

•

You Can't See The Whole When You're Deep In A Hole

THE DRIVER DROPPED ME OFF on a road that would connect me with the highway to Lubbock, some 340 miles east. From there it would be about 105 miles north to Canyon. I got a ride to the main highway by noon, but then had a long wait. Fortunately, I had a ball cap with me, however I didn't have sunscreen. The sun and heat were brutal. I'm fair skinned and was fried to a crisp by the end of the afternoon. I bought a large soda at a convenience store and kept going back to refill the cup with water. $1 was left in my pocket. I had to keep facing the west into the afternoon sun in order to catch a ride going east. It became so hot that I had to get off the shoulder of the road and sit in the shade of the building a few times before I passed out.

It wasn't until early in the evening that a car stopped. I had been standing there with my thumb out for six hours. It was a small sedan driven by a young serviceman. He already had luggage and two young kids in the car.

"I sure appreciate this, but you're pretty full. Are you sure you want to give me a ride?"

"Not a problem, Sir. You – um, really look like you could use a lift."

With that he rearranged the luggage to fit in my bags and moved one of his kids into the back seat. They both complained, but he told them to shush. We got on the road, and he offered me some cookies. We made small talk about the service, Vietnam, and the trucking business. I was having trouble tracking the conversation.

"It's OK if you want to sleep. Go ahead if you want."

I slumped in the seat and was in and out of consciousness for the rest of our ride to Lubbock. The young gentleman made the extra effort to take me to a truck stop that I was familiar with and dropped me off. He said that if he didn't have the kids along, he would have taken me all the way to Canyon. He wished me well, and I thanked him and his children sincerely. Thank you again, Sir! With one duffel bag over each shoulder I went inside. It was about 1 a.m., and no one else was sitting in the lounge. I tried to make myself comfortable and started to drift off to sleep. A few minutes later I was prodded by the night manager.

"What are you doing here?"

"Lost my ride, Sir. (That's trucker-speak for "got fired.") I'm just trying to get some sleep."

"Well, you can't sleep here. The management doesn't allow it."

"OK."

I got up and tried to pull myself together.

"I'm sorry, Sir, but is there any way I can talk you folks out of a shower? I can't pay for it, but I would really be grateful."

He frowned and looked me over for a minute.

"Hold on. Let me check."

He returned a few minutes later and gave me a key, some soap and a towel.

"This bathroom hasn't been cleaned, but the maid said you can use it if you want. Just be quick and don't leave a mess."

I thanked the man gratefully. Cleaning myself up made me feel somewhat human again. When I was done, I left my last $1 on the counter for the maid and carried my bags outside. What the hell! She would make better use of it than I would. The time was about 2 a.m. There were two cops leaning up against their patrol car, chatting with each other when I walked out. One was the local sheriff – an older man – and the other was a young lady with the prettiest face I had seen in a long time.

"Excuse me, folks. I'm trying to hitchhike up to Canyon. I know we're a ways from the freeway, and I've got these bags. Could you possibly give me a lift to a good spot to get a ride?"

The guy grunted and looked at his partner. They both shrugged.

"Climb in the back. Why don't you tell us what's going on?"

I told them about the job that didn't happen and my efforts to get up to my storage locker. The guy did the talking.

"What's in the bags? They look pretty heavy."

"I've got my CB radio and trucking gear, a camera, all my clothes, bedding and a laptop with a couple thousand photos that I've taken – just about everything."

He looked over the seat and tried hard to evaluate who he had sitting in the back of his patrol car.

"Hitchhiking is not as safe as it used to be. We find some really strange types out on the highway. You don't impress me as someone who should be out there."

"Thank you, Sheriff. I don't intend to make this a habit."

The gal was driving, and she pulled the patrol car up to an overpass where two freeways intersect. Then she reached beneath her seat and pulled out a plastic container. It had a sandwich and some fruit in it. She turned around and handed it to me.

"Here. I want you to have this."

"But that's your meal! Thank you, but I really can't take that."

"When was the last time you ate something?"

I had to think.

"I had some cookies last night and a granola bar yesterday morning."

"Come on – take this. It's nothing. You need to get some food in you."

Damn. She gave me a dazzling smile as I gratefully accepted the sandwich.

"When you need an endorsement for Sheriff, please let me know!"

I thanked them both for the lift and got out of the car. I swore to myself that I would never take peoples' amazing generosity for granted again. I looked around, and there was a level spot under the beams of the overpass. I climbed up and got out of view from the traffic. I sat with my bags and slowly ate my meal. Sleep overcame me as I ate the last bite.

The sun had risen a few hours before I woke up. The Saturday morning traffic was light. I hiked a few hundred yards to where the traffic merged and headed north to Canyon. It was already a warm day. I soon discovered that I had made the bad mistake of leaving my water cup on the counter of the bathroom. All I could do was stand there and hope for a lift. But no one needs a good reason to pass up a hitchhiker. You don't know who he is or what trouble may come from your generosity.

Big trucks roared past. Pickups, SUVs, and vans whipped by. I stood at the same spot for four hours. The heat was bearing down unmercifully. I was hot, thirsty, and dangerously dehydrated. I began getting dizzy and had to sit on my bags and lower my head until the spells calmed down. The sun was directly overhead now. When it moved to the west and sank lower, I would be in more serious trouble.

The hopelessness of the situation began to overwhelm me. My thoughts turned to suicide again. Why not just run out in front of a truck? It actually happens frequently, but I didn't like that idea. It was too messy, I did not want to end my life with a moment of pain, and it also wouldn't be fair to the driver. Pills would be an answer, however I didn't have any. I became focused on getting a gun, but I did not have the money. OK – I'll steal one.

Then a Jeep Wagoneer stopped. There were three guys in it – all dressed in tuxedos on their way to a wedding in Amarillo. The driver was the groom and the other two were his best men. I tried to lift my bags into the back, but did not have the strength. One of the guys got out to help me.

"You OK, Bud?"

"I've got to get out of this sun. It hit me a little bit back there."

I could not hide the tremors in my hands.

"We've got some beer in the back. How 'bout a cold one?"

The alcohol would have finished me off.

"I better not, thanks. Would you have some water or a soda?"

"Nope. Sorry, but we have to make a pit stop in a few minutes. You can pick something up then."

We went down the road, and they were all drinking beer and having a wonderful time. I wasn't much up for the party, however, and would have nodded off except that they kept asking me questions. The noisiest of the three was the groom.

"You ever been married?"

"Twice."

"What happened? You didn't like it?"

I didn't want to talk negatively about marriage on his wedding day.

"Oh, it was good. Things – just didn't work out."

One of the best men tossed his beer can out on the highway and turned to me.

"So, what advice would you give to our budding groom?"

If he only knew how bad a choice of marriage counselors I was.

"Well, first pick the right woman, but I presume you've already done that. Then do everything possible to keep her happy."

"Do you have kids?"

This question always came up with the subject of marriage.

"No. It didn't happen."

If there was one way to destroy a conversation or kill a good mood, it was to tell someone about my kids. Fortunately, we pulled into the convenience store, and that was the end of the questions.

I was beginning to feel nauseous. I went in anyway, and the guys were getting some good-humored jeers for being dressed so formally. They were boisterous and having fun, however, and none of the jabs mattered to them. I went up to the motherly lady behind the counter and asked if I could have a large cup for water. She studied me for a minute.

"You're not with those guys are you? You're red as a beet."

"No, Ma'am. I'm hitchhiking and got too much sun."

"Hitchhiking! Help yourself. Have a soda if you want."

She handed me her largest cup.

"Thanks. I really appreciate it Ma'am."

The air conditioning was running at full blast, and I started to shiver when I stood under a vent. I felt the cold ice as it dropped into the cup. The soda splashed over the ice like a cool mountain stream bubbling over rocks. I could feel the chill all the way down to my toes as I drank each swallow. It was glorious.

The guys came out of the restroom, and we went outside. A large thermometer dial mounted on a post was wavering over 105 degrees. The asphalt was soft under my feet. They took more beers out of the cooler, and we piled back into the Jeep. Canyon was only one hour away. When we got to my exit, the driver said they were too far behind to take me to my storage locker. It would not be a good thing to miss his own wedding.

"Just drop me off at the interchange, please. I can see the units from here. Have a great wedding, folks. I appreciate the ride."

The lockers were less than a mile away. I could make it from the exit. I was feeling somewhat relieved to finally be this far. I gave the happy crew an appreciative wave as they pulled away. I knew I was in trouble, however, the moment I tried to pick up the bags. I could hardly sling them over my shoulders. The sun was getting lower with the full force of the heat hitting me in the face. I trudged down the highway about ten yards before I had to stop to catch my breath. Sweat was streaming into my eyes. I sat on the shoulder and tried to hitchhike. Nobody stopped, however. I had to keep moving. I thought of hiding one bag in the grass and coming back for it, but that seemed like more work. I was getting more unsteady each time I tried to go a few yards. My skin became clammy, and I started to shiver. I sat down again and put my head in my hands.

I looked at the storage locker, but it didn't seem any closer than when I started. I looked back and I had, in fact, gone about half way. I looked ahead of me again and the storage units now seemed even farther away.

"I'm goddamn losing it."

I now had to carry the bags up hill. I might as well have been scaling Mt. Everest. Every step was painful and my stops became even more frequent. My heart was racing, and I was gasping for breath. My back started to cramp every time I lifted a bag. I sat for several minutes. I wasn't going to make it. What was the use anyway? I didn't have anything to do even if I did get there. I looked at my arms, which were flaming red. I became nauseous. I walked into the grass to wretch up what little fluids I had in me. I straightened up painfully and stumbled over to my bags.

"This isn't worth it. Why not get it over with? Hell, I've lived long enough. It didn't work out. So what?"

Wal-Mart was a few miles beyond my locker. Do they sell guns at Wal-Mart, I wondered? I knew they used to. Go there, get a damn gun and end this bullshit. That became the plan regardless of the bags.

Why not drop the crap here and forget about it? I could, but I didn't want some idiot picking them up and stealing all my stories and photos. I hadn't been able to do anything with them, but I sure as hell didn't want anybody else to. That would piss me off even after I was dead and gone.

I sat there looking at the ground. The heat was fierce. I looked up, and at least I wasn't sweating any more. But I wasn't getting any further by sitting there. I stood up and struggled to lift the two bags on my shoulders again.

"Get the bags into the locker. Get a gun. That's the plan."

I kept repeating that mantra again and again. I looked over at a small tree standing in the field. I didn't see the tree so much as the shade. I was getting awfully tired.

"After the storage locker – after the storage locker, I'll go under the tree and lie down. Then I'll get the gun."

I looked up at the storage complex. There was less than a hundred yards to go.

"Just a little more – after the storage locker ..."

Finally, I reached the entrance. I pulled the code out of my wallet to open the gate. I dragged one bag to the locker at a time, opened the lock, and pushed open the door. Furnace-hot air and clouds of dust blew out at me. I pushed the bags on top of some boxes and looked at the stacks that held what amounted to what was left of my life. I locked the door and left it behind.

"That's the last I'll ever see of them."

I remembered the tree out in the field. The tall grass was comfortable, but it was brutally hot even in the shade. I lay there until I became aware of being bitten on my back by some kind of insect. The bites burned like hell, so I got up and urgently brushed a few bugs out of my shirt. Time to get moving again, so I walked back out to the highway.

The sun was hitting me head on, and I felt my skin getting toasted. The air shimmered with waves of heat rising from the asphalt. Suddenly the sky began to swirl, my legs became limp, and I collapsed on the gravel by the side of the road. I was on my knees struggling to stand up when a highway patrol car drove past. It whipped around over the center divider and came up behind me. The officer was a young, bull of a man who looked like he was born to be a cop. He slipped his arms beneath my shoulders and lifted me to my feet.

"You're in pretty bad shape, Sir."

"I'm OK – just a little too much sun."

I wondered, why does everyone kept calling me "Sir" when I looked and felt like crap?

"Just a little? Let's get you in the car, and we'll talk about it."

I was dizzy and had to steady myself against him. He put his arm around my waist and got me to sit on the back seat with the door open. I would have passed out if it wasn't for the air conditioning and shade. My skin felt like it was on fire, I was shaking, and my speech was practically incoherent. I could not begin to make any sense of the situation.

"OK Sir. I'm going to take you to a convenience store up the road. The owner's a friend of mine. I'm sure he can find you some help. It's against regulations to let you die on my highway, so let's get moving."

The policeman helped me inside the store and explained to the owner how he had found me. Could he track down someone from his church to give me a hand? I was still trembling as he sat me down in a booth. He said goodbye, and I shook his hand weakly.

"I can't thank you enough, Officer. I appreciate it!"

"Glad to be of assistance, Sir."

The owner patted me on the shoulder.

"What kind of a soda would you like?"

"Lemonade – if you have it, please."

The cashier brought it over to me.

295

"That's very kind, Miss. Thanks."

I emptied the drink and tried to get up for a refill, but the gal took the cup and brought it to me.

"Keep your seat, Sir. If you want more, let me know."

I started to nod back and forth in the seat. I was trying to figure out how to get out of there and go on to Wal-Mart. The duffle bags had been taken care of. Someone in the family would find them somehow. I didn't have to deal with them anymore. I was exhausted, my head felt like it would explode any minute, and I was weak. I didn't want to beg for my next meal. Better to end everything as soon as possible.

The owner interrupted my thoughts, and asked who I was and what had happened. I told him my name and attempted to run through the events of the day. Much of what I tried to say was confused. He had to ask several questions before I got things straight. He said he would take a few minutes to make some calls. When he came back, I was sitting with my eyes closed, drifting off to sleep. He leaned over and put his hand on my shoulder.

"Unfortunately, we don't have an ambulance service in Canyon. However, an alderman from our church is coming over, and he will take you to Amarillo."

"It's Saturday evening! I can't ask anyone to do that."

"It's OK, Mr. Blake. He's already on his way."

The gentleman soon arrived and sat down next to me.

"How are you feeling, Sir?"

I took a moment to take stock of myself.

"Better, thanks, but I really hurt all over. I've got the worst headache I can remember – it's almost making me blind."

I recalled that he was an alderman, so I refrained from more colorful adjectives.

"You should be in a hospital. Do you have any insurance?"

"No – no insurance."

"Well, I suppose we could take you to the emergency room. Hmm – we have a Veteran's Hospital in Amarillo. Are you a veteran, Roger?"

I looked at him and tears came to my eyes. Proud images of time in the Navy passed through my mind.

"Yes Sir. I am a veteran."

•

Kindness is contagious. Feel free to infect the world!

•

Caring Is The Chicken Soup Of The Cure

I REMEMBER LITTLE of our 20 mile drive to Amarillo. I would snap back from my drifting thoughts only when the driver asked me a question. Immediate events or timeframes were already slipping beyond my ability to recall. My answers didn't matter, however. He was asking questions primarily to keep me from falling off to sleep. We arrived at the hospital's emergency room, and I was able to shuffle to the admissions desk with the driver's assistance. I painfully lowered myself into a seat in front of the clerk.

"What is the problem, Sir?"

I did not know where to start.

"My head – it feels like it's split in half – my back aches something terrible – I'm weak and feel shaky all over."

The gentleman who had brought me there explained how I was found on the highway and had been talking about suicide. The clerk raised an eyebrow.

"Suicide – are you depressed?"

I hated my life and everything about myself.

"Yes – damn depressed."

"So, how were you going to commit suicide?"

I looked at him grimly.

"Get a gun, walk out in a field, and shoot myself. If that didn't work, I would do it some other way."

He deliberated for a moment and seemed to soften his skepticism.

"OK Mr. Blake, do you have your VA card?"

I searched through my wallet and, my gosh – I found it! I had forgotten I even had it. I handed it across the desk.

"Excellent, Sir. That saves us a lot of problems. Can I have your current address, please?"

"Don't have one."

My last address was where my last trucking job had been. Admitting to my suicidal thoughts and being homeless was utterly humiliating. My inability to lift myself above these problems displayed weakness that was distasteful to every fiber of my character. I had been beaten by myself. Dejection worsened my depression as I sank deeper into my world of despair.

"You're homeless?"

"Yes – homeless."

I guess I didn't look like I should be. I still despised myself for being so weak and destitute.

"I hate to make you wait so long, Sir, but the psychiatric nurse who will have to admit you is out. It's Saturday, and we only have a minimum staff working now. She might not be back for an hour or so. Please have a seat in the reception area."

"I may be dead by then."

"You have no idea how many times I've heard that, Sir."

He turned with a frown and started to process my admission papers. My driver helped me over to a chair and bought me a soda from a vending machine.

"You'll be OK now, Roger. Just wait for the nurse. I wish you all the best."

I thanked him emotionally and sat there trying hard not to become too anxious. Once again, I had been helped by the generosity of a total stranger. I couldn't keep doing this. I kept thinking that my life had amounted to a total waste and the only way to escape was to end it all. I bent over and put my hands on the sides of my head. The nurse found me in that position when she finally arrived over an hour later. She had to shake my shoulder to bring me back from my scattered thoughts.

The next thing I recall was partially waking up around mid-morning the following day. I wouldn't recommend this experience to anyone. I was staring at a white ceiling and glaring fluorescent lights. The walls were glossy white and the floor was a light, beige tile. I was only remotely aware of someone in a white, hospital jacket who was talking to me. Other people in long white coats were standing off to one side. I slowly drifted out of my medicated slumber.

My gosh – I'm dead. It's true what they say about men in white coats, I thought seriously. These people are here to carry my body away! A nurse was now shaking my shoulder.

"You can't have me."

If I was going to die, it had to be on my terms.

"You're OK, Mr. Blake. We gave you pills to help you sleep."

She put her hand on my arm to reassure me. It felt cool and strange against my sunburned skin, but the contact was welcome and comforting. I will always remember that soft touch. When you are depressed, the simplest gesture of genuine concern can make a world of difference. I had worked my mind into such a state that I felt unfit for such personal interaction. She had changed all that.

"Do you know where you are?"

I tried, but still could not remember.

"No – sorry."

I was totally disoriented and did not have a clue. I had some disjointed memories of the events of the day before, but could not put them together. I noticed an IV plugged into my arm. One of the doctors stepped forward.

"That's to give you some pain meds and get you hydrated again, Mr. Blake. You're in the Psychiatric Ward at the VA Hospital in Amarillo. Do you recall being admitted here?"

"Just bits and pieces."

I was still struggling to remember.

"Well Sir – your memory will come back. We'll be helping you with that. Right now, the important question is – how do you feel?"

I had to take stock of all the aches and pains.

"My lower back is the worst. My head feels like a cracked coconut – and my side is itching like crazy. Would you check it, please?"

"Sit up, Mr. Blake, and we'll take a look."

I painfully pulled myself up, and the nurse opened my robe.

"Chigger bites! Good God – there're all over! How did you get those?"

It took a moment, but the memory came back.

"Ah – I was resting under a tree, and they must have got under my shirt."

"Nothing's worse than chigger bites! There are a lot of bumps and rashes starting where they bit you. Whatever you do, don't scratch them. That will just make the itching worse and cause infections."

She hustled out to get some cortisone cream while the doctor continued with his summary.

"We've given you oxycodone, Sir. It will make you drowsy, but should relieve most of your pain. We've also been applying a cream that will help ease your sunburn."

"The oxy – whatever it is – is not doing much for my back, Doctor. And why is my head hurting so much?"

"Heat exhaustion, dehydration, stress, or maybe a reaction to the pills, Mr. Blake. It's difficult to tell at this point. You had a pretty rough time. We'll try some different medications and see if they help. Do you still feel depressed and suicidal?"

I sighed. I hated having to talk about this to anyone. I looked at the concerned group circling my bed and decided that there was no point in denying my problems.

"Yes, Doctor. There's nothing I want to live for. I really don't give a damn!"

"OK, I guess we can agree you're depressed. Do you think you might attempt suicide here, Mr. Blake?"

I sighed and took time mulling the question over before I finally replied.

"No, not here – too many people. It is something I would do in private."

"As long as you are suicidal, Sir, we can't release you. It sounds like you will be with us for a while. We have group therapy sessions in the afternoons, which you are required to participate in. We will also schedule one-on-one discussions with you on a regular basis and be trying other medications to relieve your depression and pain. How does that sound?"

I bristled at being "required" to do anything. How could anyone begin to understand? The thought of exposing myself to the scrutiny of total strangers – particularly those who had no professional training or interest – was totally distasteful. Why make myself the object of their idle curiosity? And talking about my problems or my pain would do nothing to make them disappear.

"I'll try any med you've got if it will make me feel better, Doctor, but I do not do well in groups. I get anxious and just want to avoid them. Is there any way I can get out of that?"

"No Sir. Everybody who stays here is required to go through the program. You will probably find it to be beneficial once you get into it."

I thought seriously for a moment. I might have to be part of the group, but my degree of participation was up to me.

"OK."

The first session came that afternoon. I listened to everyone else's sad stories of abuse, failure, loss, and despair. A few patients were angry and loud. Then, it was my turn to tell the group my problems.

"I'm sorry – I just got here. I feel very awkward with all of this. Can you give me a pass?"

The therapist was patient, but not pleased.

"We appreciate you telling us how you feel, Mr. Blake. That's OK for today, but please be prepared to join the conversation tomorrow."

I nodded gratefully.

"Thank you."

In fact, I felt threatened by the anger expressed around me. I took all the stories to heart and identified with each of those poor people. If anything, I was more depressed after the session than before. I explained my reaction to the therapist and asked again to be excused in the future.

"No Sir, group therapy is mandatory. Come tomorrow and just express your feelings. When most people get started, they want to tell us everything."

I spent the rest of that day curled up in bed, dozing off, and reliving past events of my life, as if they were on an endless movie reel unwinding in my mind. I dreamt of being in cool woods sitting beside a mountain stream as it gurgled and tumbled over the rocks. I longed for quiet mountain trails. I recalled my photography. The regimentation of the VA Hospital, however, brought back memories of the Navy, and then I would recall the accident that came close to ending everything. I ran through all the good times and resurrected the disturbing failures of my past. That inevitably led to images of my kids. I was back where I started. Whatever I did – however much I tried – the depressing moments kept coming back. Now that I was getting some care, however, my sense of desperation began to fade into the background. Perhaps there was some hope after all.

On the third day, my physical problems began to subside as a result of the powerful medications. I noticed that every hour or so during the night a nurse had opened my door and peeked in to make sure I wasn't somehow trying to commit suicide. My skin that had been blistered by the sun was now peeling off in large patches. My headache was gone, but I still had to struggle with my back. I told the doctor about it and asked for an X-ray, but he replied that we would have to address that problem later. This was a mental facility. Suicide and depression were their primary concerns, which had to be managed first.

That made no damn sense to me at all.

"This back pain is enough to make anyone commit suicide."

"Sorry, that's just the way it is."

It was time for my second group therapy session. I had not slept well for days. My anger about having to be at the meeting in the first place had become intense. The staff's response to my back problem had left me simmering. But I pulled myself together and listened again while everybody vented their problems. I still could not be that open, but I tried to offer something.

"I'm here because I had heat stroke – or as the docs are now telling me, heat exhaustion. I – um – was out on the highway hitchhiking. I've pretty much lost everything and am dealing with depression and have thoughts of suicide."

"Very good, Mr. Blake. Can you tell us how you came to be out on the highway?"

I told everybody about losing my job, not getting hired in El Paso, and having to hitchhike up to Canyon. I hadn't dealt with any of my emotional issues, and the therapist wanted to dig deeper.

"Didn't you call your family? Wasn't there anyone you could contact for support?"

His probing only heightened my anger.

"No, dammit! My family is not involved with any of this. It's my problem and no one else's."

"I don't understand, Sir. Why wouldn't you call them if you were having so much trouble?"

All of my built-up resentment at being trapped in a mental ward – at being in pain – at being drugged – at my life – at all the mistakes I had made – and now having to subject myself to personal questions in front of others – all of it exploded in my head.

"For chrissake! I just answered that question! I didn't fucking want to. Is that clear enough for you?"

I sat silently for the rest of the session. Emotional outbursts were very rare to me. I was shaking and wringing my hands. Any calm sense of reason and understanding had deserted me. My secrets hurt like open sores and I desperately wanted to keep them hidden. Disclosing my past created such mental distress that I had lost any ability to discuss it rationally. I could not cope with the overflow of emotions that surfaced as the result. Later that afternoon, my therapist, a nurse, and two other doctors came into my room. I was curled up in my bed as usual.

"Mr. Blake, please give us your attention. We need to have a talk."

I sat up and put my legs over the side of the bed. I rubbed my eyes and ran my fingers through my hair.

"I'm sorry, Doc. Everything's really fuzzy."

"I understand, Sir. I'll take this slow, and if there is anything you don't understand, we'll go back over it."

He sat in a chair opposite me.

"Mr. Blake, I think you will agree that you are resisting our attempts at group therapy."

They had finally got something right! I wondered where this conversation was going. I sat up straight and listened closer.

"After reviewing your file, we have determined that your problems are going to require long-term treatment, which we are unable to provide at this facility."

"So where does that leave me, Doctor?"

"We have contacted the regional VA Hospital in Albuquerque, Sir. The psychiatric ward there is much better staffed to diagnose your difficulties and provide proper care. They have a bed available, and we are proposing to send you there tomorrow. How does that sound?"

"That would be good ..."

Anything to get out of there.

"... but I don't have a way to get to Albuquerque – and I'm damn sure not about to hitchhike!"

"That's not a problem, Sir. In cases like this we are required by regulations to transfer you by ambulance. We have arranged for one to pick you up tomorrow morning."

I was amazed. I knew from the many times that I drove trucks over Interstate 40 that the distance was about 270 miles.

"Really? The VA would do that?"

"Absolutely. I highly recommend that you accept this arrangement."

"Very good. I accept – thank you."

"We're just doing our jobs, Mr. Blake. I hope everything gets better for you."

The next morning, I was escorted out to the waiting ambulance. It was the first fresh air I had breathed since my arrival. The driver was a tall, muscled, young man. The EMT Nurse riding with me in the back was athletic and strong in her own right. Either of them could have bent me in half like a pretzel. They both came up to introduce themselves, and the big guy squeezed most of the juice out of my hand while grinning broadly at the same time.

"You're not going to give us any problem, are you?"

"I might want to, but I don't think I could get away with much."

I had to shake the pain out of my fingers.

"Very good, Sir. But the transfer documents say that you may be suicidal. We'll have to watch you closely."

I nodded. They helped me into the ambulance and strapped me to the gurney. I remarked that I felt guilty accepting this ride at taxpayer expense.

"We do this run all the time. You need the ride, so take advantage of it."

We made a brief pit stop in Santa Rosa. The driver had to follow me into the bathroom while I took a leak.

"Goddamn. Do you have to hold my pecker too?"

"No Sir! Just have to watch. Sorry."

I was still looking for some way to get even with the guy for squeezing my hand.

"That's almost as bad. Don't get too close – I spray."

The grounds of the VA Hospital in Albuquerque presented a pleasant atmosphere that reminded me of a college campus. The grass was green, and old elm and sycamore trees provided friendly shade along the walkways. It looked like a place that I wouldn't mind coming to for treatment. I was admitted through the emergency room, which was busy and efficient. Soon, a pair of male nurses took control of me and dismissed the ambulance crew. They walked me over to Ward 7, which housed the psychiatric facility for in-patient cases.

My positive expectations came to a quick end. We took the elevator to the second floor and got off in what immediately felt like a prison. I wanted to bolt and get as far from there as possible. It had the same sterile walls and ceilings as the facility in Amarillo. The stern nurses explained the rules of behavior – including more group sessions and the hours that I was expected to be in the recreation room. I felt as if I had been locked in a cage. Oh, gawd! What the hell had I got myself into now?

They took me to my room. It was for double occupancy, but for the moment, I had it to myself. That was a very good thing. I couldn't imagine being in the same room with someone who had similar, unpredictable problems. I had to undress and trade my clothes for a gown. If I wanted to brush my teeth, I had to check out a small brush and tube of paste at a window that was only open for a few hours a day. Even small, travel-sized bars of soap had to be controlled by the supply room. Everything that I didn't use had to be returned – including the unused sliver of soap. I objected, but "rules are rules."

I spent the rest of the day just lying on the bed, which had a mattress about as hard as a stainless-steel food-prep table. I did not interact with anyone, and no one spoke to me. That was fine. I just withdrew into my own private world to wait for what would happen next. Late in the afternoon, a psychiatrist came in and sat next to me.

"How do you feel, Mr. Blake?"

"Sore from this stupid bed. Doesn't the VA know what a mattress is?"

"Patients have tried to kill others by suffocating them with soft mattresses. We can't have anything in the ward that someone might try to use as a weapon. I'm sorry, but you'll have to make the best of it. So – how do you feel emotionally?"

I sat up and lowered my head.

"Honestly, Doctor, I feel worse for being here. I haven't been able to sleep. I did not expect all the restrictions and regimentation. I'm rotten depressed and can't see the end of this."

"I'll order some sleeping meds for you, Mr. Blake. But I've looked through your file and apparently you have thoughts of suicide. Is that still a problem?"

"Yes, I think about it all the time, but I have no plans to do it at the moment. If my depression doesn't get any better, however, I might have to change my mind."

"We'll try very hard to prevent that, Sir. Can you tell me what's making you so distressed?"

I looked at the young doctor and wondered how deep I would have to go this time.

"Pardon me, doctor, but these memories are very hurtful and private. It is very difficult for me to discuss them, and I would prefer not to go there if you don't mind."

He studied me seriously for a few moments.

"Mr. Blake, you will eventually have to bring them all out. That's why you are here. It's the only way we can help you. We need to know what's going on in your mind before we can begin to fix it."

"I'm sorry, Doctor. I understand what you're saying, but I'll have to work myself up for that. Just the thought of having my past scrutinized is stressful. Can you give me some time to think about it?"

"Fair enough, Mr. Blake. I'll visit with you again tomorrow. I have to repeat, however, that you must do this sometime and the sooner the better – and the sooner we can get you out of here."

The next day, I shuffled down the hall in my red hospital socks for breakfast and returned quickly to bed. As before, I just lay there feeling sorry for myself. I didn't want to be there. I needed some freedom to walk by myself in the sun and feel the breeze through my hair. I couldn't believe that I had agreed to have myself locked up in a psych ward in the first place.

The therapy session that morning was easy enough. I told the group about the recent events that brought me there. When we were wrapping up, the therapist asked if I thought the session had been valuable.

"I can't figure out why this crap keeps happening to me, Doctor. It's like I'm snake bit or something."

"We will be working to get to the bottom of these problems, and you've made a positive start, Mr. Blake."

I went down to the rec room for lunch and dinner, but only picked at my meals to find the edible pieces. I said nothing to the other patients and only glanced up now and then to keep tabs on some of the more belligerent ones who might become threatening. Being in the same space as others who were more mentally disturbed than me was giving me problems. I was only dangerous to myself, but who knew about the others? I finished as soon as possible and went back to my room to lie down again. Despite the meds they were giving me, I was exhausted from not sleeping the previous nights. It was impossible to get comfortable on that damn rack.

The next morning I went down for breakfast, but felt even less like doing anything. My thought processes were suffering from days of fatigue. I went back to my room and lay there dozing fitfully. One of the nurses opened the door quietly and slipped in. She leaned over and gently shook my shoulder to get my attention. She was almost talking into my ear.

"Mr. Blake. Please listen to me."

I rolled over and looked up at her. We were very close.

"You will never get out of here if all you do is stay in bed. You need to get on your feet. Walk the hall if that's all you can do. The best thing would be to spend time in the rec room. Read a magazine or a book. Talk with somebody. Just sit there. It doesn't matter."

"But I'm so damn tired."

I was almost in tears.

"Force yourself out of this bed, Mr. Blake. I can't believe you want to stay here forever."

I studied her face. She was not a young woman, but still very attractive. She gave me a reassuring smile. Everything she said was absolutely true. The advice was just so damn difficult for me to act upon.

"OK – I get it, thanks."

She could have most certainly gotten herself into trouble. Nevertheless, it was the best counsel I had heard from anyone there. She left as cautiously as she had come in. This was indeed not the way I wanted to spend the rest of my life. I was there to get some help. Get up, Blake. You can move beyond this!

I felt like Humpty-Dumpty lying in a shattered pile next to the wall. All the king's horses and all the king's men – all the professional therapists and psychiatrists in the world – couldn't put me together again. Their impersonal diagnosis had not been enough. All it took, however, was one soft touch of the nurse in Amarillo, and now the genuine concern of this lady, to bring me back from the brink. Their humanity proved more effective than all the other treatments and therapies.

So, what was I doing just lying there waiting for something to happen? I stood and shuffled down to the rec room. There were a few patients sitting around, but it was mostly quiet. I went over to a large window that looked out over the trees and courtyard below. I imagined myself in the green fields of my youth. I recalled the gentle summer winds blowing through the tall grasses. I closed my eyes and could almost smell the fragrant air before a thunderstorm. I remembered running through meadows with wildflowers, dragon flies, and buzzing bumblebees ... then someone was talking to me. I had to struggle to come back to reality.

"Sir – Mr. Blake! I'm sorry to disturb you, but we have a team of psychiatrists who would like to talk with you. Let's go back to your room – if you don't mind."

I nodded and followed him down the hall. Three doctors stood around me who I had not seen before. One of them opened a file and flipped through it for a moment.

"We see from your records that your shoulder and back injuries came from an accident in the Navy. Would you tell us about that, please?"

OK. I had dodged these questions long enough. I was tired of holding everything inside, and the time had come to open up. I sighed and told them the whole story down to the livid details of my imminent death, being hopelessly trapped in the cockpit, and having been frightened out of my mind.

The doctors looked at each other.

"That was over 40 years ago. Would you say that you are still bothered by the accident?"

"Oh yes. It can surface at any time in my thoughts – or sometimes in nightmares."

"So – you expected to die?"

"Worse than that, Doctor. I was certain I was going to die. I was watching it happen, and – truthfully – I ought to be dead."

He nodded and turned to one of the other doctors. This man was tall with crisp features like the creases in his white hospital jacket. His voice was measured to say only what was necessary.

"Mr. Blake – have you ever been evaluated for PTSD?"

I looked at him with a blank expression.

"I'm sorry, but I don't know what that is. P-T – what?"

"P-T-S-D or Post-traumatic Stress Disorder. You've never heard the term?"

"No Sir."

The doctor paused and looked at the others. They all nodded their heads in return.

"As the name implies – PTSD is a serious condition. It affects many of our service people. It can cause serious difficulties in social behavior and professional performance. We have an expert team here who would like to conduct a series of tests and interviews with you. In your case, PTSD may have been latent since your accident. Once we develop a definitive diagnosis of what's going on, we will be able to determine a plan for treatment. You may find this process difficult, but it could have a positive impact on the rest of your life. I strongly recommend that you submit yourself to this evaluation. Would you allow us to do that?"

"... latent since the accident ..."

I repeated the phrase to myself. I was shocked and struggled to comprehend the implications of what the doctor had just said.

"Yes Sir, of course. I would like that."

The next week was spent being examined, evaluated, interrogated, and psychoanalyzed. One battery of questions led to the next. The doctors tested my mobility and balance. Cognitive exams determined my abilities to remember and analyze. My back and shoulder were X-rayed. They looked deep into my eyes and ears. I was given new prescriptions for muscle relaxers and pain killers. I recounted time and again the significant events of my life, including details of the accident.

During this period, I became more cooperative with the medical teams, but my deep-seated problems remained. However, the more I came to understand PTSD, the more I understood my difficulties and could better deal with them. When the psychiatrists were done, I was told that I had a "well developed" case of PTSD that seriously impacted my ability to function in society. Treatment would require a series of anti-depressants, muscle relaxers, pain medications, and personal therapy. After ten days, the psychs asked if I still felt like committing suicide. My answer was "no." The urgency of that idea was in the past. I was let out to build another life for myself, but the VA still kept a tight rein on me.

There was a sequence of psychiatrists after I was released who were tremendously helpful. Each of them was well-meaning, but they came and went more frequently than I had changed trucking jobs. Every time I had to break in a new one, we had to start at the beginning. I would get them up to speed only to have them retire, move on to other jobs, quit because of health reasons, or be let go for lack of government funding.

The one professional at the VA who knew me since the first days of my release was a psychiatric nurse named Charlie, whose specialty was PTSD. He was also from the East Coast and an artist. I related to him on a personal level and always looked forward to our sessions. At first we met every two weeks, then once a month, and finally bi-monthly or so.

Charlie was a teddy bear of a man, with bushy hair and a beard that matched his cobbled appearance. He wore high-top canvas sneakers that had the effect of drawing a smile out of me, regardless of how bad my mood was that day. Charlie's quick, dry sense of humor matched his friendly disposition – all of which disarmed my defenses. He was easy to talk with, and I became comfortable telling him anything I wanted. I was also plugged into the VA Pain Clinic for my back problems and could now come to the VA for all my medical needs.

Finally, I was advised to submit the hospital's findings to Social Security and the VA administrative offices, and make claims for additional disability beyond what I was already receiving for my shoulder.

•

The cost of our safety-nets is great,
but the cost of not having them would be unacceptable.

•

Chapter *35*

2005 – Late Summer

The Past Is Cast In Stone – The Future Has Wings

I WALKED OUT AND STOOD under the tree that I had gazed upon from the window upstairs. I let the early morning air flow around me and scuffed at a clump of grass. I was free and damn – it felt good! On the downside, the lingering effects from my meds left me noticeably unsteady and groggy. My freedom was all that mattered, however.

I had an airline ticket in my hand for a flight back to Amarillo provided by the Veterans Administration. The government was obligated to get me back to the location where I had first been admitted. My Social Security payment should have been deposited in the bank, so my first order of business was to visit the ATM in front of the hospital. Life was coming together. I was enjoying every moment of my getaway from Ward 7 and looking forward to whatever the future had for me.

A taxi arrived to take me to the airport. The ride was paid for by the VA, but the driver refused to take a tip.

"I'm glad anytime I can help a veteran!"

I remained amazed at the kindness that I received from total strangers every time I turned around. I grabbed my file, got out, and gave the man a wave. He drove off, and I went to check in at the airline counter. Unfortunately, I had left my ticket on the back seat of the taxi. After some anxious minutes, I was able to reach the dispatcher of the cab company, and she contacted the driver. I was embarrassed when he swung back through the drop off area and handed me the ticket with an understanding smile. He would still not accept a tip. OK, I still wasn't functioning at 100%. I resolved to be more careful.

My immediate goal was to collect my baggage from my storage locker and get settled temporarily back in Albuquerque. I needed to be close to the VA Hospital for my frequent out-patient treatments and therapy appointments. The Social Security payment of about $1175 per month was the only income I would have for a while, so I couldn't afford to spend time and money in motels while I found a place. My least favorite pastime, of course, was flying. I was so medicated, however, that the flight didn't matter. At the Amarillo

Airport, a veteran volunteer met the plane and drove me to the nearest U-Haul lot. Thank you, Sir. I rented a small van and drove to Canyon to pick up my belongings. It was still morning, and I was on schedule to drive back to Albuquerque that afternoon. That meant making the four hour drive, getting unloaded in another storage locker, finding an apartment, and returning the rental – all before the business offices closed. The plan was doable, but only if I pushed and everything fell into place.

Interstate 40 is like a race on a Hot Wheels track. Driving through Los Angeles at 75 miles an hour in a semi-truck on a Friday afternoon would have been easier than this. Trucks and RVs used their size to muscle us smaller vehicles out of the way. Faster cars jockeyed to get around the slower ones. I did my best, but was not doing well. I caught myself swerving out of my lane and reacting slowly. I was still groggy from the meds and kept having to shake myself back to attention as I sped along. Horns blasted at me as big trucks roared past. I drifted so close to one truck that I came within inches of tangling myself underneath its trailer. I usually take pride in my safe driving, but this time I scared myself out of my wits. I was shaking badly by the time I took the first Albuquerque exit, and had to pull off on the shoulder until I got hold of myself.

Change of plans. I was too nervous to do any looking around. There was a storage locker a few blocks from the exit, so I stopped and emptied out all my belongings. I rented the first crummy room that I looked at in a cheap apartment complex across the street. I drove to a U-Haul lot, backed into a dumpster as I tried to park, and couldn't get rid of the van fast enough. The bus ride back to my apartment finally gave me time to calm down. I had survived the beginning of the rest of my life, but it was less than a glorious start.

Other problems soon became evident. Besides therapy sessions, the standard medical treatments for PTSD are anti-depressant drugs. I also had to take prescription sleeping pills and industrial-strength pain killers for my back. Unfortunately, I was allergic to many of the medications that the VA tried on me. Narcotic-based drugs gave me splitting headaches and anxiety attacks that sent me to the emergency room twice. Such extreme pain was more than I could manage. I once had to call 911 because my head felt like it was about to explode. I was delirious, waving a kitchen knife in the air, trying to figure out how much it would hurt, and how long I would take to die. Dealing with my meds was a crap-shoot with the dice loaded against me. Months went by before my doctors worked out a trial-and-error combination of drugs that my body could tolerate.

My first meeting with Charlie, however, came right after my call to 911. I was a psychotic train wreck. I was tightly withdrawn on the chair trying hard to behave normally, but could not stop shaking. My head was splitting apart from a reaction to my meds. He listened to all my problems and then calmly switched to the positive things that I had accomplished.

"Well, Roger, you've made the trip to Amarillo and got your things – that must feel good to have them again."

"You're right, Charlie. It feels like I'm a little more whole again."

"You've got your own place now. At least you're not sleeping out in some field."

And so on. By the end of each of our sessions, Charlie had me looking on the bright side of my life again.

Soon after being released from the Ward, I emailed everyone on my list to explain that I had "been in the hospital." It would be a while before any more daily photos would be sent out. To those who inquired more deeply, my response was that I had gotten heat stroke, but would be OK. I was too embarrassed to tell my family or anyone else what had actually happened. I eventually called Cuzin' Connie and filled her in with all the details.

"I suspected something was going on, Roger. I hope you're doing better."

"Thanks, Cuz'. This last month has not been much fun. I'm improving but still have a ways to go."

"It would be good to see you, Roger. Are you up for coming over for dinner or going out somewhere?"

I had to decline.

"Not yet, Connie. I'm really more comfortable being by myself for now."

"I understand. But if you need anything or just want to talk – give me a holler."

"I will, Cuz'. Thanks a lot."

I did not call, so after a few weeks, she finally phoned me.

"We're going 4-wheeling on the dirt roads around Ladron Peak about 50 miles south of Albuquerque. I'll pick you up about 9 a.m. – so be ready. OK?"

I had to chuckle.

"I guess I have to go then?"

"Yup – and bring your camera. There's lots to shoot."

Her timing was perfect. I had been longing to see a bit of the world beyond the shell that I had built around myself. Connie is the perfect New Mexico tour guide. She has stacks of picture albums, maps, and stories about early settlements and ghost towns – some that have already crumbled to dust and no longer exist except in her extensive files and encyclopedic mind.

She picked me up, and we spent the morning poking around the fallen-down adobe walls of a hideout used by a notorious Albuquerque cop-killer, "Bronco Bill" Walters. We had a picnic beside an old school house and spent the rest of the afternoon climbing on the tailings of an abandoned mine. I lost myself photographing the timeworn timbers and rusted equipment that had been left behind. By the end of the day I was anxious to get back into photography.

My camera and creative compulsions led me out of my darkness once again. It would be months before I could buy a car, so the city bus became my mode of transportation. I wandered the streets and alleys of Albuquerque looking for any shot that I found unusual or interesting. Cityscapes replaced landscapes. Captions and stories came to mind to go with the photos. I began to write and send out my photo/emails again.

I also submitted claims to Social Security and the Veterans Administration for additional disability compensation, as my doctors had suggested. After a year filled with redundant tests, evaluations, and diagnosis, both of my requests were approved.

Progress was not without setbacks, however. One afternoon, I was walking across a street at a busy intersection. A car was stopped in front of me, waiting for a break in the heavy traffic in order to make a left turn. The driver and I looked at each other, and I was sure that she knew that I was going to cross in front of her. She turned back to watch the oncoming vehicles from her left.

I was directly in front of her hood when she gunned the accelerator. WHAM! The car knocked me 10 feet into the oncoming traffic. Tires were screeching and cars were swerving around me as I sat up and held my arm to my body. My left shoulder was jammed, and my back muscles were painfully sprained. Instead of scrambling to get out of the way, I remained on the pavement with my head between my knees wanting to be run over.

"Just hit me for chrissake! Put me out of my misery! Please! Come on – do me a goddamn favor!"

I definitely had some distance to go before I was out of my psychological woods.

The driver jumped out to help me, and bystanders waved off the traffic until the police came. My physical injuries were minor compared to the damage done to my emotional recovery. I was a mental wreck. Every time I made progress, I was thrown back to the point where I had started. Life didn't matter if this was what I had to look forward to.

I tried to find an attorney to represent me in a case against the driver, but no one was interested because I was: 1) already on government disability and could not claim loss of income; 2) already had mental problems, so there would have been no way to prove additional "pain and suffering"; and 3) my physical injuries were "soft tissue" that would heal. I was simply not worth an attorney's time. I personally negotiated a settlement with the woman's insurance company that gave me enough to buy a higher-end camera, rent a better apartment, and get myself into a used car.

My first trip was to visit my friends Jerry Lee and Catherine outside of Austin, Texas. JL and I had talked about our military experiences before, but we had more in common now that I had been diagnosed with PTSD. The hot Texas sun was setting after a full day of JL's horse clinics and my photography. We sat on his porch, sipped good whiskey, and quietly talked about the Vietnam War. He showed me one of his favorite books, *Achilles in Vietnam* by Jonathan Shay. When he opened the cover, a sheet of paper fell out. On it were Jerry Lee's thoughts written about 25 years after he left Vietnam. One note in particular captured the essence of his grim experience:

> "This book belongs to Gerald Sewell, who died in Vietnam,
> but lived to have his character undone, his honor stolen, his
> heart broken by the cruel war he left there and the cruel
> betrayal he found on his return."

Tears soon fell freely as JL spoke of the horrific events that had changed his life. His memories had never released their grip on his mind. I was overwhelmed with sadness that such a strong and talented man had to suffer so greatly. After I returned home, I wrote this story for Jerry Lee:

•

FACES

Early morning fog still slumbers over the river and canyons in the rugged wilderness. An old soldier stands high on a rocky outcropping, his lean figure silhouetted by the rising sun. He still carries himself with the tight grace of a military man, as precise in his movements as the orders he used to give. He is as craggy and rough as the ledge he stands on. The soldier has visited this spot many times, searching for answers and a peace that will not come. This is a hard man – harder on himself than most others – a fighter and warrior.

He looks out over the quiet rolling hills, but despite the beauty before him, he sees only the grim faces of men he killed in battle and those who died fighting by his side. He lowers his head and weeps for his friends and enemies alike. He would have gladly died rather than live with the memories of the War that have tortured him all these years. He wishes he had died and not the others.

His tears finally dry, and he looks out sadly over the bright, new day. The morning light is crystal clear. The air is fresh and cool. A hawk riding on thermals above the valley floor cries a lonely call that breaks the silence and echoes through the hills. Suddenly, a jay thrashes out of the brush nearby as it squawks an alarm. The soldier catches another movement in the corner of his eye. One shadow passes in front of another. A mesquite branch rustles as it is pushed aside. He hears the low, rumbling snarl that can only be made by a big cat. Mountain lions roam these hills. The soldier has noticed their tracks on the trail, but they keep to themselves and are seldom seen. He reaches to his side and slips his Ranger's knife from its sheath. His old instincts return, and he braces himself, ready for whatever might come. The light catches a pair of eyes watching from the shadows.

"Come on out, Cat," the soldier says. "If you are looking for breakfast, you best move on. I may not be in a mood for living, but I won't let the mangy likes of you make a meal of me."

The mountain lion looks some more, then rises from his crouch and ambles forward with no tension in its body.

"You spoke to me, so I will speak with you."

The big cat stops and sits.

"I'm not too hungry yet. Do you mind if I ask what bothers you so?"

The soldier stares and makes no reply.

"I do not know much about human emotions," it adds, "but I've watched you on this ledge many times. Your sadness has always puzzled me."

"Well now," mutters the soldier. "I've finally tipped my rocker."

Nightmares and hallucinations are nothing new to this man. He shakes his head, looks again, and sure enough the great cat is sitting there, looking inquisitively, and waiting for a reply. The thought that this particular cat is somehow familiar, flashes through his mind.

"I know nothing of sadness," it continues. "I am just curious what could possibly matter so much that you hike miles to come here, and all you do is cry."

The soldier shakes his head. He is used to talking with voices that ramble through his mind, but this is different.

"Good question," he finally sighs. "You see, I was a soldier – a man who ordered others into battle. They trusted me, but I led many to their deaths. I killed many of the enemy and civilians too. I don't think I can live with their memories any longer."

The mountain lion thinks for a moment.

"I too am a killer," he says reflectively. "If you were protecting yourself, your men, and your country, what is the problem with that? I think you should be revered as a great patriot and hero."

"The war was contrived and unjust. The sacrifice of so many should not have happened. Civilians died who cared only to live their lives – not about politics, nationality, or someone else's conflict. I should have known better and simply said no.

"Still, you were a soldier," the cat says thoughtfully. "You followed orders. You fought with your men in battle and led them well. You were willing to die for them. It is not your fault they died and you survived."

"The people at home turned against us," says the old warrior sadly, looking down and searching for his words. "I thought I was fighting for them, but I was wrong. They burned the flag and spat on me and every value I was fighting for. They made me a symbol of war, but all I fought for was justice and peace. My men and I were betrayed."

These ideas were strange to the cat, and it looked out over the valley, deep in thought until it spoke again.

"The people were wrong. Humans have fought many conflicts for bad reasons. You were caught in events that required you to fight for your country. You should not bother your mind with what others think. Certainly not with those who do not know you or care what is in a soldier's heart."

"I've thought that many times," he replies. "But I still feel their hate. I can't help it."

"Consider this," says the great cat as it licks his paw. "That was years ago, and you are older now. There is nothing you can change. No one hates you now. You are just a fragment of history – no different from millions of soldiers who have returned with memories they want to forget."

The two silently look out over the serenity below.

"It's the faces," says the soldier finally. "I can't forget the faces."

"Ah – it's the faces!" repeats the great lion.

With that, it stands and shakes the morning stiffness from its body. It stretches and twitches its tail nervously.

"I do not look at faces."

The cat starts pacing around as though it is distracted.

"You are poorly suited to be a killer. You are a warrior that cannot kill without remorse and guilt. That is a bad combination."

"That is the difference between you and me. Killing comes naturally to a predator like you, but not to a human being."

"This has been an interesting conversation," purrs the cat as it circles back, "but it is time I found some breakfast. You take care."

"I will, and you best do the same," replies the soldier.

The cat's mood has changed. The old warrior watches it carefully. It flicks its tail back and forth and looks at him sideways. It measures in its mind the distance between them, and runs its tongue slowly over its lips. The hair on its back is tense and raised. It starts to prowl in a wide circle, waiting for an opening or something that might distract the soldier. It paws absently at a rock, all the while carefully judging the man's attention and response.

Adrenaline pumps through the soldier's veins, and the familiar feel of combat returns. Their eyes lock together – unblinking, unafraid. He grips his knife tight. The cat's eyes get dark and red, and in a flash the warrior recognizes it as the same demon that appears in his nightmares; the same beast with red-hot eyes and blood dripping from its claws and fangs; the same ferocious fiend that leaps out of the explosions, smoke, and fire, as the faces drift by in an endless river of blood; the same vicious, mindless passions of war and terror that torture his own thoughts and grip his heart; the same violent passions that wake him, thrashing at the sheets, and desperately trying to drive them from his mind and soul.

The lion paces, waiting for an opening, then turns and paces back again. It growls and snarls and stares menacingly. The soldier keeps his stance wide, one leg behind the other for balance, leaning slightly forward, knife raised in front ready to strike. Sunlight flashes off the razor-sharp blade. He keeps his other arm moving to distract the cat's attention. The cat jumps to the side. The soldier follows just as fast, but his back foot catches on a root and shifts his weight off balance.

Fast as lightning the cat bounds forward out of the blazing sun. It gathers speed and leaps into the air with deadly claws and fangs spread wide, ready to rip apart the soft flesh of its prey. The soldier ducks aside and slashes viciously at the lion's face with his knife. Blood flows from a wound across its eye and cheek, but the taste of its own hot blood only urges it on. There is no retreat. The best one wins. It is the time to kill or time to die.

The cat lunges forward – low to the ground this time. It swerves to avoid the blade and hits the warrior chest-to-chest, driving them both to the ground. It howls in victory, but the soldier rams his forearm into the lion's mouth as it strikes to make the fatal blow. He stabs it in the shoulder with his knife, as the cat clamps its jaws with all its might. It shakes the arm and hears the satisfying crunch of splintered bone. They roll over and over on the hard rocks. The soldier has his legs locked around its body and keeps close to avoid the slashing claws. He stabs again and again – driving the blade deep until the hard steel finds the lion's cold heart. The great cat screams, then rolls its eyes, goes limp, and falls aside.

The battered warrior slowly stands, his heart pounding in his chest as he gulps for air. His arm is hanging limp and throbbing at his side. He looks at the cat lying at his feet.

"Damn you, cat!" he yells. Then quietly, "Damn you to Hell!"

As he watches, its body fades away. The soldier blinks, thinking it might be the light – but no, the cat's body has vanished. The blood on the soldier's arm and body also slowly disappears. All that is left is the cat's face. Then it is not the cat, however. It rises up to greet him, and becomes one of the faces of the enemy he remembers so well. But instead of pain and fear of death, the face is serene and smiling. It is the eyes that speak.

"I understand. It is all right."

Soon the face becomes another. This one the soldier remembered was burned and anguished, but now is clear and calm.

"It is not your fault," the eyes say.

Then another face and another and more until they all pass before him. Each has a message - some with a friendly nod, others with a smile.

"You were a soldier." "We were soldiers, too." "You were very good – better than me." "It was war." "You are not to blame."

He sees the lieutenant he killed in fierce hand-to-hand combat. The battle was at night and explosions framed their bodies in the smoke and fires. The lieutenant bows his head and comes up with a jaunty grin.

"If I had to die – I'm glad it was by the likes of you."

The faces of civilians pass before him – villagers, refugees, peasants, old people, and children too. Some had been caught in the line of fire. Some died in their homes. All died needlessly in the curse of war.

"It was war." "We understand." "We forgive," they say.

His troops now come to him one by one. Each face he knew, and some come with their families beside them. Each is glad to see the old soldier again.

"I understand." "I respect you." "I would serve with you again." "I would follow you anywhere, Sir."

Finally, it is the man who the old soldier knew and loved so well. It is his comrade who had shared their traumas of ordering men to battle and their deaths. This was the man who happened by a fate of protocol to be a step ahead of the soldier as they went out a door into the light. It is the face of his commander who was ripped apart by a mortar round that happened to land at his feet, and whose body shielded the old soldier from most of the blast. His face comes close.

"You have honored our deaths well. Honor us now by living with the happiness and joy that we will never know. Forgive yourself – for a life of sorrow and pain is just another wasted life."

The commander's face begins to fade. The soldier wants to go to him, but he can't respond. Before his face is gone, all the others are there with him. They raise their hands in solemn salute and then finally disappear into the quiet shadows. The old soldier tries to say "thank you" or "yes Sir" but his throat is dry, and no words come. He watches the woods for a long time after the faces are gone. Instead of their gruesome images, he remembers only those who had just appeared.

He looks to the sky. The afternoon sun is getting low. The hawk now circles high above the distant hills. The warrior still holds the knife, but it is clean, and he sets it back in its scabbard. He bends his injured arm and closes his fingers. There are scars, but the wound has healed. There is no pain. His step is lighter. He no longer feels the heavy burden in his heart. He stands at attention on the rocks and raises his arm in a solitary salute, then slowly lowers it to his side.

"Farewell," the old soldier says. "I best get down the trail. Tomorrow is another day."

•

Jerry Lee and I could go months without talking. However, when we got together the conversation picked up right where we left off. Many of our emotions and feelings went unspoken, but were understood between us. We were always supportive of each other regardless of what we had been up to. We both had our medical and emotional issues. Many things were too painful to discuss and not worth the effort to bring up. The story "FACES" was one of those subjects. It was my hope, when I wrote the story, that it might bring my friend some comfort. That was not the case, however. No amount of reason or good intentions could ever change the facts – or his memories of them. I suspect most PTSD victims are the same way. I certainly am. The only reliable therapy I have found is to keep my mind occupied with other things.

My activities in Albuquerque started to expand into broader circles. An email recipient, whom I had met while photographing a trail ride with Jerry Lee, referred me to Cathy, an Albuquerque publisher of a monthly horseman's magazine. She was looking for someone who could take pictures and write brief descriptions of rodeos, horsemanship clinics, and other events. The pay would be a small amount based on whatever material she published. I needed a creative project and would benefit a great deal from the experience. Even the few extra dollars would be a tremendous help. It was a perfect arrangement for the moment, and who knew what would happen when I got credit in the magazine for my material. The work was easy and fun.

Cathy had a friend, Sandy, who was an active board member on several community and non-profit organizations. Cathy told me that Sandy needed a photographer, and that she had given her my name and phone number. Sandy would be contacting me soon.

"Hi Roger, it's Sandy. I think Cathy told you I would be calling."

"Yes she did. Tell me – what is it you are working on."

"Of course. I'm on the board of a cancer support group that is having its annual fund raiser coming up. In past years, we have had a person who has been kind enough to take photographs of the people at the luncheon that we honor. He won't be doing it this year, so we are looking for someone else. Cathy tells me you are doing a fine job for her magazine, and I was hoping you could help us out."

I knew I would be awkward at the event, but it seemed like a worthwhile cause.

"I would be glad to help, Sandy. What else can you tell me about it?"

"That's great, Roger! The people include doctors, nurses, care-givers, volunteers, and cancer survivors. There are 55 honorees ..."

"Oops! That's an awful lot Sandy, and I don't have the right equipment for formal, indoor portraits. My work is much more spontaneous. I was thinking there would be about a half dozen people."

The indoor shots were definitely not something I wanted to do, however maybe there was another way.

"Maybe I could take the photos in their office or at home. Then I could spend more time with each subject, and the photos would be much more interesting."

325

"We could probably arrange that, but these people are located all over the state, Roger."

"I don't mind the travel, Sandy. So, the other question is – when do you need the photos?"

"The luncheon is only five weeks away."

I was silent for a moment.

"I don't know if Cathy told you, Sandy, but I have some serious issues with PTSD. I – um – had a breakdown and was recently released from the VA hospital. I have great difficulty with this kind of pressure."

"No, she did not tell me that, Roger."

"Honestly, I don't think I can handle all this. Taking the photographs is just the start. Then there will be hours spent editing, proofing, and organizing the work. I cannot do that, make the appointments, manage the schedule, and even get all the directions."

"I will help as much as I can. You just do the photography, and I'll do all the coordination. Would that be OK?"

"Really? Do you realize how much work that will be?"

"Sounds like fun to me, Roger. So, you'll do it?"

The fact that she would place that much positive confidence in me provided the encouragement that I needed despite my apprehensions.

"OK, Sandy. I'll do the best I can."

There were many times when I was about to throw up my hands and bail out of the arrangement. Despite Sandy's detailed schedule of appointments and directions, I couldn't keep track of who I had seen, where I had to go for my next portrait, or even what damn day it was. When I was discouraged, she was always there to tell me, "You can do it, Roger." I could not possibly have completed the work without her. I was still editing and printing photos on the morning of the event.

I finally met Sandy and her husband Ron, a retired attorney, at the awards luncheon. I watched proudly as a slide show cycled through my images on a huge screen in front of hundreds of attendees. I had never doubted the

2006 – Late Summer

quality of my work, but to have it appreciated by so many was a new and gratifying experience.

Sandy pulled me aside and asked if we could get together sometime. She said she wanted to help. We met for a pleasant lunch at a café a week later. Our conversation drifted from the program that we had just completed to what my plans were for the future. I told her about my dreams to be a fine artist or photographer, but those had to be on hold indefinitely. Sandy was sympathetic and at the end of our meal, she invited me to their house for dinner. I told her I was not ready, but she persisted – like only Sandy can – and in the end I had no choice other than accept.

That first meal with Ron and Sandy set the course of the rest of my life. I went from feeling nervous and awkward – like I should excuse myself for imposing on them and return to my apartment – to finally enjoying the evening and telling them bits of my background and recent history. Sandy plied me with a fine meal (why does this sound familiar?) and we promised to do it again soon. I had a delightful time – but much more important – it was the beginning of my steep climb back to social confidence.

Sandy and Ron became benefactors and collectors of my work. One evening, they invited me again for dinner at their sprawling adobe home. I had just finished hanging a dozen of my photographs that they had purchased, and we were admiring the new look of the walls.

"Well, what do you think, Roger?"

I looked around and felt that something was definitely wrong. When someone asks my opinion, I have never been able to hold back from delivering it.

"The photos look great, (I had to say that) but they are not well lit."

We were not finished until new track lighting had been installed, the entire house was repainted, redecorated, re-stuccoed, and their one acre yard was re-landscaped. I even moved in with them for about a year while the improvements were in progress. I provided the design, some labor, and supervised the work. Moderation was not one of the criteria – although poor Ron choked on the cost every time I came up with a new idea. All of the work was successful, however, and the end result was a much more comfortable home. I was immensely proud – and my photographs were now properly lit!

I became one of Sandy's projects. She continued to gently – but very persistently – open doors for me throughout Albuquerque. She introduced me to worthwhile contacts and pushed me to become involved in activities.

Through her, I met an art dealer who accepted my photography in an on-going show, and a few photographs sold from time to time. I put together brochures and slide shows for another organization that she served on as a board member. If I had never met Sandy, none of this would have happened.

Other promising opportunities started to present themselves. Through my younger brother Tony, and the photo/emails, I was invited to give a presentation and be the judge at the monthly meeting of the Charlottesville, Virginia, Camera Club – one of the most active photography groups in the country. The club president, Pete, had been receiving my emails for some time.

"I can talk about my own work, Pete, but I do not want to critique any other photographer's art. Who the hell am I to place myself at a level to evaluate anyone else's images?"

"The judging is an integral part of the presentation, Roger. You can't do one without the other."

Damn. I was flattered by the invitation and really wanted to show my photos, so I accepted. When the date arrived, my nerves were rapidly disintegrating, and all I wanted to do was escape back home to New Mexico. Tony picked me up at the motel to make sure I didn't cop out on the whole affair. I got through the event, but my insecurity showed, and I promised myself I would just stick to creativity in the future.

Jerry Lee and Catherine introduced me to a woman named Pebbles who was Director of the University of Texas Performing Arts Center at Austin. There was some wonderful space in the waiting area of the hall where art was displayed, and she invited me to hang some of my photos. As before, I could not pass up the chance to display my work. One of my pieces was accepted into the University's permanent art collection. That was an honor worth all the effort.

I also participated in juried shows with the New Mexico Veterans Art Association. Two of my photographs won awards. I was meeting people and getting recognition for my work. All these would appear to be positive developments, however the exposure and pressure of presenting my photographs became too demanding. My anxieties were irrational and self-destructive, but they became more than I could handle. I stopped participating in art shows and finally said no to further work for Sandy's organizations.

I had moved out of Ron and Sandy's and was now looking for a larger place of my own. They owned a rental house that had become vacant and kindly offered it to me. I only lasted there a few weeks before I got into a fight with a neighbor about the noise coming into my yard from his outdoor, hot tub/entertainment center. I had to move out before I did something I might regret. I needed a place away from the hassles of urban life – with room to breathe, enough space that neighbors wouldn't bother me, and a view that went beyond my back fence. I had lived in cities before and was happiest when I got away from them.

I spent a few months searching the area for something that met my criteria and was also affordable. When I found it, there was no turning back. It was a comfortable modular home on one acre in the Jemez Mountains about a two hour drive northwest of Albuquerque. It came with a separate 1000 square foot metal building which I could convert into an art studio (if I ever found the money) or could use for anything else I wanted. The deck looked out at an 11,000 foot mountain less than ten miles from my front door. There were ponderosa pines, aspen trees, granite rocks, clear streams, and back-country hiking trails. I closed escrow in January, 2008 – just months before the real estate bubble burst. I was pleased with the deal, however, and am still pleased with it now.

A few months after I moved in, I received an email from my old girl friend, Cia. I had lost track of her after she moved to California from my gallery in Madrid over ten years before. She found me through my photography website. It turned out that she had gotten herself into an abusive relationship and was not doing well. I'm a sucker for a damsel in distress.

"Do you need to be rescued?"

Cia thought about it for a few days and finally agreed. I soon arrived in Ashland, Oregon and hooked up a U-Haul trailer. Cia was packed and ready to go. It was snowing in the passes of the Cascade Mountains, so we cut out to the coast and then – what the hell – we drove down to see her family in Southern California. Eventually, we made it to my place and set up housekeeping. I did everything I could think of to make her happy, but couldn't make it last. Maybe I tried too hard. Maybe I didn't try hard enough. Maybe it just wasn't meant to be. I honestly don't know, but we were still living on divergent spiritual wavelengths.

Cia referred me to a "spiritual thinker" whose writings she thought I might find inspirational. I read a few chapters and stopped because the pain he was talking about was only emotional and psychological. I had already tried this type of healing with VA "mindfulness exercises." We would lie on thin mats, practice deep breathing, and listen to calming tapes with suggestive messages about living in the present. There was nothing wrong with the program, except that in a few minutes my back pain would overcome my peaceful state of mind, and I would have to move around. The spell was broken. I would spend the rest of the session miserably sitting in a chair. In my case, depression and physical pain have always fed on each other.

She became unhappy and announced one day that we would no longer be lovers. I became depressed. Cia became more distant. It was a bad combination that fed upon itself and only got worse. After about a year and a half, I finally asked her to leave. She told me later that she was distressed by my depression and knew that she was adding to it.

"But you were not doing anything to grow beyond it, Roger."

Anyway, Cia left. The butterfly of romance fluttered away in search of a brighter flower. I became increasingly despondent and gloomy. My back pain became debilitating. It was so bad that I couldn't even lift my camera to take a picture. I had to quit doing photography and sending out my daily emails. When I wasn't gazing out my window, I was staring at my computer and waiting for the next cycle of bad news. Occasional emails from friends like Ron and Sandy and family were my main source of contact with the outside world.

One group that was after me, however, was from Pomfret School, my prep school alma mater. Our 50th class reunion would be in a few months and it was time – my old friends and classmates, Clark and Steve, informed me – to send in a biography for the reunion book. Of course, they encouraged me to attend. I gave their request a few seconds thought and could not come up with anything positive to write. Their messages were easy to delete, but they kept resending their requests anyway. Clark tracked my phone number down and finally called.

"Why haven't we heard anything from you, Roger?"

"I have some medical problems, Clark. I've also got some mental issues – specifically PTSD going back to my time in the Navy. I won't be able to make it back for the reunion."

Clark was uncharacteristically quiet for a moment.

"I'm really sorry to hear that, Roger. I have no idea what it must be like, but it has to be tough. But please send a biography. Everybody would love to hear what you've been up to."

"I'll think about it."

I ended the conversation as quickly as possible.

I tried writing something up over the next few days, but everything always came out negative, and always raised more questions than it answered. I decided not to send anything at all. Clark finally called again to see how I was doing.

"I've been looking forward to receiving something from you, Roger. You know – just hit the highlights. Whatever you care to send will be OK."

"I don't think so, Clark. I've tried, but I'm not doing well with this."

Clark gave his East Coast, full-court press.

"I realize it's a hassle, Roger, but it will only take a few minutes ..."

"Uh, Clark, it's not that writing it is a hassle, and I have plenty of time. Let's see. How can I express this so that you will understand? – I just don't want to do it!"

Clark understood that. I no longer received requests for the bio, but messages about the reunion events kept coming in. The more personal ones from Clark and Steve continued to urge me to come. They assured me that everybody would be glad to provide any assistance I needed. That was not my problem, however. I couldn't bear the thought of having to answer all the questions about my history and PTSD. It was easier to stay home. I ignored all further attempts to get me involved.

●

Saying "No" is an act of self-defense.

●

331

Don't Go There

Life Is A War Of Reason Vs. Reality

THE IMPORTANT CONSTANTS IN MY LIFE were Sandy and Ron, Cathy, my family on the East Coast, Jerry Lee and Catherine, Charlie, and the staff at the Veterans Hospital. My back rapidly deteriorated to the point that I needed a cane to get around and sometimes even a walker. Multiple surgical procedures were required to keep me on my feet. I became known on a first name basis with the VA pain management staff.

"You again, Roger!"

"How about a lower lumbar lobotomy, Doc?"

"That's not on my list of approved treatments – regretfully."

Sometimes, Charlie would act as a cheerleader encouraging me to expand my activities; other times he provided a cautionary note when he felt I should step back from what I was doing. I had not felt suicidal for a long time, but we both knew that some event – like my worsening levels of pain, or losing Cia, or my increasing isolation – could trigger a precipitous, downward slide at any time.

One day, I was sitting in the waiting area for my next psych appointment with Charlie. As usual, I had taken a seat in the back row, so I could observe everybody as they checked in with the receptionist. Even though we each shared similar backgrounds and were there for the same reason, we seldom communicated amongst ourselves. In my case, anyway, I just found it too difficult to introduce strangers to my problems. I felt deep empathy, however, for the others in the room – especially for the younger vets. My own mental and physical problems gave me a new level of compassion for those who also suffer and are incapacitated. Our preference was certainly not to be there, but the undeniable fact was that each of us needed the support and counsel.

The door to the doctors' offices swung open, and Charlie appeared. Today his high-top tennies were red.

"Come in, Roger. Sorry I'm running late."

I pushed myself up from the chair, put my weight on my cane, and waited for the muscle spasms to pass through my legs as they always did after sitting for some time. I made my way across the room while Charlie patiently held the door open for me. We shook hands, and he looked me over.

"So, how's the back today?"

"Not so bad, Charlie."

In fact, my back was in rough shape, but it had been much worse before the last steroid injection a few weeks ago. We walked down the hall past a maze of small offices. I was doing fairly well by the time we reached Charlie's cluttered cubbyhole. He gestured for me to take a seat and closed the door.

"So, what have you been up to, Roger?"

Charlie settled into his chair. He already knew that Cia had left, and that I had given up my photography.

"I'm just trying to survive. Frankly, Charlie, it's not getting any easier."

"Doing any writing? Any painting?"

I looked down blankly at the floor.

"Nothing's worked – I don't have a creative thought in my head."

Charlie rocked back in his chair and studied me thoughtfully.

"You're damn good, you know, Roger. 'FACES' was one of the best stories about PTSD that I've read. If you just applied yourself, I'm sure something good would come of it. We've talked about this before. You are aware of how much satisfaction you get from doing anything creative. It's the most constructive thing you could be doing right now."

"All that happens, Charlie, is I get frustrated and stop in the middle of what I'm doing. I can't force creativity to happen when I'm in this level of pain."

Charlie gave up on that subject.

"Anything new with Cia? Any chance you can turn that around?"

"No, she's gone. I can't imagine that she would want to come back."

"Do you think the breakup was related to PTSD, Roger?"

"Sure. Between that and the pain, I haven't been much fun to be around lately. She couldn't understand why I'm not bright and cheery all the time."

"Well, the holidays are behind you. At least, you should feel good about that."

I had to smile. Charlie had found something I was happy about.

"Yes. Now I don't have to worry about them for another year."

Charlie was getting impatient.

"You're not helping, Roger. Something positive must be going on in your life. Tell me – what do you do all day?"

I looked at him and tried to think of something positive, but couldn't think of anything.

"I just sit around. Sometimes I read or get on my computer. I'll catch up on the news or check my emails. Some days, it's like I just sit and wait for emails to come in just so I can delete them."

I sighed and sat silently for a moment. Charlie waited for more.

"I've been getting emails about my 50th class reunion that's coming up. They want me to send a bio and commit to being there, but I'm not going to do that."

"Why not, Roger? That kind of activity would be great for you!"

I shook my head.

"Nah. I haven't seen or heard from them for 50 years and now I'm expected to act like we're best buddies? I don't have anything in common with those folks anymore."

It was Charlie's turn to shake his head.

"For Pete's sake, Roger! You should listen to yourself. You've got a reason for not doing everything. Forget all that garbage. Surely there will be some old friends there who you would enjoy. Mingle with your public for once. Grit your teeth – get off your ass – and go!"

"I would always have to be explaining myself, Charlie. Then everyone would discover that they didn't really want to know about any of this crap – like my kids. I run into that reaction all the time. They would be embarrassed, and so would I."

Charlie sighed. It was time to wrap things up.

"I'm concerned, Roger. You are even more depressed and withdrawn than usual. You were doing much better not so long ago. I understand about the back pain, but you can't let that shut down your entire life. And you are never going to have another 50th reunion. It would be a real shame if you missed it."

I nodded. It was good advice. Whether or not I would take it was another matter.

"OK, Charlie. I'll give it some thought. Thanks again for the encouragement."

"You know how to get hold of me if you have to. Give me a call, Roger – whenever you want."

We shook hands, and I hobbled back down the corridor. I was sick of myself and disgusted with my life. I would have kicked myself out the door if that was possible.

Yes – Charlie was right about the reunion. I should go and would probably do fine once I got past the initial awkwardness. But no – I really did not want to put myself or the others through those moments. My sense of embarrassment, inadequacy, insecurity – or whatever – would last as long as I was there. I agonized with these arguments for weeks. I lost sleep over the dilemma and became progressively angry with my inability to make a decision one way or the other.

I would have gone on like this forever except that the day of the event was approaching. I missed the time when I could have bought a reasonably priced airline ticket, but was not about to go through the hassle and expense of flying anyway – not to mention the trauma that consigning my life to an airplane always put me through.

I could still drive if I wanted, and the trip itself was an attractive option. It had been years since I had been across the country. I woke up on the last day that I could leave, told myself, "What the hell," packed a suitcase, and took off down the highway. I did not tell anyone I was coming – not even my family –

because I had no idea what condition I would be in before or after I arrived. Or I might turn around half-way there and come back.

Events had been scheduled all weekend. My plans, however, were to arrive on Saturday morning, stay the day, and make my escape when I felt like it. I could honestly say my back was hurting and had to leave. The farther I drove, the more comfortable I became with the idea. My reticence was nonsense – I kept telling myself – so why not relax and enjoy the gathering? Just go and do whatever I wanted afterwards – like drop in on my brothers, continue on to Maine, or go to museums. If I felt awkward or distressed, I could bail out at any time.

Pomfret School is located in a picturesque rural area of northeast Connecticut. The inevitable subdivisions and commercial developments have not detracted from its splendid New England charm. Majestic maple trees – that were already old 50 years ago when I was there – framed the buildings and lined the winding walkways. The crystal-clear morning was a perfect promise of summer after the long winter. The grass seemed even greener than I remembered as a student. I sat in my car and watched the many groups of alumni and their families wandering the grounds. I was some distance away, but I saw my classmates organizing themselves for their reunion picture on the marble steps of the sundial – the traditional spot at Pomfret for group photos.

I drove closer. Some of the people looked familiar, but I had only vague recollections of the names that went with the faces. I became nervous and felt terribly out of place. My sketchy memories of the experiences that we had together were uncomfortably incomplete. All of my PTSD inhibitions and anxieties welled up in my mind. What was the sense of reliving those happier times if they would only open every old scar in my past? What the hell was I doing here?

A car came up behind mine and waited for me to move out of its way. My foot pressed down on the accelerator. I could not get away fast enough.

Purpose Breeds Progress

EXCUSES FOR MY FAILURE to make an appearance flooded my thoughts. I was distressed and conflicted all the way back to New Mexico. I had thought I was better able to manage my reactions to social situations, but clearly I was not. My mind kept grinding away about this after I got home. Even my initial rejection of the idea of going back to Pomfret was an excellent example of how PTSD influenced every decision I had to make.

The problem I had of sending a biography for the class book also continued to bother me. I still felt that a few brief paragraphs would not have made any sense. It had, in fact, been better not to send anything at all. This decision, combined with my rapid escape from the reunion, inspired me to write *RAMJET*. I had unleashed a deep desire to tell people what had happened in my life and why I had become who I was.

I wrote a few pages, starting with my last counseling session with Charlie, but still had no real plans beyond dabbling with the events to occupy my time. There were no expectations of finishing a story or doing anything other than maybe filing my thoughts away with the other short stories I have written. Three and a half months later, however, I had an initial draft of my autobiography. I had poured out my soul on paper for anyone who would care to read it.

Dredging up my life from the buried recesses of my mind has been extraordinarily traumatic. Editing and proofing the drafts was intensely difficult as well. Re-living each event brought it to the forefront of my thoughts and left the memories – like wounds – exposed and raw. If I had known how demanding the writing would become, or had spent any time thinking about the task ahead, I doubt that I would have attempted the project. But after I sat down and got started, the words would not stop flowing.

If recovery means to heal completely, then I can't say that I have ever healed or returned to normal – whatever normal is at this point. I doubt that I ever will. For me, that would be to move beyond myself – or become someone new. I have never been able to deny the existence of my negative thoughts – PTSD – or rid them from my mind. The same has been true of my anxieties and fears. They can be made less significant, however, by a series of positive events and actions that leave no time for negative thinking. Action has always been my best therapy.

Accordingly, my creative nature has led me out of depression and non-productive isolation once again. I am glad to report that *RAMJET* is certainly my most significant creative achievement. A tremendous burden has been lifted from my mind just by getting it finished and behind me. The impact of the book on me has been entirely positive. Writing this story has given me new confidence and purpose. Maybe now, time will fade these events into the dim, forgotten pages of this book. At least I can no longer claim that I am depressed because there is nothing in my life to be happy about.

Perhaps *RAMJET* will lead me to a better life. Now I can hope.

Self-Portrait

CPSIA information can be obtained at www.ICGtesting.com
Printed in the USA
LVOW110646100113

314919LV00003B/6/P